Colección Támesis

SERIE A: MONOGRAFÍAS, 177

THE POETRY OF LUIS CERNUDA

ORDER IN A WORLD OF CHAOS

NEIL C. McKINLAY

THE POETRY OF LUIS CERNUDA
ORDER IN A WORLD OF CHAOS

TAMESIS

First published 1999 by Tamesis, London

ISBN 1 85566 063 6

Tamesis is an imprint of Boydell & Brewer Ltd
PO Box 9, Woodbridge, Suffolk IP12 3DF, UK
and of Boydell & Brewer Inc.
PO Box 41026, Rochester, NY 14604–4126, USA
website: http://www.boydell.co.uk

A catalogue record for this book is available
from the British Library

Library of Congress Cataloging-in-Publication Data
McKinlay, Neil C. (Neil Charles), 1968–
    The poetry of Luis Cernuda : order in a world of chaos / Neil C.
McKinlay.
        p.   cm. – (Colección Támesis. Serie A, Monografías ; 177)
    Includes bibliographical references and index.
    ISBN 1–85566–063–6 (alk. paper)
    1. Cernuda, Luis – Criticism and interpretation.   I. Title.
PQ6605.E7Z775   1999
861'.62 – dc21   99–18395

This publication is printed on acid-free paper

Printed in Great Britain by
St Edmundsbury Press Limited, Bury St Edmunds, Suffolk

TABLE OF CONTENTS

vi

ACKNOWLEDGEMENTS

The original basis for this book was my Ph.D. thesis, 'Order in a World of Chaos: A Comparative Study of a Central Dialectic in Works of Thomas Mann, Franz Kafka and Luis Cernuda', accepted by Glasgow University in November, 1996. I should therefore like to thank above all my two supervisors, Professor D. Gareth Walters and Mr Bernard Ashbrook, as well as their colleague Professor Roger Stephenson and former colleague Professor Nicholas Round, who provided me with a wealth of inspiration and encouragement. Since then Professor Walters in particular has continued to assist and encourage me, and for that I am particularly grateful. In addition I am much obliged to Dr Ángel María Yanguas Cernuda for granting permission to quote extensively from Cernuda's poetry.

My greatest debt of gratitude is however due to my parents, who have suffered and supported me with exceptional patience throughout the time that this work has been in preparation.

N.C.M.

For my parents

CHAPTER ONE

THE CRISIS OF FAITH

The trend towards a non-theistic world view has characterised Western thinking in the last two centuries. Scientific research, especially since Darwin's landmark work *On the Origin of Species by Means of Natural Selection*, has been dominated by materialism, and its relative objectivity has been instrumental in countering the claims of the religious that the universe was created by and is still in the control of Almighty God. This trend away from theism has been mirrored in both philosophical and literary expression and, within the European context, it is present across the whole spectrum of European culture. The world has become chaotic.

An atheistic viewpoint is, however, like a theistic one, a matter of active faith and can never be definitively proved or disproved by purely rational arguments. What matters here is not the appropriateness of faith (that is the free choice of every individual), but rather the fact that atheism is much more widespread.[1] While there is insufficient space for a detailed account of philosophical ideas, it may suffice to mention some key figures whose philosophy has been particularly decisive in shaping twentieth-century thinking, in order to appreciate more fully the way that faith has changed. One of the most influential philosophers of the nineteenth century is Arthur Schopenhauer, who speaks, in *Die Welt als Wille und Vorstellung* (*The World as Will and Representation*), of life as a 'ganze Tragikomödie' ('complete tragi-comedy'),[2] and Janaway succinctly sums up Schopenhauer's ideas by saying that, 'The old ideas of the immortal soul, the divine purpose, and the dignity of man have died ... and should not be revived'.[3] It is perhaps this attitude of the ultimate purposelessness of the world that is seized upon most vigorously by one of Schopenhauer's successors, Friedrich Nietzsche, of whose work there appears to have been a new and different

---

[1] It should be stressed that this study is not intended as a philosophical or theological discussion. The objective is purely to document a trend from as neutral a perspective as possible.

[2] Arthur Schopenhauer, *Die Welt als Wille und Vorstellung, Band II*, Vol. II of *Sämtliche Werke* (Wiesbaden: Eberhard Brockhaus, 1949), p. 407.

[3] Christopher Janaway, *Schopenhauer* (Oxford: Oxford University Press, 1994), p. 100.

interpretation with every generation.[4] (The misinterpretation of his work by the Nazis to suit their own Fascist ends earned him singular notoriety.) The major reason for this diversity of interpretation is that Nietzsche frequently cannot be taken literally: his complex and even self-contradictory style makes interpretation infamously difficult. Nietzsche will be remembered most of all for his declaration of the 'death of God'[5] and for his preaching of the 'Übermensch' ('Superman') who 'overcomes'[6] Europe's stagnant society. We might also mention here Søren Kierkegaard, considered the 'father' of modern Existentialist philosophy, who, unlike Schopenhauer and Nietzsche, was a Christian believer. This different perspective allows him profound insights into the consequences for the individual who is unable or unwilling to believe in God. Kierkegaard's analysis of 'anxiety' (or, in its German translation, *Angst*) in *The Concept of Anxiety*[7] and of 'despair' in *The Sickness unto Death*[8] points forward to commonplaces of twentieth-century literature, where individuals find themselves lost in a meaningless existence.

These ideas about life and the order of the universe are current also in literature. The sense of a world divorced from an Absolute rapidly becomes a *topos* in Romanticism: in the German context, for example, Heinrich von Kleist laments that 'das Paradies ist verriegelt'[9] ('Paradise is locked'). It is also worth mentioning the poetry of Friedrich Hölderlin, of which Cernuda was very fond.[10] Hölderlin's poetry frequently gives expression to his being

---

[4] For an overview of this, see Peter Pütz, *Friedrich Nietzsche* (Stuttgart: J. B. Metzlersche Verlagsbuchhandlung, 1967), pp. 6–16.

[5] For example, in *Die fröhliche Wissenschaft* (*The Gay Science*), section 125, we read 'Gott ist tot! Gott bleibt tot!' ('God is dead! God remains dead!') (Friedrich Nietzsche, *Werke in drei Bänden*, ed. Karl Schlechta (München: Carl Hanser, 1954–56), II, p. 127).

[6] In *Also sprach Zarathustra* we read (*Werke*, II, p. 279):

Ich lehre euch den Übermenschen. Der Mensch ist etwas, das überwunden werden soll.

(*Mine is the doctrine of the superman.* Man is something to be overcome.)

[7] Kierkegaard defines 'anxiety' as 'the dizziness of freedom, which emerges when the spirit wants to posit the synthesis and freedom looks down into its own possibility, laying hold of finiteness to support itself' (Søren Kierkegaard, *Kierkegaard's Writings*, ed. and trans. H. V. Hong and E. H. Hong (Princeton: Princeton University Press, 1980), VIII, p. 61). See also Patrick Gardiner, *Kierkegaard* (Oxford: Oxford University Press, 1988), pp. 108–09, and Alastair Hannay, *Kierkegaard* (London: Routledge, 1991), pp. 164–65.

[8] As Hannay comments (p. 34), 'The sickness of *despair* ... is not to face death in the expectation of eternal life.'

[9] Heinrich von Kleist, 'Über das Marionettentheater', in *Werke in einem Band*, ed. Helmut Sembdner (München: Carl Hanser, 1966), p. 804.

[10] Luis Cernuda, 'Historial de un libro', in *Prosa I*, Vol. II of *Obra completa*, ed. Derek Harris and Luis Maristany (Madrid: Ediciones Siruela, 1993–94), p. 640. All subsequent

caught between two opposing poles: religious faith and doubt. The 'mystery of divine love'[11] is explored for example in 'Patmos',[12] while the sense of humanity as distanced from an unattainable Absolute is clear in 'Brot und Wein' ('Bread and Wine'):

> Aber Freund! wir kommen zu spät. Zwar leben die Götter,
> Aber über dem Haupt droben in anderer Welt.

> (But, my friend, we have come too late. True, the gods are living, but above our heads, up there in a different world.)[13]

This is an idea which particularly attracted Cernuda,[14] but we should take care not to forget that such religious doubts are becoming commonplace. It is therefore not surprising to find a parallel process within the Spanish literary context. The hold of religion has however been stronger in Spain than in northern Europe, and thus the Romantic literature of Spain is rather slower to abandon entirely a Christian world view. Rosalía de Castro, for example, gives voice to a combination of despair, doubt and faith.[15] Similarly, the writings of the earlier Duque de Rivas express a comparable degree of despair, and a greater degree of doubt than Rosalía's poetry. In the play *Don Álvaro o la fuerza del sino*, for example, Don Álvaro speaks in Act III, scene iii, of 'el cielo' 'con su ceño furibundo',[16] suggesting a God who is distant and uninterested in humanity. Much more radical, although still never abandoning theology, is the later writer Miguel de Unamuno, who,

---

references to Cernuda's work will be to this edition. For convenience, only the title of the relevant volume will subsequently be given.

[11] L. S. Salzberger, *Hölderlin* (Cambridge: Bowes and Bowes, 1952), p. 41.

[12] Friedrich Hölderlin, *Selected Verse*, ed. and trans. Michael Hamburger (London: Anvil Press Poetry, 1986), pp. 193–203.

[13] Hölderlin, p. 111.

[14] See for example 'A las estatuas de los dioses' from *Invocaciones*, discussed below, pp. 16–18.

[15] Evidence of this tension can be seen in for example poem 109 of *En las orillas del Sar* (Rosalía de Castro, *En las orillas del Sar*, ed. Marina Mayoral, 3rd ed. (Madrid: Castalia, 1989), p. 172):

> Y alzando al cielo la mirada ansiosa
> busco a tu Padre en el espacio inmenso,
> como el piloto en la tormenta busca
> la luz del faro que le guíe al puerto.

[16] Duque de Rivas, *Don Álvaro o la fuerza del sino*, ed. Donald L. Shaw (Madrid: Castalia, 1986), pp. 116–17. See also Richard A. Cardwell, '*Don Álvaro* or the Force of Cosmic Injustice', *Studies in Romanticism*, 12 (1973), especially 562.

devastated by the tragic death of his son in 1904, was terrified of dying himself. A recurrent theme of his writing is the desperate desire for onto-logical security which ultimately could only be found in a Christianity he was unable unquestioningly to accept. The protagonist of his novel *Niebla*, Augusto Pérez, for example, suffers from a Kierkegaardian 'ansia de inmortalidad'.[17] Particularly disturbing in Unamuno's work is the profusion of philosophical, theological and psychological questions which find no real answers, a feature particularly common in twentieth-century writers.

This is no more than the briefest overview of the general trend towards the abandonment of faith in an ordered universe, and the examples chosen will inevitably appear somewhat arbitrary. More important is the fact that it is into this context of doubt which the writings of Luis Cernuda should be placed. Before turning to Luis Cernuda, however, we should not ignore his contemporaries. It is amongst the writers of his own generation, usually re-ferred to as the Generation of 1927, that we find the most fertile period of poetic achievement in the early part of the twentieth century in Spain. Nonetheless, even a superficial understanding of the poetry of the 1927 Generation is enough to illustrate the greater value in analysing Cernuda's poetry against a more general background of a European crisis of faith than as a part of his own contemporary poetic circle. This is due to the fact that, despite their being referred to as a 'Generation', there is little which could be said to unite them. Comparative studies of their poetry are likely to con-centrate almost as much on the differences between them as they are on the similarities. Three elements in particular are however frequently cited as central to their being considered a 'Generation': the influence of Juan Ramón Jiménez, the date of 1927, and the relative influence of literary fash-ion in more general terms. Juan Ramón Jiménez did exert some influence on the early poetry of various members of the Generation, although such an in-fluence requires, variable as it is, to be assessed on an individual basis rather than on the group as a whole.[18] As far as the date of 1927 is concerned, it is significant, first, in that it marks the tercentenary of Góngora's death: many commemorative activities were organised by members of the Generation.

---

[17] Miguel de Unamuno, *Niebla*, 18th ed. (Madrid: Espasa-Calpe, 1980), p. 154.

[18] Perhaps the most obvious points of contact between Juan Ramón and the 1927 Genera-tion are introspection, formal rigour and, above all, Symbolism. As Michael P. Predmore comments about the rôle of Symbolism, 'una nueva modalidad de ordenar y estructurar los poemas dentro de un conjunto más amplio, dentro de un sistema simbólico: tal es el legado del *Diario* a la generación que le sigue' (*La poesía hermética de Juan Ramón Jiménez. El 'Diario' como centro de su mundo poético* (Madrid: Gredos, 1973), p. 230). We should not however forget that French poetry also had its part to play in all of these areas, and it is difficult to make any useful global statements about direct lines of in-fluence.

Second, Juan Ramón Jiménez publicly refused to attend the celebrations, and the resentment this engendered caused a marked conscious decrease of his influence, such as it was, on their poetry. This change in influence has resulted in the popular understanding of the date as a watershed in many of their poetic careers.[19] This is however far too convenient and simplistic, first, because it tends to exaggerate the influence of Juan Ramón,[20] and second, because it suggests there was a sudden marked change in the Generation's poetic development in 1927, which is simply inaccurate. The pre-1927 poetry is certainly not all uniform in its conception and execution, and the changes which are visible in individual poets' later collections can frequently be traced as developing from the earlier poetry.[21]

More important than such questions is the relative influence of literary fashion. There are two fashions which found most widespread acceptance: the return to traditional verse forms,[22] followed by an adoption of the almost diametrically opposed movement of Surrealism. Such formal issues do however reveal little about the concerns of the individual poets. As far as themes are concerned, they are rather less similar. In the broadest terms, the earlier poetry is frequently more joyful, while the later poetry more tragic and tortured. There are however so many exceptions to the rule that it is debatable whether such a generalisation is really of any use at all.[23] Perhaps more common than anything else in the poetry of the Generation of 1927 is however an inward-looking tendency, where it is either the individual, or even purely aesthetic concerns, which matter most. Those who did broaden the scope of their interest, especially in their Surrealist poetry, tended to do so

[19] See Geoffrey W. Connell, 'Introduction', in *Spanish Poetry of the Grupo Poético de 1927* (Oxford: Pergamon, 1977), p. 14.

[20] As Amancio Sabugo Abril comments, 'Juan Ramón ... tiene seguidores de su poesía en poetas del 27, pero no discípulos' ('Teoría y práctica de la poesía. (De Juan Ramón a Cernuda)', *Cuadernos Hispanoamericanos*, No. 536 (1995), 131). For an informative overview of the far-from-easy relationship between Juan Ramón and the 1927 poets, see C. B. Morris, *A Generation of Spanish Poets 1920–1936* (Cambridge: Cambridge University Press, 1969), pp. 5–11.

[21] There is not the space to embark upon an analysis of such a major topic here, but, to take one brief example, the powerful expression of the loss of paradise in Alberti's *Sobre los ángeles* is surely more of a progression from the attitude of wistful longing present in much of his earlier *Marinero en tierra* than a new beginning.

[22] Some of this may well be attributable to Juan Ramón Jiménez, but French influences also had their part to play.

[23] Guillén, for example, throughout his poetic career, expressed his joy in life and the world, while Alberti's persona in *Marinero en tierra*, as mentioned, is both joyful and wistfully longing for escape, and then in *Sobre los ángeles* mourning the loss of paradise. Aleixandre, meanwhile, speaks of pleasurable fulfilment and of pain in *La destrucción o el amor*. There are no constants.

more on a social or political level. These various aspects, and especially the degree of introspection, perhaps account for the fact that it is hard to make useful comparisons between them and, more importantly for the present study, to fit them neatly into the context of the crisis of faith.

The poetry of Luis Cernuda is, as suggested, even for a group of poets as loosely connected as the Generation of 1927, more on the margins of that generation. Cernuda had plenty of reason to be on its fringes, as a brief glance at his biography will establish. Born on the 21st of September, 1902 in Seville, where he also grew up, he was geographically on the literary fringes of Spain. In addition, his first collection of poetry, *Perfil del Aire*, published in 1927, received a rather lukewarm reception by critics. In particular the comparisons made with Guillén were a source of considerable disillusionment for the young poet, who found his poetic identity cast more in terms of Guillén than as an individual in his own right.[24] The bitterness this instilled in him alienated and marginalised him still further.

Cernuda did however become more integrated into literary circles when he moved to Madrid in 1928, where he stayed until 1938, apart from six months in Toulouse in 1929. It was however at the end of the 1920s that he realised that he was a homosexual, and this distanced him irreconcilably from mainstream society. He did however continue to write, and the first edition of *La realidad y el deseo* was published in 1936, to much more favourable critical acclaim than *Perfil del Aire*.

Cernuda's isolation was however to increase substantially in the years that followed. In February, 1938, he left Spain to give a series of lectures in England, but he was never to return. On his journey back, news of the development of the Civil War prevented his return, and he went back to England, before moving to Glasgow in 1939 where he worked as a *lector* at Glasgow University until 1943. Both the city and the university he loathed, and he was delighted to leave Glasgow in 1943 to take up a post at Cambridge University before moving to London in 1945 and then the United States in 1947, which initially he did prefer to the United Kingdom. Greatest respite did however come when he moved to Mexico in 1952 where he felt at home, but by this time his poetic achievements were beginning to wane,

---

[24] Cernuda's poetry has been read as the creation of a 'mito personal' (see for example Luis Maristany, *La realidad y el deseo. Luis Cernuda* (Barcelona: Laia, 1982), p. 33, or César Real Ramos, 'La raíz de *la diferencia* de Luis Cernuda: La visión mítica de la realidad', *Anales de la Literatura Española Contemporánea*, 15 (1990), 117), whereby the act of creation is in itself a creation of an individual identity. This explains to an extent his sense of anguish at being compared so closely with Guillén, although it is debatable whether Cernuda's poetic identity and actual identity can be equated, and restrictive to understand the whole of *La realidad y el deseo* in such terms.

and his divorcement from the Generation of 1927 was now total. Visa problems forced him to return to the United States, which after Mexico had little to offer Cernuda, and he spent as much time as possible in Mexico, where he died suddenly on the 5th of November, 1963.

In stressing the philosophical, literary and biographical backgrounds against which Cernuda's poetry was written, we have inevitably concentrated on thematic concerns rather than formal ones, but formal concerns are just as important. In particular there is a methodological background against which the reading of Cernuda's, or indeed any, poetry must be set. Just as a crisis of faith has changed the way people look at the world, so too linguistic philosophy and literary theory have changed forever the way we approach literary texts. The writings of a range of theoreticians, such as Derrida, Abrams, Iser, Bloom, Miller, etc., have in their various ways highlighted the problems inherent in the interpretative process. The Post-Structuralists in particular have emphasised the problematic and even arbitrary nature of language and meaning. The problems are compounded by the fact that, even although an author's creation is a product of the intellectual and cultural background in which it was written, it is folly to imagine that the exact parameters of that background can be known precisely by the reader. By the same token, every reader is a product of his or her own culture and background, and this will in turn affect the way in which he or she responds to a literary text. A definitive reading therefore does not exist. Whatever the poet's attitude to the crisis of faith, there is a 'crisis of interpretation' which no reader can avoid. It is however too extreme to suggest that reading 'is always a misreading'.[25] Certainty and security of meaning cannot be guaranteed, but there is at least a large degree of semantic common ground. After all, if there were none, any act of reading would logically be pointless. While there is a range of signification, that range is, in my opinion, finite, not infinite. Nonetheless, the complexity of interpretation which this engenders must never be underestimated.

It is into the context of crisis of faith which our reading of Cernuda's poetry may now be placed, beginning with the way in which that crisis of faith finds its expression. That crisis is however only one aspect of the poetry. Just as important is the desire to rebuild order in the face of the chaos of the modern world, seeking both absolute order and also order in the material world, in the realms of 'love' and the erotic, and in art. As the overview of Cernuda's life and background suggests, however, the searches for order will always be problematic.

---

[25] Harold Bloom, *A Map of Misreading* (Oxford: Oxford University Press, 1975), p. 3. Bloom is discussing in the first place the creative process, but the principle would appear to apply to all acts of reading.

CHAPTER TWO

ORDER INTO CHAOS: THE LOSS OF THE ABSOLUTE

Luis Cernuda: Poet of Eros, *Ethics or Crisis of Faith?*

We have chosen to foreground the crisis and loss of faith as central to *La realidad y el deseo*. At first sight this may seem curious, for probably its most obvious thematic concern centres, not around such overtly existential matters, as around love and erotic interest. Certainly the French subtitle 'À mon seul désir' points towards an erotic import. Furthermore, the centrality of *Eros* to Cernuda's own existence, from which his poetry assuredly springs,[1] is beyond question. Harris is able to go so far as to claim that, in poem VII of *Primeras Poesías*, there can be found 'the emphatic proclamation of love's dream as the sole aim and purpose of his existence'.[2] In the context of *La realidad y el deseo* as a whole, however, Harris sees *Eros* as subordinate to an 'ethical' concern, whereby the poet creates his own persona and identity, true to himself, in poetry, which then becomes the 'truth of himself'.[3] Silver on the other hand sums up the entire collection as the expression of Cernuda's 'thirst for eternity',[4] although Silver does not argue so much for existential or metaphysical concerns *per se* as for a Romantic nostalgic longing for a lost Edenic paradise of pre-adolescent innocence, where eroticism is still a key issue.

---

[1] María Cristina C. Mabrey, in *La obra poética de Luis Cernuda: entre mito y deseo* (Madrid: Pliegos, 1996), sets out consciously to depart from the 'biographical' approach to Cernuda's poetry, stating categorically that Cernuda's 'intención al escribir poesía no era dar la crónica de su vida' (p. 42) and that 'se ha propuesto ... abandonar los procedimientos de la crítica tradicional que tiende a ilustrar la obra con la biografía del autor' (p. 173). Mabrey is right to state that this sort of approach creates 'una visión muy limitada' (p. 41), but it is pointless to ignore Cernuda's biography, not least because, in the opening sentence of 'Historial de un libro', he speaks of 'la historia del acontecer personal que se halla tras los versos de *La realidad y el deseo*' (*Prosa I*, p. 625).

[2] Derek Harris, *Luis Cernuda. A Study of the Poetry* (London: Tamesis, 1973), p. 26.

[3] Harris, pp. 148–79. In particular Harris stresses the 'search for an environment where his personality can be fully realised' which the poetry reflects (p. 176).

[4] Philip W. Silver, *Et in Arcadia Ego: A Study of the Poetry of Luis Cernuda* (London: Tamesis, 1965), p. 27.

The problem with both Harris' and Silver's approaches is essentially the same: a desire to unite and simplify Cernuda's poetry under a general heading. While it is undeniable that his poetry tells of the problems when the dream of desire ('deseo') encounters 'la realidad', it is crucial to establish that, fundamental to any thorough understanding of *La realidad y el deseo* is not so much an insistence on its unity as an appreciation of its complexity and even at times contradiction. While we can uphold Harris' interpretation of Cernuda's poetry as an ethical concern inasmuch as he remains true to himself throughout his creative career, we must be careful not to exaggerate this beyond the broadest of categories.[5]

To what extent then is it fair to highlight the crisis of faith as central to *La realidad y el deseo*? Is such an approach not open to the same charge of generalisation and simplification? Oddly enough it is that which helps to illustrate the complexity, because it foregrounds both order and chaos, which coexist in dialectical opposition throughout *La realidad y el deseo*. Not only that, it also demonstrates, first, the interplay of erotic and existential concerns, and second, the steady emergence of the existential as a theme in its own right. While the 'ethical concern' is more of a preoccupation or motivating force lying behind the poetry than a theme proper and can therefore be placed to one side, our first obligation must be to establish more precisely the relative significance of *Eros* and more general existential issues. It is admittedly the erotic impulse which predominates in Cernuda's first collection, *Primeras Poesías*. This collection is concerned with the experiences of Cernuda's adolescent persona. The poems of *Primeras Poesías* are broadly similar, with confinement, indolence and lack of fulfilment appearing time and again throughout the collection. Poem XVI is a good example of the main thrust of *Primeras Poesías* in general:

> La noche a la ventana.
> Ya la luz se ha dormido.
> Guardada está la dicha
> En el aire vacío.
>
> Levanta entre las hojas,
> Tú, mi aurora futura;

---

[5] Harris does acknowledge that the 'complexity and contradiction of Cernuda's character are reflected faithfully in his poetry', but insists that 'the poetry itself absorbs these contradictions into an organic unity' (p. 179). What is perhaps most stimulating about *La realidad y el deseo* is that, considered as a whole, it presents a thoroughly disunited, fragmentary picture.

No dejes que me anegue
El sueño entre sus plumas.

Pero escapa el deseo
Por la noche entreabierta,
Y en límpido reposo
El cuerpo se contempla.

Acreciente la noche
Sus sombras y su calma,
Que a su rosal la rosa
Volverá la mañana.

Y una vaga promesa
Acunando va el cuerpo.
En vano dichas busca
Por el aire el deseo.[6]

Running through this poem are conflicting positive and negative emotions. On the one hand there is an impression of promise, hope and vitality, but on the other there is frustration and confinement. Frustration and confinement are both conveyed succinctly in the first line: 'noche' points to lack of light and the lack of daytime vitality, while 'la ventana' is representative throughout *Primeras Poesías* of the barrier which exists between the adolescent persona and the world upon which he gazes. Yet in this stanza there is also hope, for 'la dicha' is 'guardada', although the fact that the 'aire' is 'vacío' again injects a sinister aura. The principal focus of hope for the persona is then made more explicit in the second stanza, with the reference to 'Tú, mi aurora futura', although the exact nature of this 'tú' is never defined very closely. Does it refer to another person? To nature? To a dream? Ultimately we cannot say with any real certainty, but what matters most is the very existence of hope as a counterpart to frustration.

Once the conflict between hope and frustration is set up, it continues and develops throughout the rest of the poem. In the third stanza, when the erotic element comes to the fore, the sense of the persona's isolation is painfully apparent, for he is now forced into sterile self-contemplation. The tension then remains unresolved right to the end of the poem: in the fourth stanza 'las sombras' of night contrast with 'su calma', while the final stanza

---

[6] Cernuda, *Poesía completa*, pp. 117–18. Page references to this volume of the *Obra completa* will hereafter be cited parenthetically in the text.

somewhat enigmatically speaks of a 'vaga promesa', contrasting with the vanity of seeking happiness 'por el aire'. It is difficult to draw definitive conclusions as to the nature of the 'vaga promesa', but more important is the impression of someone dreaming hopefully of some kind of meaningful interaction and fulfilment who, while he is isolated, has not yet experienced enough of the chaos of the world to give in to despair.

Therein lies the main focus of *Primeras Poesías*. Despite this, there are suggestions of a significance in these adolescent experiences which extends beyond the primary concerns of sexual awakening, hope and indolence to encompass more general existential ideas. (This is a preparation for the later poetry, where there is a development towards quite specifically existential and metaphysical concerns *per se*.) Poem VII of *Primeras Poesías* is a good illustration of this duality. At first sight it is a typical example of this collection: an unfulfilled erotic impulse, combined with a sense of confinement, indolence and alienation:

> Existo, bien lo sé,
> Porque le transparenta
> El mundo a mis sentidos
> Su amorosa presencia.
>
> Mas no quiero estos muros,
> Aire infiel a sí mismo,
> Ni esas ramas que cantan
> En el aire dormido. (111)

This poem contains again an element of conflict between positive and negative emotions. In the first stanza the 'amorosa presencia' is the confirmation of existence and thus evidently a sign of hope and expectation, although the verb 'existir' does not suggest as great a degree of vibrant vitality as 'vivir'. There is however a considerable tension between stanza one and stanza two, for the second stanza is suffused with a deep sense of frustration, isolation and alienation. The persona needs genuine experience and interaction and cannot be satisfied by mere vicarious excitement. All of this is however still very much consonant with what has already been seen in *Primeras Poesías*. The wording of the closing stanza of the poem on the other hand lends it a much broader scope:

> Soy memoria de hombre;
> Luego, nada. Divinas,
> La sombra y la luz siguen
> Con la tierra que gira. (112)

The sense of alienation and despair in these lines is obvious, although the phrasing is rather enigmatic. Interpretation of the stanza can however be aided if it is considered in terms of potential Neo-Platonic overtones. In Platonic terms, 'The soul before birth ... was acquainted with the world of Ideas; knowledge of the Ideas in this life is achieved through the soul's recollection of what it has previously known'.[7] There could be an echo of this in the line 'Soy memoria de hombre': while superficially the meaning is surely that his existence is so pointless that vibrant vitality is, even in adolescence, no more than a distant memory, on a deeper level the relationship between present life and past memories is analogous with the relationship of imperfect human life to the perfect glory of the soul's former life in the world of Ideas. In addition, the phrases 'Divinas,/La sombra y la luz siguen/Con la tierra que gira' lend a kind of cosmic or universal dimension, where there is a split between the world and the persona. If light and shadow are 'divine', then they could represent that world of Ideas which the persona can only recollect. Thus the *world* appears more ordered at this stage, an idea which is reinforced by the phrasing 'la tierra que gira', 'girar' suggesting the harmonious movement of the Platonic spheres. The *persona* however has no access to this order, although this ordered world is in itself no more than a very temporary perception. It must be stressed that this constitutes no more than an evocation at this stage, but these lines do nonetheless demonstrate that we are witnessing the beginnings of the expression of Cernuda's more general world view.[8]

Indications of such a broad scope for Cernuda's poetry are admittedly vague in the earliest collections. It is not until the third collection, *Un río, un amor*, that the way in which Cernuda expresses his world view really begins to become clear. While it is certainly true that this collection and the fourth, *Los placeres prohibidos* (both influenced by Surrealism), were written as the result of a disastrous amatory experience,[9] to understand them only in those terms is severely limiting. 'Decidme anoche', in *Un río, un amor*, gives a clear expression to the fact that Cernuda deems the failed amatory experience to have an existential, metaphysical significance. It is evident

---

[7] *The Concise Oxford Companion to Classical Literature*, ed. Margaret C. Howatson and Ian Chilvers (Oxford: Oxford University Press, 1993), p. 429. I am indebted to Professor D. Gareth Walters of Glasgow University for this suggestion.

[8] Terence McMullan informs us that 'Soy memoria de hombre' also recalls a Reverdy poem 'Mémoire d'homme', but that Cernuda 'makes a metaphor of it', but gives no explanation of this metaphor ('Luis Cernuda and the Emerging Influence of Pierre Reverdy', *Revue de Littérature Comparée*, 49 (1975), 138).

[9] See Harris, p. 34.

from the very beginning of the poem that Cernuda's intention is to reformulate his experience into a much more generalised poetic statement:

> La presencia del frío junto al miedo invisible
> Hiela a gotas oscuras la sangre entre la niebla,
> Entre la niebla viva, hacia la niebla vaga
> Por un espacio ciego de rígidas espinas. (148)

The emotional torment is instantly apparent. The freezing of the blood, symbol of life itself, constructs an image of death, and the only thing said to be alive is the 'niebla', heightening the sense of unreality about the persona's existence. Furthermore, there is a preponderance of words denoting dimness and darkness, creating an atmosphere of gloom, while the presence of the 'rígidas espinas' conveys the pain and anguish of living in a hostile environment. The persona himself however has only the vaguest presence in this opening stanza: 'miedo' and 'sangre' are the only two elements which suggest his existence. This vagueness creates an abstraction; it draws the poem towards a more general statement about humanity. The human presence then does become more explicit in the second stanza:

> Con vida misteriosa quizá los hombres duermen
> Mientras desiertos blancos representan el mundo;
> Son espacios pequeños como tímida mano,
> Silenciosos, vacíos bajo una luz sin vida. (149)

We must recognise the human presence as 'los hombres' rather than a specific individual. Cernuda has moved away from talking about himself and his situation to meditate upon the situation of humanity in general. It is interesting to note at this stage the degree of uncertainty conveyed: the fact that the 'vida' is said to be 'misteriosa', and that subject and main verb are prefaced by the indefinite 'quizá', lends an aura of a persona musing bewildered upon human life. 'Decidme anoche' is in no way intended as 'amateur philosophy', but rather a poetic statement whereby it does not matter if definitive answers cannot be found. More important is the way that Cernuda has constructed his poem so as to transcend his specific situation. In addition to 'los hombres', we have in this second stanza the evocation of 'desiertos blancos' as representative of the world, surely an image of dryness and sterility, reinforced by the image of a scorching sun which damages and dries up ('luz *sin* vida') rather than brings life and hope. Furthermore, the fact that the second and last words of the stanza are both 'vida' lends it prominence and is therefore demonstrative that it is a general concept which is paramount.

In 'Decidme anoche' there is an interplay of two basic themes: grief and alienation on the one hand and human life and a world without direction on the other. The concentration on life and the world in the second stanza continues in the third stanza, and then the fourth stanza returns to the theme of grief:

> El dolor también busca, errante entre la noche,
> Tras la sombra fugaz de algún gozo indefenso;
> Y sus pálidos pasos callados se entrelazan,
> Incesante fantasma con mirada de hastío. (149)

This stanza has a complex grammatical construction. The subject of the verb 'busca' in line one is postponed until line four ('Incesante fantasma'). We are therefore only told in line one that 'something' is seeking 'dolor'. (On an initial reading we could imagine that 'dolor' is in fact the subject of 'busca'.) The result is a vagueness, which draws the focus away from the specific to the general. When we finally encounter the subject, this generalising process is continued, because it is no more than a vague 'fantasma', not an identifiable individual: we are now explicitly invited to assume that this experience has a significance beyond the circumstances of one individual.

The process of moving beyond the circumstances of one individual to a more general statement about the world reaches its climax with the incorporation into the poem of a specifically supra-human level. This is first suggested in the third stanza, and is made explicit three stanzas later:

> Sí, la tierra está sola; a solas canta, habla,
> Con una voz tan débil que no la alcanza el cielo;
> Canta risas o plumas atravesando espacio
> Bajo un sol calcinante reflejado en la arena. (149)

There is a vivid picture of a world divorced from the harmonious, transcendent order which once held sway. The poem has now moved definitively from the circumstances of a tortured individual to a vision of the whole world. It should however be stressed that, since this is poetry and not philosophy, this is not a particularly systematic process of individual experience leading to metaphysical contemplation. All the various spheres of concern are present together as integral parts of a single complex expression. The 'ethical' concern is there in the genesis of the poem, imbuing it with Cernuda's own personal experiences, but at the same time completely transcending those individual circumstances to meditate upon and convey an impression of the pain which *Eros* can cause, not just to Luis Cernuda, but to any member of society so afflicted. Beyond this lies the poet of the 'crisis of faith' who muses bewildered upon a senseless world. As *La realidad y el deseo* then progresses, the desire to give expression to metaphysical ideas and questions steadily increases. Indeed, in some of the later poetry, when Cernuda was in exile (most especially collections VII, *Las nubes,* and VIII, *Como quien espera el alba*), the erotic theme all but disappears altogether, with poems which deal exclusively with the problems of man's existence and with his relationship to the Absolute. It is however important to be aware that those later poems in which existential matters are of primary importance are but a development and intensification of traits already in evidence in the earlier poetry.

The Age of Order

Existential and metaphysical concerns are therefore a primary focus within *La realidad y el deseo.* It is appropriate now to embark upon the analysis proper of Cernuda's depiction of the crisis of faith. But what is it first of all that becomes lost? While it is necessary to bear in mind that Cernuda starts out from the premise that the universe is without order, this does not mean that there is no indication of a bygone era of order, divorced as it is from modern reality. On the contrary, we are provided with many insights into this bygone era.

The keynote in Cernuda's portrayal of a former age of order is nostalgia for what is gone. There is indeed a very strong sense of a Romantic yearning for the past. What is more, when Cernuda looks towards an age of order and more specifically towards a time when there was widespread belief in abso-lute order (i.e., where the cosmos is ultimately controlled by an Absolute), his image is always extremely positive, contrasting starkly with the chaos of the modern world. It is a theme which is explored with greatest intensity in the poetry of *Invocaciones,* which shows a marked influence of the German Romantic poet Friedrich Hölderlin. One prominent area of overlap between the two poets is in reference to the gods of Antiquity. Hölderlin's 'Diotima' is a good example of his exploitation of the theme:

> Komm und besänftige mir, die du einst Elemente versöhntest
> Wonne der himmlischen Muse das Chaos der Zeit,
> Ordne den tobenden Kampf mit Friedenstönen des Himmels
> Bis in der sterblichen Brust sich das entzweite vereint,
> ...
> Denn Diotima lebt, wie die zarten Blüten im Winter,
> Reich an eigenem Geist sucht sie die Sonne doch auch.
> Aber die Sonne des Geists, die schöne Welt ist hinunter,
> Und in frostiger Nacht zanken Orkane sich nur.

(Bliss of the heavenly muse, now come and soothe for me, as once you reconciled elements, the chaos of this age! Temper the raging battle with Heaven's peaceful music until in the mortal heart all that is severed unites, ... For Diotima lives, like delicate blossoms in winter, rich in inherent spirit, yet she seeks the sun. But the sun of the spirit, the lovelier world, has gone down, and only quarrelling gales clash in the frosty night.)[10]

This poem is structured fundamentally around a binary opposition set up between a former age on the one hand, when Diotima exerted her peaceful and harmonious influence upon the world, and the 'tobenden Kampf' which is modern life on the other. It is clear that, without the gods, there is only chaos. All that is positive is related to Diotima (in particular 'versöhnen', 'Wonne', 'Friedenstönen', 'die zarten Blüten'), while what the persona experiences is steeped in negativity: 'das entzweite', 'die frostige Nacht', 'Orkane', 'sich zanken'. It is particularly interesting that Diotima is said to be alive, but now indifferent to the fate of humanity: this in itself intensifies the personal sense of tragedy and loss.

The various ideas of former order, present chaos and divine indifference[11] all find their counterparts in *La realidad y el deseo*. In the last poem of *Invocaciones*, 'A las estatuas de los dioses', Cernuda makes use of imagery which has much in common with Hölderlin's picture of the gods of Antiquity. The opening of the poem is concerned primarily with what that bygone era was like:

Hermosas y vencidas soñáis,
Vueltos los ciegos ojos hacia el cielo,
Mirando las remotas edades
De titánicos hombres,
Cuyo amor os daba ligeras guirnaldas
Y la olorosa llama se alzaba
Hacia la luz divina, su hermana celeste.

Reflejo de vuestra verdad, las criaturas
Adictas y libres como el agua iban;
Aún no había mordido la brillante maldad
Sus cuerpos llenos de majestad y gracia. (246)

---

[10] Hölderlin, pp. 10–11.
[11] The question of indifference will be discussed later. See below, p. 29.

The sense of nostalgia is very strong in this poem, lending it a definite aura of Romantic longings for the unattainable ideal. This is not insignificant, for *Invocaciones*, influenced as it is by Hölderlin, is probably the most overtly 'Romantic' of all the collections of *La realidad y el deseo*.[12] As with Hölderlin's 'Diotima', then, this longed-for era is remote: since the loss of order has already taken place, it is a world to which the persona has no access. It is interesting that the persona in the initial stanzas of the poem largely leaves himself out of the situation. (It is only really the use of the second person which alerts us to his presence at all.) It is only in the final stanza that his presence is obvious. This clearly has considerable affinity with the process of generalisation in 'Decidme anoche', for it is given to the statues themselves rather than a human presence to evoke the bygone era. This suggests two rather conflicting ideas: on the one hand 'statues of the gods' must have a more direct link with the period when they were worshipped. On the other hand they are no more than inanimate objects, thus emphasising the sheer unreality of this age of order and its total divorcement from modernity. It is a myth and can never be more than such.

This mythical world is not merely remote. It is a Golden Age, a paradise, where 'titánicos hombres' lived, where 'amor' and 'luz divina' existed. Moreover, the opening lines of the second stanza refer not just to the 'dioses' but also to the 'criaturas': in this former age of order individuals lived in security and harmony.[13] The choice of epithets linked to 'criaturas' is also striking: while 'libres' is a positive quality, the significance of 'adictas' is less immediately apparent, especially since there appears to be nothing in particular to which they might be 'adictas'. Does it suggest a state

---

[12] Care should be taken not to overestimate the Romanticism in Cernuda's poetry. Certainly it frequently has much in common with Romantic ideas, but it is something of an overstatement to suggest that 'Cernuda also fits M. H. Abrams' romantic paradigm more perfectly than any previous "romantic" poet' (Silver, 'Cernuda and Spanish Romanticism: Prolegomena to a Genealogy', *Revista Hispánica Moderna*, 43 (1990), 112). See also Silver, *De la mano de Cernuda: Invitación a la poesía* (Madrid: Cátedra, 1989) for a longer discussion of the same topic. Similar, if less fully developed, ideas are also held by Robert K. Newman ('Luis Cernuda: El hombre visto a través de su poesía', *Ínsula*, Año 19, No. 207 (1964), 6), and Rafael Argullol ('Cernuda romántico', *Quimera*, 15-I-1982, pp. 29–32). Cernuda, while frequently heir to Romanticism, often transcends the boundaries of a 'romantic paradigm' with a sense of *desengaño* and radical alienation, *Angst* and even blatant cynicism. Even in *Invocaciones*, Agustín Delgado recognises that Cernuda is 'mucho más moderno que Hölderlin', noting in particular the 'soledad ... radical', although his term 'neoromántico' may equally be too restrictive, for the use of any literary categorisation is not particularly helpful (*La poética de Luis Cernuda* (Madrid: Editora Nacional, 1975), p. 179).

[13] Salvador Jiménez-Fajardo (*Luis Cernuda* (Boston: Twayne, 1978), p. 48), describes it as a 'state of grace'.

of near-intoxication with this idyll of which they (and by extension also Cernuda's dreaming persona, shadowy presence as he is at this stage in the poem) are a part? If this is the case, then there is a degree of *desengaño* in the following two lines when the 'cuerpos llenos de majestad y gracia' are contrasted with 'la brillante maldad' of modern times. This phrasing is in fact ironic in two ways: the reference to 'maldad' contrasts starkly with the glorious myth and thus to a certain extent deflates it, but curiously, the use of the adjective 'brillante' applied to 'maldad' is also unsettling. It hints that there could be something *positive* about the 'maldad': the poet is attached to the modern world, despite its chaos.[14] In the main, though, the poet is looking back to when the age of order was genuine. As mentioned above, of course, it is only genuine in a mythical world.

In the latter part of the second stanza of this poem Cernuda expresses succinctly his perception of this age of order. The strands of thought in the opening eleven lines (the gods and their effect on the community) are brought together in the last two lines of this second stanza:

En vosotros [los dioses] creían [las criaturas] y vosotros existíais;
La vida no era un delirio sombrío. (246)

The concept of faith highlights the fundamental difference between the mythical era and the modern one: the world was ordered because the world in general believed in the gods. That faith allows the gods to affect the world: without it they effectively disappear. (This does of course imply that faith itself is more important than the entity, extant or not, in which faith is placed.) This is certainly an overtly religious vision, although it is clearly not related to any specific dogma. This is not however untypical of the religiosity to be found in *La realidad y el deseo*, for Cernuda does tend to be rather vague and indiscriminate about matters of faith. In *Las nubes* he addresses the specifically Christian God in 'La visita de Dios', but that is followed by 'Resaca en Sansueña', which deals in part with a pagan god of Antiquity.[15] It is not therefore unfair to situate Cernuda's attitude towards matters religious within a general context of a crisis of faith.

---

[14] Ángel Sahuquillo postulates that the gods 'podían tener pasiones homosexuales' and therefore 'la maldad' refers to 'el saber cristiano' which has ruined the homosexual paradise. This is just plausible, and there are certainly homoerotic overtones discernible, but completely ignores the metaphysical resonances (*Federico García Lorca y la cultura de la homosexualidad. Lorca, Dalí, Cernuda, Gil-Albert, Prados y la voz silenciada del amor homosexual* (Stockholm: Stockholms universitet, 1986), p. 100).

[15] See also Harris, p. 79.

When looking towards a former ordered universe, Cernuda's vision is not limited to specifically religious concepts. While the religious element is certainly important, it is complemented by an equally important concern with the depiction of a lost primitivity, of an era lacking the 'sophistication' of the modern world (in the sense in which 'to sophisticate' means 'to deprive (a person or thing) of its natural simplicity'[16]). While this has something in common with the mythical world already discussed, there are subtle differences. In the second collection *Égloga, Elegía, Oda*, what is predominant is the image of a primitive paradise. The 'Égloga' describes an idyllic pastoral vision:

> Tan alta, sí, tan alta
> En revuelo sin brío,
> La rama el cielo prometido anhela,
> Que ni la luz asalta
> Este espacio sombrío
> Ni su divina soledad desvela.
> Hasta el pájaro cela
> Al absorto reposo
> Su delgada armonía. (128)

All is beauty, peace, order and harmony in this idyllic environment. This is the age of order evoked without reference to modernity and its 'brillante maldad' as clearly depicted in 'A las estatuas de los dioses'. It is interesting to note the lack of human presence in these lines, a feature largely maintained throughout the poem. ('Ninfas' do make an appearance, but they if anything stress the mythical aura of the scene.) This lack of significant human presence is noteworthy for at least two reasons: first, as yet another illustration of Cernuda's desire to generalise his poetry rather than to be overtly egocentric, and second, to emphasise the degree to which the whole of the natural world is in unified harmony with itself before the intrusive corrupting presence of a degenerate humanity which knows little, if anything, of prelapsarian innocence.[17] At the same time, however, it is difficult to maintain that the 'Égloga' is Cernuda's best: this first stanza, and the

---

[16] *The Concise Oxford Dictionary of Current English*, ed. R. E. Allen, 8th ed. (Oxford: Clarendon Press, 1990), p. 1160.

[17] As Catherine C. Bellver remarks, all the poems of this collection 'radiate a sense of suspended serenity identifiable with a young man still untouched by loss and failure' ('Luis Cernuda's Paragons of Mythical Beauty', *Revista Hispánica Moderna*, 43 (1990), 33).

poem as a whole, is rather quaintly over-written, marked by a rather cloyingly effusive lyricism.

Much of the 'Égloga' then proceeds in a similar vein to the first stanza,
steadily fleshing out the description of the primeval idyll with a quite remarkable lack of activity or narrative movement (so much so as to become
rather wearisome in a poem of 130 lines). The seventh stanza is however
pivotal:

> Idílico paraje
> De dulzor tan primero,
> Nativamente digno de los dioses.
> Mas ¿qué frío celaje
> Se levanta ligero,
> En cenicientas ráfagas veloces?
> Unas secretas voces
> Este júbilo ofenden
> Desde gris lontananza; (131)

The overriding impression of these lines is once again one of the paradise.
More important than this is the adjective in line two, namely 'primero',
which is the very crux of the entire poem: this is an evocation of an Edenic,
primeval age where the world is not merely beautiful and harmonic, but
magnificent in its newness. The degree of Cernuda's devotion to such a vision is underscored by the way in which he dedicates such a lengthy poem to
a description of it. It should however be stressed that, while there is a reference in line three to 'los dioses', it is not a semi-religious poem in the vein of
'A las estatuas de los dioses': rather, the reference here emphasises the picture of primeval splendour. But is there only idyll in 'Égloga'? A slightly
discordant note is in fact sounded in line four with the reference to a 'frío
celaje'. At this point the question of nostalgia starts to come into play once
again. It is a vision of an age of primitive order, certainly, but it is no more
than a vision, and as the poem draws to a close it is the contrast between the
vision and present reality which comes to the fore:

> Silencio. Ya decrecen
> Las luces que lucían.
> Ni la brisa ni el viento al aire oscuro
> Vanamente estremecen
> Con sus ondas, que abrían
> Surcos tan indolentes de azul puro.
> ¿Y qué invisible muro
> Su frontera más triste

> Gravemente levanta?
> El cielo ya no canta,
> Ni su celeste eternidad asiste
> A la luz y a las rosas,
> Sino al horror nocturno de las cosas. (132)

The suggestion of the close of the day underlines that this vision is definitively over, returning the persona to his own world. The three-line question provides an image of confinement, the 'invisible muro' cutting the persona off from the natural world of which he could only dream he was a part. At this point the nostalgia is again particularly evident. The closing four lines however add a further dimension. Ostensibly these lines refer to the darkness of nightfall, but, in his choice of the words 'cielo' and 'celeste eternidad', Cernuda points towards an almost metaphysical significance. This effectively combines the ideas of primitivity and an ordered universe into the one vision, with the result that a whole world has been created, in dream, which is not available in reality. While this is suggestive of an evasive, escapist tendency, it does not mean that Cernuda does not know what reality is: the lack of involvement of the 'cielo' and the 'celeste eternidad' at the end of the 'Égloga' are an indication of the separation between humanity and eternity,[18] which marks the return of the persona (who has been all but invisible in the poem) to the realms of 'realidad'.

There is one further aspect of the portrayal of the age of order which demands attention. In *Las nubes* there is an explicit desire for Christian faith, although it is never actually found. Thereafter there are still isolated references to a bygone age of order, but by then the sense of loss is even more irrevocable than in 'A las estatuas de los dioses'. A good example of this rather more distanced and sceptical stance is to be found in 'Hacia la tierra' from *Como quien espera el alba*, the eighth collection, where the persona not only looks back over a former age of order but also over his life:

> Cuando tiempo y distancia
> Engañan los recuerdos,
> ¿Quién lo ignora?, es amargo
> Volver. Porque interpuesto

---

[18] Manuel Ballestero discusses the whole of *Égloga, Elegía, Oda*, finding evidence that there is 'demasiada consciencia para dejarle [a Cernuda] sucumbir o a una atemporal ingenuidad restauradora o a una exquisitez esteticista' (*Poesía y reflexión: La palabra en el tiempo* (Madrid: Taurus, 1980), p. 120).

> Algo está entre los ojos
> Y la imagen primera,
> Mudando duramente
> Amor en extrañeza. (361)

The note of nostalgia is at least as strong as it is in 'A las estatuas de los dioses', but there is a bitterness in the face of loss which adds a new dimension to the idyllic presentation encountered in both *Invocaciones* and *Égloga, Elegía, Oda*. The power of the dream of adolescence is evoked in the phrases 'recuerdos', 'la imagen primera' and 'amor', but they are now transfigured beyond all recognition, destroyed by 'tiempo y distancia'. The depiction of an age of order is now no more than the vaguest presence, merging into all dreams of adolescence and innocence. This marks however a logical progression from the early poetry, for the seeds of doubt, illustrated by the disparity between dream and reality, were already evident then. Now in the closing stanzas of this poem the persona has still more to say about the age of order and his relationship to it:

> Posibles paraísos
> O infiernos ya no entiende
> El alma sino en tierra.
> Por eso el alma quiere,
>
> Cansada de los sueños
> Y los delirios tristes,
> Volver a la morada
> Suya antigua. Y unirse,
>
> Como se une la piedra
> Al fondo de su agua,
> Fatal, oscuramente,
> Con una tierra amada. (362)

These stanzas are a more direct confrontation with the tendency to dream. Now the dreams become 'de-mythified': 'Posibles paraísos/O infiernos ya no entiende/El alma *sino en tierra*.' The paradises of the 'Égloga' and of 'A las estatuas de los dioses' are divorced spatially and temporally from the persona's existence. Now there is a reorientation 'hacia la tierra': the age of order, if it is genuinely to mean anything, must exist *here and now*. The fact that there are 'paraísos *o infiernos*' is nevertheless confirmation of the debased and degenerate nature of the modern world. To a certain extent this reorientation towards the world of today could be regarded as a positive, affirmative step, but in 'Hacia la tierra' there is rather more of the abandon-ment of the vision of a bygone order than a discovery of a new one. The age of order is therefore but a distant memory.

The Loss of Order

Since the age of order is depicted as something so divorced from the modern world, there can be no question that chaos now reigns. It is however on the chaos itself that *La realidad y el deseo* dwells, rather than on the disintegration of order. This nonetheless does not exclude the poetry from providing insights into the causes of that disintegration, although there is never any systematic, straightforward presentation of linear decline. What we witness is a series of clues and hints which can be pieced together to form a cohesive picture, where it is above all the sense of loss which pre-dominates.

It must be admitted that there are few clues and hints as to the process of decline in the earliest poetry. This is not surprising: while the early poetry is distanced from the specific individual Luis Cernuda, it is still 'egocentric' and introspective inasmuch as each poem unquestionably focusses on a sin-gle adolescent persona (although he is never named and is often a very shadowy presence). It is with the more mature poetry, from *Un río, un amor* onwards, that the desire to look far beyond the individual manifests itself most clearly. That said, tiny indications do exist of the problems which will arise. As we know, the confinement and isolation of the adolescent per-sona(e) from the world outside form the crux of the early collections. It is in this relationship between persona and world that there emerge the first glimpses of disintegration and loss. In the first place, the persona's exclusion from the outside world is analogous, in poem VII of *Primeras Poesías*, with the Platonic soul's earthly exclusion from heaven.[19] In addition, this sense of exclusion suggests that the persona (and by extension humanity also) has only a minor status in the natural world as a whole. The natural world reap-pears spasmodically throughout *La realidad y el deseo*, and the attitudes towards it tend to be fairly similar. The predominant emphasis is on the positive, secure, vibrant quality which nature is seen to possess,[20] as poem I of *Primeras Poesías* illustrates:

[19] See above, pp. 11–12.
[20] See for example Andrew P. Debicki, *Estudios sobre poesía española contemporánea. La generación de 1924–1925* (Madrid: Gredos, 1968), p. 296, and also Silver, 'Cernuda, poeta ontológico', in *Luis Cernuda*, ed. Harris (Madrid: Taurus, 1977), p. 210.

Va la brisa reciente
Por el espacio esbelta,
Y en las hojas cantando
Abre una primavera.

Sobre el límpido abismo
Del cielo se divisan,
Como dichas primeras,
Primeras golondrinas.

...

En su paz la ventana
Restituye a diario
Las estrellas, el aire
Y el que estaba soñando. (107)

This poem is one of the most positive in *Primeras Poesías*, imbued with an optimism on the part of the persona for the future which the encounter with reality only serves to dismantle. Nature here has it own, confident existence. It has had complete freedom to grow in harmony with itself. In fact, the human presence is not even mentioned until the last line, and even then is only a vague 'el que ...'. The impression is that nature has no particular need of humanity. Thus, even in such an apparently optimistic poem, there are hints of the persona's exclusion rather than inclusion. This is emphasised by the reference to the window in the final stanza: the window may well be the means by which the persona sees nature framed before him, but it is supremely ironic that it also separates him from it. He has no more than a vicarious part in its vitality. This can of course at the same time suggest that nature here is itself a kind of Absolute, representative of an ordered world rather than a chaotic one,[21] but there is no indication of God reigning supreme in this poem. On the contrary, there is a distinct impression that nature is so complete in itself that, in the same way that it has no need of humanity, so too it has no need of God. Not only that, in a traditional theocratic understanding of the world, God is above man, who in turn is above nature. That is far from the case here: even if nature does not need man, *he* needs nature, for the note of hope and promise is based on the persona's ability to take part (albeit vicariously) in the natural world. Most disconcerting of all, however, is the very last word of the poem, 'soñando'. What will

---

[21] There are certainly occasions when Cernuda's view of nature can border on the pantheistic. See for example 'El viento de septiembre entre los chopos' (225–27) or 'Jardín' (332–34).

happen when the persona wakes up? It seems more than likely that the seeds of destruction are already sown.

Whatever man's status in the world as a whole, he nonetheless takes centre stage when the loss of order is explored in greatest depth. Above all it is the question of man's doubt and faithlessness which has a major rôle to play. In 'A las estatuas de los dioses', the key-note of the bygone 'Golden Age' is the faith of the 'criaturas'. One of the most telling steps in the decline from order into chaos is taken when faith disintegrates. It is relevant to return to a stanza of 'Decidme anoche' quoted earlier:[22]

> Sí, la tierra está sola; a solas canta, habla,
> Con una voz tan débil que no la alcanza el cielo;
> Canta risas o plumas atravesando espacio
> Bajo un sol calcinante reflejado en la arena. (149)

For Cernuda, the earth, and thus all those on it, is now alone. Humans only have each other with whom to communicate and their efforts to reach out to another realm are feeble and ineffective. Furthermore, the very fact that 'el cielo' 'no alcanza' the earth's voice suggests that heaven takes no part in the communicative process either. In addition, while the phrase 'Canta risas o plumas' could sound optimistic, the sense of a lack of ultimate order to the universe prevails,[23] as can be seen in the closing stanza of the poem:

> Se detiene la sangre por los miembros de piedra
> Como al coral sombrío fija el mar enemigo,
> Como coral helado en el cuerpo deshecho,
> En la noche sin luz, en el cielo sin nadie. (150)

The reference to 'sangre' in line one, and the adjective 'helado' in line three, remind us of the negative imagery of the opening stanza, where 'La presencia del frío ... /Hiela ... la sangre' (148). Despite the fact that a love relationship inspired the poem, it finishes with the metaphysical image that, as the night sky is devoid of light[24] (with light's positive connotations of un-

---

[22] See above, p. 14.

[23] See also Richard K. Curry, 'Between Platonism and Modernity: The Double "Fall" in the Poetry of Luis Cernuda', in *The Word and the Mirror: Critical Essays on the Poetry of Luis Cernuda*, ed. Salvador Jiménez-Fajardo (Toronto: Associated University Presses, 1989), p. 122.

[24] Shelley A. De Laurentis also comments how 'sombra' and darkness in Cernuda represent 'los aspectos múltiples de la realidad' ('Luz y sombra en la poesía de Cernuda', *Sin Nombre*, 6, No. 4 (1976), 15).

derstanding, enlightenment, etc.), so the sky (or 'heaven') is devoid of people. This is a poetic and emotional evocation of metaphysical doubt, of the disintegration of faith. The loss of order is now inevitable.

The matter of doubt versus faith is not stated definitively in 'Decidme anoche'. It is an issue to which Cernuda returns time and again, reaching a climax of intensity in *Las nubes*. Before reaching this state of desperation, however, signs of the desire to dream continue to be in evidence. An interesting poem which lies somewhere between this desire to dream of order and confrontation with existential chaos is 'Soñando la muerte' from *Las nubes*. It affords us valuable insights into the interplay of dreams, faith and doubt:

> Como una blanca rosa
> Cuyo halo en lo oscuro los ojos no perciben;
> Como un blanco deseo
> Que ante el amor caído invisible se alzara;
> Como una blanca llama
> Que en aire torna siempre la mentira del cuerpo,
> Por el día solitario y la noche callada
> Pasas tú, sombra eterna,
> Con un dedo en los labios. (264)

This stanza is given over to an exploration of the meaning of death for the persona. The fact that the persona is 'soñando' of death is in itself suggestive that death is a source of escape from the tyranny of the world, and this attitude is largely supported by the sense of peace and release which is conveyed. The most obvious feature of this initial stanza is the adjective 'white': 'blanca rosa', 'blanco deseo', 'blanca llama'. White flowers are often associated with funerals, but white is also a common symbol of purity and innocence. The conjunction of these two ideas would appear to unite death with an absence of corruption and decay, and there is an evident desire to escape 'la mentira del cuerpo'. The direct address to death in the last two lines, where it is referred to as a 'sombra eterna', contrasting with the whiteness of the three entities with which it is compared, then paves the way for the central idea of the poem. This is explored in most detail in the third and final stanza:

> Cuando la blanca juventud miro caída,
> Manchada y rota entre las grises horas;
> Cuando la blanca verdad veo traicionada
> Por manos ambiciosas y bocas elocuentes;
> Cuando la blanca inspiración siento perdida

> Ante los duros siglos en el dolor pasados,
> Sólo en ti creo entonces, vasta sombra,
> Tras los sombríos mirtos de tu pórtico
> Única realidad clara del mundo. (264)

The structure clearly forms a parallel with that of the first stanza, with the three entities 'juventud', 'verdad' and 'inspiración', also all white, placed in the same relative positions as 'rosa', 'deseo' and 'llama'. Whereas however in the first stanza the 'rosa', 'deseo' and 'llama' are all compared with death, in order to suggest that that is the way to avoid corruption and decay, here we see the opposite situation, whereby positive elements of life have been corrupted and negated by the influence of the world. For that reason the persona's belief in death as a means of escape is intensified. This is different from the scepticism of 'Decidme anoche', for there is certainly more in the way of hope and belief. At the same time however there is clearly no thought of God or after-life but rather the eternal peace of total extinction. It is implicit rather than explicit atheism. Death is then defined as the 'Única realidad clara del mundo': if this is hope, it is no more than the tragedy of desperate hope in the ultimate annihilation of the self, for life and the world have no meaning.

In addition to the scepticism of 'Decidme anoche' and the very negative 'faith', if it can be called such, of 'Soñando la muerte', there is, curiously enough, an idea of a notional existence of God or some kind of Absolute, but that, contrary to the Christian message, there is once more a gulf between the Absolute and humanity. This is illustrated in the later stanzas of 'A las estatuas de los dioses'. While the opening stanzas reflect upon the age of order when the gods reigned supreme and people believed in them, the focus of the fourth stanza then shifts in order to concentrate more on the present:

> Eran tiempos heroicos y frágiles,
> Deshechos con vuestro poder como un sueño feliz.
> Hoy yacéis, mutiladas y oscuras,
> Entre los grises jardines de las ciudades,
> Piedra inútil que el soplo celeste no anima,
> Abandonadas de la súplica y la humana esperanza. (247)

The stanza opens with another wistful glance towards the past mythical age of order before shifting abruptly to the present. The choice of the verb 'yacer' in line three, with its connotations of tombstone inscriptions, encapsulates the entire message: all that remains of the gods is decaying statues, surrounded by the aura of death. (The fact that the statues are themselves

made of stone also links them with tombs.) Paradoxically their aura of death
is not so much indicative of the non-existence of the gods as it is symbolic of
the end of faith. There is nothing there to vivify the statues, certainly, but the
primary reason for this is that they are 'abandonadas de la súplica y la
humana esperanza': just as the age of order depended on faith, so the age of
chaos is dependent on the lack of that faith. The paradox of the existence of
faith in an Absolute being more important than the existence of that Absolute is explored further in the last two stanzas of the poem:

> Tal vez su fe os devuelva el cielo.
> Más no juzguéis por el rayo, la guerra o la plaga
> Una triste humanidad decaída;
> Impasibles reinad en el divino espacio.
> Distraiga con su gracia el copero solícito
> La cólera de vuestro poder que despierta.
>
> En tanto el poeta, en la noche otoñal,
> Bajo el blanco embeleso lunático,
> Mira las ramas que el verdor abandona
> Nevarse de luz beatamente,
> Y sueña con vuestro trono de oro
> Y vuestra faz cegadora,
> Lejos de los hombres,
> Allá en la altura impenetrable. (247–48)

The first line of this penultimate stanza is ambiguous: will faith return the
sky/heaven to the statues or will heaven return faith to them? Either interpretation is possible. If the first is correct, then the creatures' (and by
extension the gods') existence is entirely dependent on the people's belief in
them. If the second, then they have their own existence, but for that
existence to be meaningful, it must be confirmed or completed by a
relationship between the human and celestial spheres. There is therefore a
tension in *La realidad y el deseo* between the acute metaphysical doubt of
'Decidme anoche' and the hope of 'A las estatuas de los dioses' of the gods'
existence. This tension is underscored in the later poem by the way that hope
is juxtaposed with despair: humanity is irreconcilably separated from the
gods by its own faithlessness. This realisation is then followed in line four of
this penultimate stanza by the rather bizarre injunction 'Impasibles reinad en
el divino espacio'. If the gods were to reign, this may suggest a possible
return to an age of order, but that possibility is negated by the use of
'impasibles', stressing the gulf between them and humanity. Why should the
persona wish the gods to reign impassively? The solution to this may lie in

the final stanza. The persona is now gazing into the night, his vision over. All that he can see is the sky and nature, beautiful though they undeniably are. What Absolute there is, or may have been, is by contrast entirely separate and divorced from the human sphere ('Lejos de los hombres'). There can be no direct means of perceiving the gods, for where they reign is 'impenetrable',[25] and yet the poet is able to dream of this 'trono de oro'. Thus if the gods reign, even impassively, at least there can be some kind of contact between them through the visionary experience. In the midst of the perception of such a gap between the two realms of the temporal and the eternal, there is therefore still a tiny glimmer of hope, although the very fact that the poem, and indeed the entire collection of *Invocaciones*, ends with the negatively charged word 'impenetrable', surely limits the scope of any optimism.

As mentioned above, it is with *Las nubes* that Cernuda's existential meditations reach their climax. In this collection there is added a further dimension to the issue of faith and the gulf between the Absolute and humanity. In 'A las estatuas de los dioses', the Absolute apparently has some kind of existence (although it is none too clear exactly how it exists), but is ignored by the world. In the poem 'La visita de Dios' from *Las nubes*, specifically the Christian God this time is extant, but does not care about the fate of mankind. The bulk of this poem is given over to expressions of the persona's metaphysical despair and will be analysed in greater detail later,[26] but what is relevant at this juncture is the direct address made to God in the last stanza:

> Compadécete al fin, escucha este murmullo
> Que ascendiendo llega como una ola
> Al pie de tu divina indiferencia. (276)

The persona has been deserted by God and made to dwell a stranger in the world without prospect of mercy. The gulf between the Absolute and humanity therefore encompasses two things: both humanity's inability through lack of faith to penetrate the realms of the Absolute and God's apparent inability or disinclination to intervene in humanity's distress.

Concentration thus far has been on the individual's world view and the relationship (or more accurately the non-relationship) between the individual and the Absolute. One further dimension which is apparent, albeit to a relatively limited extent, is the status of the world itself. The eighth poem of the

---

[25] This is also reminiscent of Diotima's passivity and indifference in Hölderlin's poem. (See above, pp. 15–16.)
[26] See below, pp. 46–50.

fifth collection *Donde habite el olvido* is a fine illustration of this. While this
poem, following as it does the two Surrealist-influenced collections, was
also originally influenced by the disastrous amatory experience, nevertheless
the distance from that experience is much greater and it is consequently
much less obvious than in *Un río, un amor* and *Los placeres prohibidos*.
Moreover, the terms in which the eighth poem is couched illustrate that it is
intended to have a significance far wider than an erotic encounter:

> Nocturno, esgrimes horas
> Sordamente profundas;
> En esas horas fulgen
> Luces de ojos absortos.
>
> Bajo el cielo de hierro
> Da hojas la amargura,
> Lenta entre las cadenas
> Que sostienen la vida.
>
> Hechos vibrante fuego
> O filo inextinguible,
> Los condenados tuercen
> Sus cuerpos en la sombra. (206)

There is some evidence here of the erotic relationship, most especially with
the reference to 'ojos absortos' in line four of the first stanza and the clause
'Los condenados tuercen/Sus cuerpos' in the third stanza, but the intention
noted so frequently already to give the poetry a broader scope than merely
personal erotic encounters is also striking here. It is really only a knowledge
of the biographical background to this poem that provides a clear indication
that an amatory experience lies behind it. While the amatory experience
should not be ignored, nevertheless it must be recognised that the poem
does work on two levels, and the metaphysical import is at least as significant as anything else.[27] The overriding picture in this poem is not just of the
agony caused by failed love, but also of a world where very little makes any
sense, where nights are endless, the sky is 'de hierro', 'amargura' abounds

---

[27] Harris (*Luis Cernuda. A Study*, p. 55) is very restrictive in his interpretation when he
says that there is 'little presence of exterior reality'. Charles Christopher Soufas, Jr., in
turn suggests the 'dios póstumo' 'could also refer to that other, more significant self into
which Cernuda desired to be transformed' ('Agents of Power in the Poetry of Luis
Cernuda', unpublished dissertation Duke 1979, p. 155). Cernuda encapsulates an *entire
world view* into this poem.

and *all* people are 'condenados'. What is more, life is sustained by 'cadenas', a powerful image of both physical and emotional entrapment and confinement. The status of the world is then made more explicit still in the last two stanzas:

> Ya no es vida ni muerte
> El tormento sin nombre,
> Es un mundo caído
> Donde silba la ira.

> Es un mar delirante,
> Clamor de todo espacio,
> Voz que de sí levanta
> Las alas de un dios póstumo. (207)

There can be no question that, not only has the individual lost contact with absolute order, the world itself has as well. It is senseless and without direction. The last line explicitly links this to the loss of the Absolute with the rather Nietzschean-sounding 'dios póstumo'. In addition, the 'mundo caído' and 'dios póstumo', taken together, are possibly suggestive of a fatalistic inevitability of the loss of order against which man is powerless to struggle, even perhaps despite any last vestiges of faith which he entertains in *Invocaciones* and *Las nubes*. Thus a complex picture has been built up of the loss of order in *La realidad y el deseo*. Man's position in nature, metaphysical chaos, the gulf between the Absolute and humanity, loss of faith, vestiges of faith, a senseless world. It is impossible to point to any one factor as the sole cause of loss. What we have instead is a mosaic made up of disparate elements, but which all point to the same conclusion: quite simply, that order is gone.

The Consequences of the Loss of Order

The consequences of the loss of order receive far more attention than the losing of order, and a complex and powerful image is established of this metaphysical tragedy. A highly emotional response to a sense of existential chaos is indeed replicated over a whole series of poems. It should be stressed that, in Cernuda's poetry, the loss of order affects the world in general, just as much as it affects the individual. An almost inevitable concomitant of this loss is that events in the world appear without sense and logical order. One such example is the poem 'El caso del pájaro asesinado' from *Un río, un amor*, which is a striking picture of a chaotic world where events take place without logical motivation:

Fue un pájaro quizá asesinado;
Nadie sabe. Por nadie
O por alguien quizá triste en las piedras,
En los muros del cielo.

Mas de ello hoy nada se sabe.
Sólo un temblor de luces levemente,
Un color de miradas en las olas o en la brisa;
También, acaso, un miedo.
Todo, es verdad, inseguro. (153)

From a biographical point of view, the world is seen as chaotic because of
failed romantic involvement rather than specifically because of a loss of
faith.[28] (Presumably the 'pájaro asesinado' is Cernuda himself.) A biographical approach is however needlessly restrictive, since the circumstances of a
failed romance are *not* explained in the poem. Once again we witness the
preference for moving away from Cernuda's own specific situation to more
generalised statements. The poem depicts an event which is an absurd part
of an absurd world.[29] The last line is particularly revealing: 'Todo, es
verdad, *inseguro*'. The juxtaposition of 'verdad' and 'inseguro' suggests
that the *only* truth of this world is insecurity. Furthermore, the comma between 'Todo' and 'es' underlines the severance of everything in the world
and the persona's life from 'verdad'. It is not really particularly important
that there is no explanation whatsoever provided for the world view which
lies behind the absurd events: it is only the absurdity itself which matters.

What receives most attention in *La realidad y el deseo* is the consequences of metaphysical chaos for individuals. 'Lázaro', from *Las nubes*, is
a particularly striking example of an exploration of acute existential alienation. It is a meditation on the Biblical story of Lazarus' resurrection, but
rather than the joy of new life, the poem expresses the near intolerable despair of a man returned to a meaningless world. The opening stanzas of the
poem set the scene and describe, from Lázaro's point of view, his raising to
life:

---

[28] See for example José María Capote Benot, *El surrealismo en la poesía de Luis
Cernuda* (Sevilla: Universidad de Sevilla, 1976), p. 108.
[29] Brian Whittaker Nield argues that the poem can be considered 'as a parable on the
human condition' ('Surrealism in Spain, with Special Reference to the Poetry of Alberti,
Aleixandre, Cernuda and Lorca, 1928–1931', unpublished thesis Cambridge 1971, p.
178).

> Era de madrugada.
> Después de retirada la piedra con trabajo,
> Porque no la materia sino el tiempo
> Pesaba sobre ella,
> Oyeron una voz tranquila
> Llamándome, como un amigo llama
> Cuando atrás queda alguno
> Fatigado de la jornada y cae la sombra.
> Hubo un silencio largo.
> Así lo cuentan ellos que lo vieron. (289)

The opening of the poem very quickly sets the scene and embarks upon the narration of the miracle of Lázaro's resurrection, although it is not long before it becomes apparent that one of the primary objects of the poem is to devalue the miracle entirely. The first hint of this objective appears in lines three to four, with the rather odd clause 'Porque no la materia sino el tiempo/Pesaba sobre ella'. Why should the weight of time be so important in sealing the tomb? It suggests that time has already moved forward from Lázaro's death, and that it cannot and should not be halted: history can only advance, it can never be reversed. After this there is a brief note of hope with the reference to the 'voz tranquila ... como un amigo', but this is swiftly negated by the image of defeat immediately following: the voice is like that of a friend calling to someone 'Fatigado de la jornada' once night is falling. In other words, the call is being made to someone whose 'day' (i.e., life) is already over, which is confirmed by the 'silencio largo' which is the only response. The poem then from this point onward sets out consciously to deflate and devalue anything that could be construed to be positive:

> Alguien dijo palabras
> De nuevo nacimiento.
> Mas no hubo allí sangre materna
> Ni vientre fecundado
> Que crea con dolor nueva vida doliente.
> Sólo anchas vendas, lienzos amarillos
> Con olor denso, desnudaban
> La carne gris y fláccida como fruto pasado;
> No el terso cuerpo oscuro, rosa de los deseos,
> Sino el cuerpo de un hijo de la muerte. (290)

This stanza is imbued with a bitter cynicism which does not welcome returning to life. The first two lines have an air of indifference about the resurrection which deflates the miracle. Furthermore, rather than the vitality of the womb (which ironically can only give birth to 'vida doliente'), all around Lázaro are the signs of death and decay: the shroud, the smell, 'carne gris y fláccida', and 'el cuerpo de un hijo de la muerte', contrasting with the fact that he has been raised by Christ, who came specifically to *conquer* death.[30] This is the resuscitation of a body which has no reason to be alive.

As 'Lázaro' progresses, it steadily becomes more and more bleak in its outlook, stressing time and again the hopelessness of human existence. The fifth stanza describes the resuscitated corpse's departure from the tomb to rejoin his friends and family, with the lack of vitality broadening out to include those supposedly still alive. The desire of others to reach out to Lázaro represents, not communication, but the gulf which exists between them. There can be no contact, not just because Lázaro is still a corpse, but because their own existence is marred by the emptiness of this chaotic world. The sheer futility of the miracle is then explored further in stanzas six and seven:

> Quise cerrar los ojos,
> Buscar la vasta sombra,
> La tiniebla primaria
> Que su venero esconde bajo el mundo
> Lavando de vergüenzas la memoria.
> Cuando un alma doliente en mis entrañas
> Gritó, por las oscuras galerías
> Del cuerpo, agria, desencajada,
> Hasta chocar contra el muro de los huesos
> Y levantar mareas febriles por la sangre.
>
> Aquel que con su mano sostenía
> La lámpara testigo del milagro,
> Mató brusco la llama,
> Porque ya el día estaba con nosotros. (291)

Lázaro's alienation is such that a desire surfaces within him to return to that state of extinction from which he has been raised, once again to 'buscar la sombra' and 'la tiniebla primaria'. That 'darkness' is assuredly Lázaro's new home from which he should never have been removed. This is reiterated by the shout of the 'alma doliente' in his 'entrañas', because it is 'agria' and 'desencajada'. The second of the two epithets is particularly powerful,

---

[30] See I Corinthians 15:22.

stressing that this entire situation is quite wrong: the soul is now literally re-moved from its fitting 'encaje' of oblivion. The disaster of the alleged miracle is then spelt out vividly when the 'testigo del milagro' symbolically 'kills' the light, ostensibly because of the dawning day, but on a deeper level without question because the less witness there is to this 'miracle' the better.

Time after time in this and the following stanzas the futility of human life is reiterated. In the eighth stanza in particular Lázaro speaks of 'el error de estar vivo' (292). The sense of alienation is so acute that the entire situation appears quite distorted and divorced from any form of sense or meaning. The revulsion indeed borders on terror, or even an inverted form of Kierkegaardian *Angst* or 'anxiety'. For Kierkegaard, 'anxiety' arises when 'freedom ... looks down into its own possibility, laying hold of finiteness to support itself.'[31] Here Lázaro is terrified by the prospect of continuing in the finite world, and desperately wishes to retreat to eternity, although it is an 'inauthentic' eternity of oblivion as a means of escape.[32] The poem then ap-proaches its climax when Lázaro and the others eventually reach a house and they go in to eat, with Christ, unnamed, as the focal point:

> Todos le rodearon en la mesa.
> Encontré el pan amargo, sin sabor las frutas,
> El agua sin frescor, los cuerpos sin deseo;
> La palabra hermandad sonaba falsa,
> Y de la imagen del amor quedaban
> Sólo recuerdos vagos bajo el viento.
> Él conocía que todo estaba muerto
> En mí, que yo era un muerto
> Andando entre los muertos. (292–93)

---

[31] Kierkegaard, *Writings*, Vol. VIII, p. 61. See also above, p. 2.

[32] There are also sporadic allusions to *Angst* in *Un río, un amor* and *Los placeres prohibidos* (see Elisabeth Müller, *Die Dichtung Luis Cernudas* (Genève: Romanisches Seminar der Universität Köln, 1962), p. 56), as well as a more fully developed allusion to it in *Ocnos*, one of Cernuda's two collections of prose poetry. In 'La eternidad', we read:

... le asaltaba [al niño] el miedo de la eternidad, del tiempo ilimitado.

La palabra siempre ... le llenaba de terror, ... Sentía su vida atacada por dos enemigos, uno frente a él y otro a sus espaldas, sin querer seguir adelante y sin poder volver atrás. Esto, de haber sido posible, es lo que hubiera preferido: volver atrás, regresar a aquella región vaga y sin memoria de donde había venido al mundo. (556)

This is much closer to genuine Kierkegaardian anxiety in the face of the limitless possi-bilities of eternity, but, oddly enough, the response is similar to that of Lázaro, i.e., to retreat, not to 'finiteness', but to an eternal oblivion, this time the security of the maternal womb. (See also James Valender, *Cernuda y el poema en prosa* (London: Tamesis, 1984), p. 32.)

This world has absolutely nothing positive whatsoever. Bread, fruit, water and human bodies are all devoid of anything worthwhile. 'Amor' is no more than a distant memory. Perhaps the ideological crux of the poem comes in the last three lines of this stanza: he is dead and amongst dead people. (It is bitterly ironic that it is given to Christ Himself, the Saviour of the world, to recognise this.) This phrase is in fact an almost exact quotation of the closing phrase of 'En medio de la multitud' from *Los placeres prohibidos* (176–77). There is however a subtle difference between the two poems. While the earlier poem is inspired by a disastrous amatory experience but couched in existential terms, this poem is fundamentally existential.[33] This is not the cry of failed love, it is despair in the face of failed life itself. What this poem proposes is that the whole of existence itself is chaotic. Not only that, in this poem, Lázaro is, after resurrection, *still* 'un muerto', i.e., Christ is depicted as having *failed* to turn round the biological cycle of life and death. This is one of the most conclusively atheistic views expressed in *La realidad y el deseo*, for it makes human existence into no more than a Darwinian biological accident.

We shall return to 'Lázaro' later, for the perspective of the poem shifts somewhat at the end. Another of the consequences of a world of chaos which the individual must face is the nature of individual identity. The sense of ontological solitude is, by the time of *Vivir sin estar viviendo*, rather more irrevocable, for the search for absolute order (discussed in the following chapter) has already taken place and failed. 'El intruso' is a particularly good example of Cernuda's growing tendency to create other personae whom he addresses as 'tú' in order to illustrate his feeling of a divided identity:[34]

> Como si equivocara el tiempo
> Su trama de los días,
> ¿Vives acaso los de otro?,
> Extrañas ya la vida.
>
> Lejos de ti, de la conciencia
> Desacordada, el centro
> Buscas afuera, entre las cosas
> Presentes un momento. (391)

---

[33] David Martínez's comment that Cernuda's scepticism is his 'inadaptación a lo que le rodea' is therefore a considerable oversimplification ('Luis Cernuda, poeta existencial', *Revista de la Universidad Nacional de Córdoba*, 5 (1964), 162).

[34] I think Adrian G. Montoro's argument that Cernuda's use of 'tú' is to construct 'una imagen coherente de sí mismo' is somewhat inadequate ('Rebeldía de Cernuda', *Sin Nombre*, 6, No. 4 (1976), 29).

Coleman comments that 'an extraneous and irrelevant being occupies his body, using it, sapping it of energies'.[35] This poem is a vivid portrayal of someone who is unable to come to terms with himself: '¿Vives acaso los de otro?' suggests confusion as to whether his own life belongs to him, reinforced by the device of addressing himself as 'tú'.[36] The following stanza reiterates this sense of dislocation, especially with the adjective 'desacordada'. The 'centro' which he now seeks is however no longer metaphysical, but his own identity.[37] As the poem progresses, the persona attempts to construct a dream about his lost youth, but fails:

> Hoy este intruso eres tú mismo,
> Tú, como el otro antes,
> Y con el cual sin gusto inicias
> Costumbre a que se allane.
>
> Para llegar al que no eres,
> Quien no eres te guía,
> Cuando el amigo es el extraño
> Y la rosa es la espina. (392)

The persona is totally isolated, emphasised by the way in which he has only himself with whom to converse. Furthermore, this interlocutor is an 'intruso', someone hostile. The persona's identity is not only split, his *alter ego* accuses him and makes him aware of the failure of his life. Then in the final stanza of the poem emphasis is placed on the hostility of the world also:

---

[35] J. Alexander Coleman, *Other Voices: A Study of the Late Poetry of Luis Cernuda* (Chapel Hill: The University of North Carolina Press, 1969), p. 177.

[36] See also Jiménez-Fajardo, *Luis Cernuda*, p. 102. José Olivio Jiménez also speaks in general terms of '[el] uso de una segunda persona ... que apuntaría a la única alteridad posible ... de un poeta que canta desde los posos más hondos de su soledad' ('Emoción y trascendencia del tiempo en la poesía de Luis Cernuda', *La Caña Gris*, Nos. 6–8 (Otoño de 1962), p. 58).

[37] James Mandrell similarly argues, in the context of 'El indolente' from *Como quien espera el alba*, that Cernuda's use of 'tú', in Freudian terms, 'betrays "a rift in the ego which never heals but which increases as time goes on"', but also contends that this other persona can be 'a means of avoiding or denying death' ('Cernuda's "El indolente": Repetition, Doubling, and the Construction of Poetic Voice', *Bulletin of Hispanic Studies*, 65 (1988), 388). Hilda Pato meanwhile makes the very interesting point in general terms that the use of 'tú' 'no aleja al lector tampoco, sino que invoca su presta presencia en el *acto del poema*, invita su actuación y su juicio' ('El «tú» (y el «otro») en la poesía de Luis Cernuda', *Anales de la Literatura Española Contemporánea*, 11 (1986), 231). In 'El intruso', however, there can be no question that alienation from self predominates.

he is 'guided' to an unknown place, friends are strangers and roses are only their thorns.[38] This is a very profound expression of ontological insecurity.[39]

The sense of ontological insecurity becomes married with still further problems when the alienated individual comes into contact with other people in this disordered world. There does however tend to be a difference between the persona on the one hand and the people with whom he comes into contact on the other. While the persona is portrayed as sensitive and emotionally troubled, the others are unfeeling and faceless. A good example of this is to be found in 'Limbo', from *Con las horas contadas*, where the persona attends a soirée:

> La plaza sola (gris el aire,
> Negros los árboles, la tierra
> Manchada por la nieve),
> Parecía, no realidad, mas copia
> Triste sin realidad. Entonces,
> Ante el umbral, dijiste:
> Viviendo aquí serías
> Fantasma de ti mismo.
>
> Inhóspita en su adorno
> Parsimonioso, porcelanas, bronces,

---

[38] There are echoes here of San Juan de la Cruz's 'Modo de subir por la senda al monte de perfección', although it is doubtful if Cernuda would be successful (*Poesía completa y comentarios en prosa*, ed. Raquel Asún, 4th ed. (Barcelona: Planeta, 1997), p. 41):

> Para venir a lo que no eres,
> has de ir por donde no eres.

Brian Hughes also sees echoes of T. S. Eliot's 'The Dry Salvages' (*Luis Cernuda and the Modern English Poets. A Study of the Influence of Browning, Yeats and Eliot on his Poetry* (Alicante: Universidad de Alicante, 1987), pp. 195–96).

[39] It is perhaps only the poem itself which is sure of its own identity. The persona is a fragmented personality, but the complete picture of that fragmentation exists as a carefully constructed, single, unique entity. The poem therefore creates anew the identity of the persona, insecure as it is, and then the reader re-creates that construct. In that way we could perhaps re-read the lines 'Para llegar al que no eres,/Quien no eres te guía' as a reflection of the process in which we as readers are engaged: the poem 'guides' us to an understanding of the existence (or more accurately non-existence) of the persona. A much more complex form of this process of creation and re-creation Jiménez-Fajardo sees as lying at the heart of '*Ninfa y pastor, por Ticiano*' from *Desolación de la Quimera*, whereby Titian's creation of the painting is reflected in Cernuda's creation of the poem and in turn reflected in the reader's reading of the poem ('Ekphrasis and Ideology in Cernuda's "*Ninfa y pastor* por Ticiano" ', *Anales de la Literatura Española Contemporánea*, 22 (1997), 29–51).

> Muebles chinos, la casa
> Oscura toda era, (460–61)

The poem opens with a rather dull and uninteresting scene. The comment which the persona makes on this scene in lines four to five, namely that it is a 'copia triste sin realidad', is intriguing. The idea of the world as a 'copia triste' has very obvious similarities with Platonic doctrine, but whereas in that philosophy the copy is of the Idea, *this* copy is '*sin* realidad'. This must surely suggest that there is no corresponding Idea. All that exists is the miserable scene before the persona's eyes. This is at once both atheistic and pessimistic in its outlook. The last two lines of this stanza then provide an early indication of the persona's loathing of the bourgeois house which he is about to enter: in echoing the idea of a 'copia triste' in the phrase 'fantasma de ti mismo', the persona suggests that any association with this society will transform him into a miserable non-person as well. The irony of this however is that, in also continuing to address himself by means of the second person, there is a strong indication that this is already what his existence is like, and that his entrance into this empty society will only be an intensification and development of his personal existence. The home in the second stanza then forms a definite parallel with the scene outside, with the emphasis on darkness and drabness suggesting society's emptiness and superficiality. The problems of involvement with that society are then brought together succinctly in the final stanzas:

> Su vida [del poeta] ya puede excusarse,
> Porque ha muerto del todo;
> Su trabajo ahora cuenta,
> Domesticado para el mundo de ellos,
> Como otro objeto vano,
> Otro ornamento inútil;
> Y tú cobarde, mudo
> Te despediste ahí, como el que asiente,
> Más allá de la muerte, a la injusticia.

> Mejor la destrucción, el fuego. (462)

Bitterness and cynicism shine through in this picture of the empty materialism of society, full of 'objetos vanos' and 'ornamentos inútiles'. Pointless triviality and empty superficiality are surely another consequence of a world without order: there is nothing of lasting value in anything in which society takes an interest, and the best thing is its total annihilation. The persona's relationship to that society is however supremely ironic. The poet's own work is compared directly with this empty superficiality: once 'domesticated', i.e., accepted by society, it 'cuenta ... como otro objeto vano'. Not only that, he is described as 'cobarde', leaving 'como el que asiente ... a la injusticia'. In other words, he appears to conform and merge pathetically and miserably into this sterile environment. Why? Clearly not because he is in implicit agreement with the vain materialistic posturings of the society, but it is at least possible, more disturbingly, that as a miserable, identity-free victim of a chaotic universe and a chaotic society, there are times when he can do little other than conform, presumably to his own revulsion.

The problem of the individual versus society has one further dimension, namely the difficulties of interpersonal relationships. They are explored most fully in 'La familia' from *Como quien espera el alba*. This poem is a very bitter reflection upon scenes round the family table from the persona's childhood. The poem makes use of the second person technique, opening with the question '¿Recuerdas tú, recuerdas aún la escena ...?' (334). The technique is however more complex here than in 'El intruso', for the 'tú' refers both to the alienated persona himself, and, presumably, to ourselves as readers as well, with the result that we are simultaneously bystanders on Cernuda's divided personality and drawn into the situation as if we are being exhorted to recall our own childhoods. After the initial scene-setting, the second and third stanzas are imbued with a loathing and revulsion for the situation which is unsettling in its intensity:

> Era a la cabecera el padre adusto,
> La madre caprichosa estaba en frente,
> Con la hermana mayor imposible y desdichada,
> Y la menor más dulce, quizá no más dichosa,
> El hogar contigo mismo componiendo,
> La casa familiar, el nido de los hombres,
> Inconsistente y rígido, tal vidrio
> Que todos quiebran, pero nadie dobla.
>
> Presidían mudos, graves, la penumbra,
> Ojos que no miraban los ojos de los otros,
> Mientras sus manos pálidas alzaban como hostia
> Un pedazo de pan, un fruto, una copa con agua,
> Y aunque entonces vivían en ellos presentiste,
> Tras la carne vestida, el doliente fantasma
> Que al rezo de los otros nunca calma
> La amargura de haber vivido inútilmente. (334–35)

There is in these lines a total lack of any kind of familial love or even concern. The parents are simply condemned out of hand, with the rather clichéd image of the remote, unfeeling patriarch and his superficial, unthinking wife. It is a degree of stereotyping which leads us to wonder if it is intended to present real individuals or instead to indicate the extent to which things in this world have gone wrong, even with the very relationships which should be closest. The sisters are appropriately miserable, and the use of the phrase 'el nido de los hombres' cynically conveys what a travesty of familial unity this is. That impression is intensified in the following stanza, where eyes do not meet each other. What links the loss of meaningful relationships most explicitly with the loss of order immediately follows, with the family joining in a travesty of a Communion service. The fact that the bread is likened to the Host is obviously ironising their pretensions, but at the same time rather more subtly perhaps suggests that this is the only significance for the Host now, coupled then with the 'copa con *agua*' rather than 'vino': there is no true Communion because there is for Cernuda no true salvation, just as, 'al rezo de los otros', there can be no salve for the 'amargura' of having lived 'inútilmente'. The whole of Cernuda's perception of metaphysical emptiness is brought together in the image of a family which does not know itself.

The persona of 'La familia' then proceeds somewhat self-righteously (and frankly somewhat unconvincingly) to absolve himself from any blame in this family disunity, and complains almost petulantly that his parents were at fault for giving birth to him. There follows a reflection on his growing up, and the third-last stanza is perhaps the climax of the poem:

> Luego con embeleso probando cuanto era
> Costumbre suya prohibir en otros
> Y a cuyo trasgresor la excomunión seguía,
> Te acordaste de ellos, sonriendo apenado.
> Cómo se engaña el hombre y cuán en vano
> Da reglas que prohiben y condenan.
> ¿Es toda acción humana, como estimas ahora,
> Fruto de imitación y de inconsciencia? (336–37)

The first lines of this stanza recall the 'Communion service' of the third stanza, and in particular the 'excomunión' is very ironic. The 'trasgresor' is presumably the persona/Cernuda himself with his deviant behaviour, but the fact that the family should 'excommunicate' him can hardly be a source of despair, for two reasons: first, because the rest of the family never communicated with each other, and second, since the family's travesty of Communion is the only one in any case, there is no salvation left which the persona can be denied. The tragedy of the poem is then summed up in the final question: lacking true foundation for behaviour, people can only 'imitate' acts from which all meaning has become lost.

There would appear to be no reason for any other response to these consequences of the loss of order than utter despair. The end of 'Lázaro' therefore, omitted from the earlier discussion, seems rather surprising compared with the rest of the poem, because the attitude changes and it is apparently much more optimistic:

> Así rogué, con lágrimas,
> Fuerza de soportar mi ignorancia resignado,
> Trabajando, no por mi vida ni mi espíritu,
> Mas por una verdad en aquellos ojos entrevista
> Ahora. La hermosura es paciencia.
> Sé que el lirio del campo,
> Tras de su humilde oscuridad en tantas noches
> Con larga espera bajo tierra,
> Del tallo verde erguido a la corola alba
> Irrumpe un día en gloria triunfante. (293)

This stanza is one of the rare glimpses of hope in *Las nubes*, although, given the bleak outlook of the rest of the poem, it is surely not unequivocally hopeful.[40] The first line of this final stanza forms an admission of defeat as far as life on earth is concerned: the desire is to work, not 'por [su] vida ni [su] espíritu', but 'por una verdad'. This would appear demonstrative of a desire to seek a religious or metaphysical answer to the problems of existence, with a direct request to Christ Himself, and the closing lines of the poem seem particularly optimistic, reminiscent of the Christian Resurrection.[41] This seems curious, for what we have been discovering is Cernuda's

---

[40] I am more in agreement with Harris (*Luis Cernuda. A Study*, p. 77) when he says that 'the poem as a whole is overshadowed by the sense of life's futility' than with Jiménez-Fajardo's greater stress on the hope (*Luis Cernuda*, pp. 65–67). Armando López Castro seems to ignore the majority of the poem altogether, seeing only the hopeful message ('Ética y poesía en Cernuda', *Cuadernos para Investigación de la Literatura Hispánica*, 8 (1987), 83).

[41] See for example I Corinthians 15:52: 'The trumpet shall sound, and the dead shall be raised incorruptible'. Incidentally, Vicente Quirarte's comment that 'La anécdota de "Lázaro" ... es también la alegoría del hombre "que espera el alba" al término de la segunda Guerra Mundial' (*La poética del hombre dividido en la obra de Luis Cernuda* (México: Universidad Nacional Autónoma de México, 1985), p. 65) is, while interesting, probably wrong: 'Lázaro', as far as we know, was completed in December, 1938 (see *Poesía completa*, p. 797), although Rafael Martínez Nadal believes it to date from 1939, for no firm reason (*Españoles en la Gran Bretaña. Luis Cernuda. El hombre y sus temas.*

lack of belief in a transcendent order, and all the consequences of that loss of order: a world which makes no sense, alienation and the chaos of existence, *Angst*, the problem of identity, the problems of interpersonal relationships. Once Cernuda's persona(e) find themselves in the midst of this despair and chaos, however, they do not simply give up or passively resign themselves to this new perception of the universe. Hope re-emerges and there surfaces an undertaking to find once more the order which has become lost.

(Madrid: Hiperión, 1983), p. 355). Cernuda himself does however state that this is the intended meaning of the title of the eighth collection, *Como quien espera el alba* (*Prosa completa I*, p. 649).

CHAPTER THREE

SEARCH FOR ABSOLUTE ORDER

The Reasons for Searching

Cernuda suffered something of a spiritual crisis when he was exiled from Spain as a result of the Civil War.[1] This was particularly acute when he was resident in the United Kingdom between 1938 and 1947: he had a bitter sense of disorientation, exile and alienation from society,[2] and as a result began to seek solace in Christianity.[3] It is in the poems dating from this period of exile that the search for absolute order finds its most powerful expression, and, while the refuge in Christianity is something of a last resort, at least from a biographical point of view, there are times when the poetry does give definite, although never unequivocal, expression to an individual's desire to find God and believe that there is a meaning behind the cosmos.

It must be admitted that the progression of events is somewhat strange. There seems to be little evidence of logic relating to the total loss of faith followed by the desire to find it again. This can be easily countered by the fact that the psychology of despair surely has little to do with logic. Moreover, from a theological point of view, if God exists, then the desire exists in everyone to find Him, and it is unquestionably in moments of greatest distress that a desire for comfort and a belief that life has a purpose manifests

---

[1] While the Civil War had a profound effect on Cernuda's life, it has a negligible presence in his poetry, despite Juventino Caminero's valiant attempts to prove otherwise ('Luis Cernuda como poeta comprometido en la guerra civil española', *Letras de Deusto*, 16, No. 35 (1986), 53–70).

[2] Dr Ivy McLelland, a colleague of Cernuda's when he was at Glasgow University, testifies both to his introversion and to his melancholy when he was in Glasgow. In addition to his loathing of the city and his misery as a result of exile, he was also apparently still deeply affected by the loss of his friend Lorca in 1936. (I am indebted to Dr McLelland for this information.)

[3] Harris, discussing 'A un poeta muerto (F.G.L.)' from *Las nubes*, reveals that drafts of the poem demonstrate that 'it is possible to antedate the concern with Christianity to the beginning of the Civil War' ('A Primitive Version of Luis Cernuda's Elegy on the Death of Lorca', *Bulletin of Hispanic Studies*, 50 (1973), 369). It still however only plays a minor rôle at that time.

itself, even in today's secular society. Nonetheless, Cernuda's degree of atheism is such that he has to develop into the situation where he can believe there is a form of absolute order to be sought. Even in *Las nubes*, the vaguest inkling of belief does not come easily to Cernuda or his personae, which perhaps makes the ending of 'Lázaro' all the more remarkable. The poem 'Cementerio en la ciudad' from *Las nubes*, written in Glasgow in 1939,[4] underlines just how extreme Cernuda's alienation was when he was contemplating the possibility of religious faith:

> Tras de la reja abierta entre los muros,
> La tierra negra sin árboles ni hierba,
> Con bancos de madera donde allá a la tarde
> Se sientan silenciosos unos viejos.
> En torno están las casas, cerca hay tiendas,
> Calles por las que juegan niños, y los trenes
> Pasan al lado de las tumbas. Es un barrio pobre. (295–96)

This stanza piles up image after image of despair, misery, deprivation and confinement with an unrelenting intensity. The opening line, with the reference to 'reja' and 'muros', conveys the impression of a prison. In the second line the ground is an infertile black and has neither 'árboles ni hierba'. When a human presence is introduced, it is no more than 'silent old men'. What is more, the trains run alongside the graveyard, a clear reminder of the juxtaposition of life and death. The intensity of this *tour de force* of human misery is then encapsulated in the last sentence: the graveyard is in a poor area, which in Glasgow immediately before the Second World War means a slum of appalling deprivation. It would appear that this is the very nadir of existence. Remarkable as it might seem, however, we have to sink lower still in the descent towards the ultimate depths of chaos. It is this final descent which is explored in the last two stanzas:

> Ni una hoja ni un pájaro. La piedra nada más. La tierra.
> ¿Es el infierno así? Hay dolor sin olvido,
> Con ruido y miseria, frío largo y sin esperanza.
> Aquí no existe el sueño silencioso
> De la muerte, que todavía la vida
> Se agita entre estas tumbas, como una prostituta
> Prosigue su negocio bajo la noche inmóvil.

4 See *Poesía completa*, p. 797.

Cuando la sombra cae desde el cielo nublado
Y el humo de las fábricas se aquieta
En polvo gris, vienen de la taberna voces,
Y luego un tren que pasa
Agita largos ecos como bronce iracundo.
No es el juicio aún, muertos anónimos.
Sosegaos, dormid; dormid si es que podéis.
Acaso Dios también se olvida de vosotros. (296)

The first line of the penultimate stanza continues with the bleak imagery of earlier in the poem, stressing the absence of leaves and birds. All that is there is earth and stone, with the earth suggesting the element to which the dead bodies have been returned, and the stone the gravestones marking their death. What is perhaps the ideological crux of the entire poem then follows with the question '¿Es el infierno así?' This is now as low as it is possible to sink: to the very source of chaos itself. While this is no more than a question rather than direct statement and surely hyperbolic, nevertheless such a devastating indictment of life cannot be overlooked. The rest of the poem then continues to expand upon this succinct expression of 'hell on earth', and we are reminded of 'Soñando la muerte', where there is a very negative faith in death as the 'Única realidad clara del mundo' (264).[5] Where however in that poem the escape of death from the world is still propounded as a possibility, here 'no existe el sueño silencioso/De la muerte': if life is hell, then tragically death is hell also. A glimmer of hope possibly emerges in the closing lines, with the exhortation to the dead to 'sleep', but that hope is dashed also with the qualifying 'dormid si es que podéis'. There will be no sleep, unless God, cynically, can forget them as well.

It is from that perspective that Cernuda can write poems which end as curiously optimistically as 'Lázaro' and explore, from the depths of absolute chaos, the possibility of a search for faith in absolute order. Cernuda's desperation is again apparent in the poem 'La visita de Dios'. It opens with Cernuda's uncanny awareness that half his life is over and the expression of his need for divine consolation:

Pasada se halla ahora la mitad de mi vida.
El cuerpo sigue en pie y las voces aún giran
Y resuenan con encanto marchito en mis oídos,
Mas los días esbeltos ya se marcharon lejos;
Sólo recuerdos pálidos de su amor me han dejado.

[5] See also above, pp. 26–27.

> Como el labrador al ver su trabajo perdido
> Vuelve al cielo los ojos esperando la lluvia,
> También quiero esperar en esta hora confusa
> Unas lágrimas divinas que aviven mi cosecha. (274)

Existential agony does not pervade this poem to quite the same extent as it does 'Cementerio en la ciudad', but that is perhaps because the persona has shifted his gaze away from total introversion and directed it, however tentatively, towards God. The attitude here is more reasoned, and the persona is able to recognise that past pleasures, while agreeable, are over and something fresh is required instead. Therefore, as the farmer longs for rain to fall on parched land,[6] so Cernuda's persona now appreciates that the freshness which is required is God. The metaphor of the 'lágrimas divinas' not only links with the rain of the previous line but also echoes the tears of Christ, for example in the Garden of Gethsemane, the supreme example of the Deity identifying with man. In its simplest terms, then, the reason for the quest is hopeless despair and its purpose is spiritual renewal.

Cernuda does not however make a complete alteration of attitude between 'Cementerio en la ciudad' and 'La visita de Dios'. In the first place, whatever the exact dates of individual poems ('Cementerio en la ciudad' is actually later than 'La visita de Dios'), Cernuda rarely completely abandons one idea in favour of another. *La realidad y el deseo* is not a single, logical, cohesive argument. The attitudes, feelings and opinions shift around, frequently somewhat incoherently, forming a complex web where conflicting attitudes are often juxtaposed, even within the context of one poem. This is precisely what happens in 'La visita de Dios', for, despite the serenity of the opening, the reasons for the search for God explored in the third stanza reveal a new bitterness:

---

[6] The imagery of these lines bears a considerable amount in common (consciously or unconsciously) with Antonio Machado's 'Poema de un día' from *Campos de Castilla*. Like 'La visita de Dios', Machado's poem opens with the persona taking stock of his life. It then continues as follows (*Poesías completas*, ed. Manuel Alvar, 17th ed. (Madrid: Espasa-Calpe, 1993), p. 218):

> Fantástico labrador,
> pienso en los campos. ¡Señor
> qué bien haces! Llueve, llueve
> tu agua constante y menuda
> sobre alcaceles y habares,

Edward M. Wilson compares 'La visita de Dios' with 'Del pasado efímero', also from *Campos de Castilla*, where the imagery is again very similar ('Cernuda's Debts', in *Studies in Modern Spanish Literature and Art Presented to Helen F. Grant*, ed. Nigel Glendinning (London: Tamesis, 1972), p. 247, and Machado, pp. 224–25).

Estoy en la ciudad alzada para su orgullo por el rico,
Adonde la miseria oculta canta por las esquinas
O expone dibujos que me arrasan de lágrimas los ojos.
Y mordiendo mis puños con tristeza impotente
Aún cuento mentalmente mis monedas escasas,
Porque un trozo de pan aquí y unos vestidos
Suponen un esfuerzo mayor para lograrlos
Que el de los viejos héroes cuando vencían
Monstruos, rompiendo encantos con su lanza. (275)

The poem at this point takes a turn towards social issues, which are rarely of major significance within *La realidad y el deseo*. The persona sees misery and injustice all around him, but he himself can only look on 'con tristeza impotente'. He knows he has not the financial wherewithal to make any substantial difference in the world. (Incidentally, the very reference to 'mis monedas escasas' is also a means of including himself in this 'miseria oculta' of poverty and injustice.) The last lines of the stanza then state that the solution to these social ills requires 'un esfuerzo mayor .../Que el de los viejos héroes cuando vencían/Monstruos'. This can be interpreted in two different ways: on the one hand, it is surely a bitter and cynical comment on the reluctance of authorities and governments to relieve the plight of the poor. On the other hand, there is also at least a suggestion that, consonant with the rôle of God in the poem as a whole, it is an 'esfuerzo mayor ... que el de los hombres', i.e., it is *divine* action which is required to end human suffering. This secondary meaning is then confirmed in the fifth stanza:

Por mi dolor comprendo que otros inmensos sufren
Hombres callados a quienes falta el ocio
Para arrojar al cielo su tormento. Mas no puedo
Copiar su enérgico silencio, que me alivia
Este consuelo de la voz, sin tierra y sin amigo,
En la profunda soledad de quien no tiene
Ya nada entre sus brazos, sino el aire en torno, (275)

With a vivid image of having nothing around him besides the air, the persona expresses the 'profunda soledad' which deprives his existence of all meaning. There is also an intensely vehement tone in the third line when he uses the phrase 'arrojar al cielo', suggesting a bitter frustration which must erupt in a demand to the heavens for intervention in human life. He cannot duplicate the 'enérgico silencio' of other people: his being depends on breaking the silence, on making supplication, not to mere earthly authorities, but to the very heavens themselves.[7] Hence in the course of 'La visita de Dios' thus far we have progressed from the depths of despair, through a recognition of a need for spiritual renewal, to a further need for divine action to end human suffering.

Direct supplication to God is begun in the sixth stanza. In the course of this supplication, we learn, not so much what the persona longs for God to do, but rather more of his complaints, problems and reasons for endeavouring to find God in the first place. The tone of this stanza is however much less bitter and angry than in the immediately preceding stanzas:

> ¿Adónde han ido las viejas compañeras del hombre?
> Mis zurcidoras de proyectos, mis tejedoras de esperanzas
> Han muerto. Sus agujas y madejas reposan
> Con polvo en un rincón, sin la melodía del trabajo.
> Como una sombra aislada al filo de los días,
> Voy repitiendo gestos y palabras mientras lejos escucho
> El inmenso bostezo de los siglos pasados. (275–76)

The initial supplication to God is sad and wistful, comparing the past with the loneliness and isolation of the present. The following lines then speak of the vanity of the persona's plans and projects. On a superficial level this can suggest no more than feeble defeat. The end of the stanza however broadens the scope substantially: by setting his own empty 'gestos y palabras' in the context of the 'siglos pasados', the persona suggests his total insignificance (and by extension man's total insignificance) in the macrocosmic process of history. This is underscored by the noun 'bostezo', indicating the world's complete indifference to the persona's miserable efforts. There are thus two further reasons for man to seek God: in his isolation man needs the company of God, while in his insignificance in the breadth of time man needs the eternal significance of God.

Just as there is a mixture of resignation and angry bitterness in 'La visita de Dios', so too the hope and faith mingle with doubt and scepticism, albeit

---

[7] These lines are reminiscent of Francisco de Aldana's sonnet 'Mil veces callo ...', although, while the images and sense of anguish are similar, in Aldana's poem it is the persona himself who is silent (*Poesías castellanas completas*, ed. José Lara Garrido (Madrid: Cátedra, 1985), p. 389):

> Mil veces callo que romper deseo
> el cielo a gritos, y otras tantas tiento
> dar a mi lengua voz y movimiento
> que en silencio mortal yacer la veo.

relatively muted scepticism when compared with 'Cementerio en la ciudad'. Nonetheless, it is sufficient to suggest that all the various reasons and motives for seeking God that we have thus far uncovered are founded more on an inward-looking desperation than on genuine faith in a supernatural God. Nowhere in the poem is the interplay of faith and scepticism greater than in the final stanza:

> Compadécete al fin, escucha este murmullo
> Que ascendiendo llega como una ola
> Al pie de tu divina indiferencia.
> Mira las tristes piedras que llevamos
> Ya sobre nuestros hombros para enterrar tus dones:
> La hermosura, la verdad, la justicia, cuyo afán imposible
> Tú sólo eras capaz de infundir en nosotros. (276–77)

The scepticism is made plain in the way that there is evidently a gulf between God and humanity, encapsulated in the phrase 'tu divina indiferencia'. At the same time, however, the despair and anger earlier in the poem have given way to a sense that only God can inspire the desire for 'beauty, truth and justice', although, crucially, the verb is in a past tense. This confirms the suspicion that this poem is a desperate cry to a Deity in which the persona has very little faith. He is weary and burdened by life and in Christianity sees potential relief from that burden. There is however a sense that, regardless of how positive the virtues of 'beauty, truth and justice' may be, the strain of life may actually be greater than the 'gifts' God once offered. This is suggested by the curious phrase 'para enterrar tus dones', which seems to propose that the pain of life in the modern world is such that it imposes a burden on man for which the knowledge of God could no longer compensate effectively. This inevitably goes a certain way towards undermining the validity of the persona's motivation for seeking God: without some degree of genuine faith that God can intervene in human life, there is little reason to seek Him.

Strange as it might seem, there is actually evidence of more genuine faith in God in the earlier parts of 'La adoración de los Magos' from *Las nubes*, which is the single poem which deals most explicitly with the search for order. It tells the story of the Magi coming to worship the Christ child (although to be precise Cernuda actually uses the legend of the three Kings as opposed to the Biblical story of an unknown number of Magi).[8] When the

---

[8] See Matthew 2. Critics have also observed echoes of Eliot's 'Journey of the Magi' (see Maristany, p. 77, and Fernando Ortiz, 'T. S. Eliot en Cernuda', *Cuadernos Hispanoamericanos*, No. 416 (1985), 104).

poem opens, we are presented with the search already underway. The narration is introduced by Melchor, who of the three characters exhibits the greatest faith and encourages the other two to continue. Melchor expresses his faith in the first section:

> Hombres que duermen
> Y de un sueño de siglos Dios despierta.
> Que enciendan las hogueras en los montes,
> Llevando el fuego rápido la nueva
> A las lindes de reinos tributarios.
> Al alba he de partir. (300)

Melchor is profoundly committed to seeking God. The enthusiasm with which he wishes the news of God's intervention to be broadcast is captured in his desire that fires be lit on the hill-tops. The sign of God's 'waking' of men from their 'slumber' suggests further that God is alive. Nothing further is required to establish the validity of Melchor's search. (The tragedy is however that this will be countered at the end of the poem.) In addition, everything else becomes subordinated to the quest, as is illustrated by the comment 'Al alba he de partir': the serene night scene of the opening stanza of the poem (298) cannot and must not be his final resting-place. What is more, just as the loss of faith was fundamental in the loss of order, so the emergence of faith is essential to a desire to find order once more. Melchor therefore appears to possess precisely what the persona of 'La visita de Dios' lacks, and he has a much more genuine basis for his quest.

Melchor's faith is however only part of the picture. While the poem deals ostensibly with three separate individuals, nevertheless 'all three project certain particular aspects of the poet's contradictory self'.[9] One early hint of the doubt which coexists with Melchor's faith appears when his long speech in section I is interrupted and deflated by the 'demonio', who mockingly says, 'Gloria a Dios en las alturas del cielo,/Tierra sobre los hombres en su infierno' (300), thus briefly recalling the 'hell on earth' standpoint of 'Cementerio en la ciudad'. It is however Baltasar, at the beginning of section II, who is the real voice of scepticism:

> Como pastores nómadas, cuando hiere la espada del invierno,
> Tras una estrella incierta vamos, atravesando de noche los desiertos,
> Acampados de día junto al muro de alguna ciudad muerta,

---

[9] Coleman, p. 105. See also Harris, *Luis Cernuda. A Study*, p. 83, and Jenaro Talens, *El espacio y las máscaras. Introducción a la lectura de Cernuda* (Barcelona: Anagrama, 1975), p. 103.

> Donde aúllan chacales: mientras, abandonada nuestra tierra,
> Sale su cetro a plaza, para ambiciosos o charlatanes que aún
>   exploten
> El viejo afán humano de atropellar la ley, el orden.
> Buscamos la verdad, aunque verdades en abstracto son cosa
>   innecesaria,
> Lujo de soñadores, cuando bastan menudas verdades acordadas.
> (301)

Baltasar lacks any real conviction, believing that the concepts of Absolutes are irrelevant. He likens their following of the star to 'pastores nómadas' because, as far as he is concerned, it is no more than wandering in a desert with no particular purpose other than survival. Man in his opinion should therefore only concern himself with the realities of immediate necessity. Gaspar, meanwhile, takes a different view again:

> Un cuerpo virgen junto al lecho aguarda desnudo, temeroso,
> Los brazos del amante, cuando a la madrugada penetra y duele el
>   gozo.
> Esto es la vida. ¿Qué importan la verdad o el poder junto a esto?
> (302)

Gaspar is happy to ignore thoughts of the eternal and be side-tracked into the indulgence of physical desires and sensuality for their own sake. More important than the three individual attitudes in themselves however is the fact that, in the early stages of the poem, there is not really one which has the upper hand. They are all accorded broadly similar prominence and weight, which produces an effect of indecision when considered together. The situation is therefore subtly different from that in 'La visita de Dios'. Whereas in that poem the reasons for seeking God are undermined by a basic lack of faith, rendering the search somewhat pointless, in 'La adoración de los Magos' *genuine* faith is juxtaposed with scepticism and there is, at least potentially, a foundation on which to build.

There is one final motivating factor behind the quest for the Absolute which demands attention. It is different again from the attitudes expressed in 'La visita de Dios' and 'La adoración de los Magos', principally because the need for faith to sustain the validity of the quest is much less apparent. In 'Atardecer en la catedral', what comes to the fore is a longing for spiritual peace and tranquillity. The persona contemplates the tranquil scene of the sanctuary. The overriding impression is one of peace:

> Como un sueño de piedra, de música callada,
> Desde la flecha erguida de la torre
> Hasta la lonja de anchas losas grises,
> La catedral extática aparece,
> Toda reposo: (282)

These lines stand in contrast to the misery and alienation in 'La visita de Dios'. The principal difference is that, whereas the primary focus of 'La visita de Dios' was the persona himself, in this poem the central point of orientation is the *cathedral*, an inanimate entity which merely represents what it in itself is not. The seed of doubt is nevertheless once again sown by the use of the words 'Como un sueño': even here there is a tinge of unreality. The poem however continues, concentrating on the peacefulness:

> Aquí encuentran la paz los hombres vivos,
> Paz de los odios, paz de los amores,
> Olvido dulce y largo,
>
> ...
>
> No hay lucha ni temor, no hay pena ni deseo.
> Todo queda aceptado hasta la muerte
> Y olvidado tras de la muerte, contemplando,
> Libres del cuerpo, y adorando,
> Necesidad del alma exenta de deleite. (283)[10]

The state for which he yearns is indicative of a particularly extreme form of evasion, where he will be free of all the bonds which tie him to the world. It is not just release from pain which is indicated in these lines, but a release from *all* feelings. The desire thus seems to be a quest for a kind of limbo or oblivion, which is not uncommon within Cernuda's poetry, and frequently has positive overtones.[11] There is nevertheless a tinge of doubt. We under-

---

[10] These lines are reminiscent of the Golden Age Neo-Platonic ideal of the 'vida retirada', escaping from the strain of the world, typified in Luis de León's poem which bears that very title (Fray Luis de León, *Poesías*, ed. Padre Ángel Custodio Vega, 7th ed. (Barcelona: Planeta, 1992), p. 10):

> Vivir quiero conmigo;
> gozar quiero del bien que debo al cielo,
> a solas, sin testigo,
> libre de amor, de celo,
> de odio, de esperanzas, de recelo.

[11] For example, in 'La música' from *Ocnos*, absorption in the music leads to 'la región última del olvido' (585). See also Kevin J[ohn] Bruton, 'The Romantic and Post-

stand his desire for peace, but nevertheless we suspect that the absence of desire and love will result in an emotional state which is no more acceptable than the pain he feels at the moment.[12] It cannot be a lasting solution. Thus there is a strong indication that, having witnessed a whole range of factors motivating the search for absolute order, from the need for spiritual renewal in the depths of despair, to the need for divine intervention in human life and for the company and eternal significance of God, tempered by a tension between faith and scepticism, we are left wondering what chances of success such a quest really has. The very fact that a simple need for peace and evasion of the world is intermingled with the quest in itself provides a clue that we are rather closer to the temporal world than to the eternal kingdom of heaven.

The Goal of the Search

Superficially at least, the goal of the search can be fairly easily defined, as an explicit desire to find God. Moreover, it is specifically the Christian God which appears most consistently (although even in *Las nubes* there is still a tendency to include and assimilate pagan concepts[13]). A closer analysis of the reasons and motivations behind the search has however revealed that such a straightforward understanding is likely to prove an oversimplification. In particular, the inter-relationship of faith and doubt does entail that the Biblical image of God ultimately appears substantially distorted.

One of the most obvious examples of distortion already discussed is the idea of divine indifference in 'La visita de Dios'. Despite this, the predominant picture of God is positive. Perhaps the most positive poem of all in *Las nubes* in its attitude towards God is 'Cordura', where the idea of divine

Romantic Theme of Poetic Space as Exemplified in the Poetry of Luis Cernuda', in *Space and Boundaries in Literature*, Vol. III of *Proceedings of the Twelfth Congress of the International Comparative Literature Association*, ed. R. Bauer, D. Fokkema and M. de Graat (München: Iudicum, 1990), pp. 353–54.

[12] The indolence in *Primeras Poesías* is matched by an equally strong desire to experience love, as for example in poem VII:

> Mas no quiero estos muros,
> Aire infiel a sí mismo,
> Ni esas ramas que cantan
> En el aire dormido.
>
> Quiero como horizonte
> Para mi muda gloria
> Tus brazos, (111)

[13] See for example 'Resaca en Sansueña' (277–81), set between two explicitly Christian-inspired poems, 'La visita de Dios' and 'Atardecer en la catedral'.

grace is accorded particular prominence. Much of 'Cordura' is written in a tone of extreme sadness, with the persona in that all too familiar pose of looking out through a window on to a world outside which is imbued with both positive and negative qualities. The poem opens bleakly with darkness and the sound of rain, the 'campo' is 'amortecido' and winter is approaching. The scene in the second stanza is perhaps slightly more encouraging, with the reference to smoke rising from the 'hogares' suggesting warmth and homeliness. The next stanzas then assume a nostalgic air:

> A veces, por los claros
> Del cielo, la amarilla
> Luz de un edén perdido
> Aún baja a las praderas.
>
> Un hondo sentimiento
> De alegrías pasadas,
> Hechas olvido bajo
> Tierra, llena la tarde. (285)

The attitude is much more serene, but, while the bitterness and cynicism are absent, there is still profound regret for the 'alegrías pasadas'. It is perhaps the reference to 'edén perdido' which is most striking, because there is none of the familiar corresponding allusions to childhood innocence, pastoral idyll, joy in nature or mythical Golden Age. Here instead it is an 'amarilla luz' revealed 'por los claros del cielo'. Superficially this obviously means the sun, but why should the sun be of a 'lost eden'? The reason may lie in the fact that the persona's eyes are turned heavenwards: not any eden but the Biblical Eden, or at least an image more closely allied to the Biblical Eden?[14] It is indeed God that is the central focus of the poem, as is then revealed after the persona meditates further upon the scene outside, graced as it is with that 'luz de un edén perdido':

> Allá, sobre la lluvia,
> Donde anidan estrellas,

---

[14] It must be admitted that the lack of a capital letter for 'edén', combined with the use of the indefinite article, maintains a degree of ambiguity. There can however be no question that the focus on the 'amarilla luz' of the sun does change the perspective from the more common images of, for example, the fall from childhood innocence, as in poem X of *Donde habite el olvido* (208–09; see also below, pp. 108–10), or the idyllic vision of primeval splendour of the 'Égloga' (128–32; see also above, pp. 19–21).

> Dios por su cielo mira
> Dulces rincones grises.
>
> Todo ha sido creado,
> Como yo, de la sombra:
> Esta tierra a mí ajena,
> Estos cuerpos ajenos.
>
> Un sueño, que conmigo
> Él puso para siempre,
> Me aísla. (285–86)

God here is in control. It is a remarkable turnaround from the anger of other poems, so much so in fact that (with good reason as it happens) we could well doubt just how much Cernuda truly believes it. (Or is the persona, like Melchor in 'La adoración de los Magos', representing someone with a faith Cernuda would *like* to possess?) Whichever is true, what matters here is that God is gazing upon His creation, and there is no suggestion that He is indifferent to it. On the contrary, the fact that the persona has been set apart by a 'sueño' which 'Él puso para siempre' could well suggest that God is reaching out towards him: God has planted a 'dream' which will only be fulfilled by faith in Himself.[15] This idea is both confirmed and explored further in the following stanza, when the poem climaxes with an image of God's grace and power:

> Duro es hallarse solo
> En medio de los cuerpos.
> Pero esa forma tiene
> Su amor: la cruz sin nadie. (286)

Again the sense of alienation is reiterated, but note there is also an indication of how the persona can be saved from it, i.e., by God's grace. This is expressed in the image of the empty Cross, the supreme symbol of God's intervention in human life.[16] The Resurrection is the expression of new life, new meaning, direct contact with absolute order. The following stanza then identifies what would result from this new perspective:

---

[15] Bruton goes so far as to say that '[reality's] existence is guaranteed by the "mirada" of ... God' ('"La mirada" in the Poetry of Luis Cernuda–The "Hedgehog on the Prowl"', *Anales de la Literatura Española Contemporánea*, 21 (1996), 31).

[16] See also Harris, *Luis Cernuda. A Study*, p. 81.

> Por ese amor espero,
> Despierto en su regazo,
> Hallar un alba pura
> Comunión con los hombres. (286)

Faith in God, the Absolute, is not purely an egocentric experience, but also represents the key to establishing new relationships with other people: the 'pure dawn' of life in a world which is harmonious, where the poet is not excluded from paradise. It is indeed this very stanza which provides the most convincing evidence that the search is indicative of a genuinely metaphysical concern. All the multitude of personal and existential problems, including the sense of loneliness and isolation, could (it is hoped) be relieved by finding faith in a personal God which would then transform the rest of his life and his contact with others. If 'Cementerio en la ciudad' bespeaks the depths of Hell, then 'Cordura' is as close to the heights of celestial glory to which Cernuda and his personae are likely to ascend.

Crucial as God's saving grace unquestionably is to an understanding of the nature of God in *La realidad y el deseo*, such a depiction is still only partial. It is expounded further in 'La adoración de los Magos' by Melchor, the one figure who truly believes:

> No hay poder sino en Dios, en Dios sólo perdura la delicia;
> El mar fuerte es su brazo, la luz alegre su sonrisa.
> Dejad que el ambicioso con sus torres alzadas oscurezca la tierra;
> Pasto serán del huracán, con polvo y sombra confundiéndolas.
> Dejad que el lujurioso bese y muerda, espasmo tras espasmo;
> Allá en lo hondo siente la indiferencia virgen de los huesos castrados.
> (302)

God embodies 'power' and 'lasting delight', i.e., a profound joy which transcends all mere earthly pleasures. The two ideas are reiterated in the second line in images: the popular images of the strength of the sea to represent power and light to represent joy. The omnipotence of God is then emphasised by contrasting it with the vanity and falseness of man's pathetic strivings. The 'torres alzadas' of line three are assuredly an allusion to the Tower of Babel, symbol of man's foolish arrogance and the sheer impossibility of reaching God by his own efforts. Melchor's attitude to such efforts is scornful, but at the same time the use of 'oscurecer' for the effect of the 'torres alzadas' on the earth should not be disregarded: they do 'darken' the earth inasmuch as they attempt to hide and detract from the truth of God's power, although ultimately they will be destroyed and exposed for the pointless vanity that they are. By the same token, the extent to which earthly pleasures are transcended is underscored in the contemptible behaviour of the 'lujurioso' of line five. (The attitude here is as scornful as it is towards 'el ambicioso' and the 'torres alzadas', slightly surprising considering Cernuda's enduring interest in erotic pleasure, but it must be remembered that Melchor's attitude is only one amongst three.) What matters most is Melchor's rejection of the world: everything on earth is inferior to God.

There is one further significant positive aspect of God's character. This is stated slightly later in the same section of this poem, again by Melchor, when his entire argument is summed up in the one word 'verdad':

> Abandonad el oro y los perfumes, que el oro pesa y los aromas
>   aniquilan.
> Adonde brilla desnuda la verdad nada se necesita. (302)

The first line here, while clearly referring to the Magi's gifts of gold, frankincense and myrrh, is also reminiscent of Christ's injunction not to 'store up for yourselves treasures on earth',[17] but instead to concentrate on the eternal, which is the realm of 'truth'. It is in this that all the various positive qualities of power, joy and saving grace are brought together, and it is only in God that everything is genuinely 'right', complete and perfect: nothing besides is required. Appropriately enough, Melchor does not require to say anything else either, and it is then Baltasar and Gaspar who reply cynically and faithlessly.

There is however a parallel negative current which exists alongside the positive endorsement of faith in God, and which should not be underestimated. The conflict between faith and doubt means that the true Christian image of God becomes distorted. This distortion manifests itself most notably in the portrayal of God as indifferent to humanity, as already commented.[18] This is in stark contrast to the attitude expressed in 'Cordura'. This idea of God's indifference is developed further in 'Las ruinas' from *Como quien espera el alba*:

> Oh Dios. Tú que nos has hecho
> Para morir, ¿por qué nos infundiste
> La sed de eternidad, que hace al poeta?
> ¿Puedes dejar así, siglo tras siglo,
> Caer como vilanos que deshace un soplo
> Los hijos de la luz en la tiniebla avara? (325)

---

[17] Matthew 6:19.
[18] See above, pp. 29 and 50.

While this poem deals primarily with the loss of faith rather than a search for it, nevertheless Cernuda's faith was a very wavering one, and *La realidad y el deseo* must be read as a single, but highly complex and disunified, vision of the world where changes and contradictions are an integral part of it. If we compare this stanza with Melchor's comments in 'La adoración de los Magos', it is striking that, whereas Melchor sees the light of joy, here man is deserted by God to wander in 'la tiniebla avara'. The understanding of the Absolute is therefore one of tension between the desire to believe in divine grace and a severe doubt that God, if He exists, cares about man. This tension is echoed in the meditation on the gods of Antiquity 'Resaca en Sansueña', interposed between 'La visita de Dios' and 'Atardecer en la catedral'. There the despairing comment is made that 'Ninguna voz responde a la pena del hombre' (281). Thus Cernuda's God is simultaneously *both* potentially the saviour of the world *and* remote and unattainable.

There is one principal element of this topic which we have as yet not discussed, and that is the idea that God is, in *La realidad y el deseo*, not so much an entity in His own right, but instead an image on to which the personae project their own desires and longings. It is an attitude which explains many of the contradictions, and is first broached at the end of 'La visita de Dios':

> Si ellas [la hermosura, la verdad, la justicia] murieran hoy, de la
>   memoria tú te borrarías
> Como un sueño remoto de los hombres que fueron. (277)

Harris interprets these lines as an 'Unamunesque God's dependence on man for His existence'.[19] The evidence of God's existence is not so much His own being, but the presence of beauty, truth and justice. If God is effaced by the lack of such virtues, then it is a short step to asserting that these virtues are not proof of His existence, but that His existence is deduced from them, i.e., God is seen as a *projection of man's desire* to interpret the universe as ordered and structured. This is a point which is explored further at the end of the long poem *'Apologia pro vita sua'* from *Como quien espera el alba*. It must be admitted that this is aesthetically not one of Cernuda's most effective poems. It illustrates a tendency to verbosity which affected him spasmodically throughout his poetic career. In the poem the persona reflects on his life and behaviour, thinking especially of friends and lovers, lamenting

---

[19] Harris, *Luis Cernuda. A Study*, p. 82. See also Eloy Sánchez Rosillo, *La fuerza del destino. Vida y poesia de Luis Cernuda* (Murcia: Universidad de Murcia, 1992), p. 132.

in the seventh stanza 'los pecados/Que la ocasión o fuerza de cometer no tuve' (347)[20] and reflecting also on death. The final stanza is probably the most intellectually stimulating one:

> Para morir el hombre de Dios no necesita,
> Mas Dios para vivir necesita del hombre.
> Cuando yo muera, ¿el polvo dirá sus alabanzas?
> Quien su verdad declare, ¿será el polvo?
> Ida la imagen queda ciego el espejo.
> No destruyas mi alma, oh Dios, si es obra de tus manos;
> Sálvala con tu amor, donde no prevalezcan
> En ella las tinieblas con su astucia profunda,
> Y témplala con tu fuego hasta que pueda un día
> Embeberse en la luz por ti creada. (349)

The ideas in this stanza are somewhat difficult to follow, for the conflict between doubt and faith seems to be particularly intense. Fundamental is the notion that God is only a projection of man's feelings. This is stated explicitly in line two, in the way that 'Dios para vivir necesita del hombre'. This is then followed by a confused arrogance which is almost amusing. The argument runs like this: if the persona dies, then there will be no-one to worship God. (We shall ignore the question of what has happened to all the other believers in the world.) God should therefore keep the persona alive ('no destruyas mi alma') so that he can worship Him, and by so doing, since God is said only to exist when people believe in Him, God will presumably keep Himself alive as well. The 'si es obra de tus manos' of line six then once again calls into question whether the persona does believe, before suggesting that the possibility of salvation exists. How are we to resolve these contradictions? The persona uses the notion of God as a means of talking about his fears of death and hopes of immortality. He does not really believe but nevertheless seems to lack the radical conviction which conscious atheism requires, because he still wants something in which to hope. Such feeble faith is however doomed to disappointment.

The concept of the projection of the individual's own ideas is developed still further in 'La adoración de los Magos'. Each character has his own perception of that which he is seeking. The search can be interpreted as little more than a reflection of each man's goals and desires. It is, perhaps surprisingly, in the character of Melchor that this can be seen most clearly. Gaspar

---

[20] I cannot help but wonder if it was Cernuda's unwillingness to repent of sin that was a primary obstacle in his search for God, perhaps even more so than his wavering faith.

and Baltasar have little faith from the very beginning, but the likelihood of
Melchor meeting with God is undermined by his own words in section I:

> ¿Será la magia,
> Ida la juventud con su deseo,
> Posible todavía? Si yo pienso
> Aquí, bajo los ojos de la noche,
> No es menor maravilla; si yo vivo,
> Bien puede un Dios vivir sobre nosotros.
> Mas nunca nos consuela un pensamiento,
> Sino la gracia muda de las cosas. (299)

The initial question, especially with its reference to 'la magia', is a strange
attitude for a believer. There are evidently doubts in Melchor's mind as well
as in Gaspar's and Baltasar's. More important than that is what follows.
Melchor makes use of logical inconsistencies based on his own existence: 'if
I can think and *I* can exist, God can as well'. Certainly the last lines stress
that he wishes to prove his premise, but it is hope, not logic, that underlies
it. The problem is that it is that very lack of logic which lies at the heart of
such a doubting faith. God either exists or does not exist. His existence cannot be 'conjured up' by contemplation of virtues, by self-contemplation or
by hope. The likelihood of failure looms ever nearer.

On the whole, then, the impression is that Cernuda's own images of God
are essentially more of a mirror of all his own highly complex and contradictory thoughts and feelings rather than genuine faith in a genuine God. God
Himself is at best of secondary importance. After offering us only rather
fragmentary evidence in 'La visita de Dios', '*Apologia pro vita sua*' and 'La
adoración de los Magos', Cernuda finally recognises it for what it is in the
ninth stanza of 'Las ruinas':

> Mas tú no existes. Eres tan sólo el nombre
> Que da el hombre a su miedo y su impotencia, (325)

This is the explicit acknowledgement that, while Cernuda has desired faith,
the concept of God is one which he uses as a means to give form and expression to what lies deep within him. The contradictory elements of grace
and indifference and the tension between doubt and faith are merely elements of his desperate struggle to come to terms emotionally and
psychologically with his isolated existence in exile. In the same way that
much of the motivation for the quest is rooted in the trials of the temporal
world, so too the vision and understanding of God is coloured and distorted
by those trials and anxieties. However much Cernuda may want to find God,

his doubt is such that he can never deal with anything other than an image which is only partially concerned with the presence of a genuine supernatural Deity and which therefore cannot have lasting significance.[21] There is thus a strong indication that the goal is in itself ephemeral. And a search for a non-existent goal is doomed inevitably to total failure from the start.

The Process of Searching

How do Cernuda's personae set about the search? Since Cernuda does not intend writing a philosophical or theological treatise but rather wishes to remodel his personal experiences in poetry, there is no single, clear, logical structure to the quest for the Absolute. Certainly there is one coherent narration of a quest, and this is to be found in 'La adoración de los Magos', but, just as this poem provides only a very partial view of the various attitudes towards the nature of God, so too would it be inadequate to take it as the sole indicator of the whole process as it is explored in *La realidad y el deseo*. Once again it is the complexities of Cernuda's poetic vision which come most strongly to the fore.

Given the importance of doubt and scepticism in this quest, it is easy to imagine that there is no real commitment to it either. This however is far from the truth, at least as far as 'La adoración de los Magos' is concerned, where Melchor's faith provides the impetus for the journey to visit the Christ-child. This is not to say that only he exhibits commitment to the search. Baltasar, the unbeliever, illustrates this:

> Como pastores nómadas, cuando hiere la espada del invierno,
> Tras una estrella incierta vamos, atravesando de noche los desiertos,
> Acampados de día junto al muro de alguna ciudad muerta,
> Donde aúllan chacales: mientras, abandonada nuestra tierra,
> Sale su cetro a plaza, (301)

The Magi have abandoned all that they know to embark on a long and difficult journey, leaving behind all certainty and not knowing if it will ever be possible to return. There is a particularly strong impression in these lines of a long, arduous, disorientating journey, with the howling of the jackals lending a note of eerie desolation. Melchor is clearly the leader of the trio. (We ac-

---

[21] There is at least a degree of truth in María Dolores Arana's comment that God 'es el ser con el que habla Cernuda cuando no habla con nadie' ('Sobre Luis Cernuda', in *Luis Cernuda*, ed. Harris, p. 181), although this still does not discount the genuine nature of Cernuda's *desire* for faith at this time. 'Las ruinas' is rather a later recognition of his own lack of faith.

tually discover later that he may have coerced the other two into joining him.) For all Baltasar's pessimism and complaints, however, even he must have some degree of commitment to it. His resistance to Melchor is, however strong, purely verbal, not physical. This is true also of Gaspar. The seriousness of the quest should therefore not be trivialised or underestimated. Moreover, there is a sense that it is only begun properly when everything is renounced in its favour.

This degree of commitment which the Magi exhibit is crucial. It is not until the third section of the poem that we learn just what trials and tests of endurance are involved in their journey. One of the tests of endurance relates to the antagonism between the three men. This is illustrated in section II, when, after each has made a long speech explaining his attitude, there is a rather more rapid interchange between them, the latter part of which is as follows:

Melchor

Locos enamorados de las sombras. ¿Olvidáis, tributarios
Como son vuestros reinos del mío, que aún puedo sujetaros
A seguir entre siervos descalzos el rumbo de mi estrella?
¿Qué es soberbia o lujuria ante el miedo, el gran pecado, la fuerza de
    la tierra?

Baltasar

Con tu verdad pudiera, si la hallamos, alzar un gran imperio.

Gaspar

Tal vez esa verdad, como una primavera, abra rojos deseos. (303)

There is precious little in this dialogue to suggest unity of purpose. Melchor, the believer, is also in human terms the most powerful and evidently can tyranically exert his will upon Baltasar and Gaspar as he pleases. (It seems more than likely that they have been forced even to embark upon the quest, although they never attempt to give up.) If we recall that Baltasar, Gaspar and Melchor can also be interpreted as different aspects of Cernuda's own personality, then it is made vividly clear how violently his feelings must oppose each other: even when placed under duress, Baltasar and Gaspar still reiterate their own convictions. This is becoming, not so much a spiritual quest, as an involved emotional struggle, even a violent psychological battle.

Not only that, it leaves us feeling that disillusionment is already more or less inevitable.

There are still more trials and tests which the Magi have to face, besides their own squabbling. While sections I and II are narrated with the journey still underway, from section III onwards the perspective changes, and the quest and its failure are already over. It is in section III that the narrative progresses towards its tragic climax. It opens with the finding of a 'choza desierta', and the second stanza tells of the physical hardship which has been endured:

> Padecíamos hambre, gran fatiga.
> Al lado de la choza hallamos una viña
> Donde un racimo quedaba todavía,
> Seco, que ni los pájaros lo habían
> Querido. Nosotros lo tomamos:
> De polvo y agrio vino el paladar teñía.
> Era bueno el descanso, pero
> En quietud la indiferencia del paisaje aísla,
> Y añoramos la marcha, la fiebre de la ida. (304)

By the time they find this place they are hungry and tired. The extent of their desperation for food is illustrated vividly by the way they are forced to eat dry, withered grapes which not even the birds would touch. The taste is particularly significant: 'polvo' on the one hand suggests the barren desert, but on the other also the substance to which mortals return on death, while the 'agrio vino' may well be reminiscent of the bitter wine which Christ was given to drink on the Cross. The quest is therefore laden with the aura of death and decay. The last line of the stanza then stresses once more its significance: despite all this pain and foreboding, they still apparently long for 'la fiebre de la ida'. This however seems curious, in the light of the bitter arguing and squabbling in section II. This tends to suggest that the narrator here is actually Melchor and it his own 'fiebre de la ida' of which he speaks. His need to hide such antagonism however only serves to increase the sense of trial and difficulty in this search.

If, in 'La adoración de los Magos', Cernuda graphically illustrates the difficulty of seeking the Absolute by referring to difficult journeys, problems and antagonism, in 'Cordura' he considers the problems in more explicitly spiritual terms:

> Por ese amor espero,
> Despierto en su regazo,

Hallar un alba pura
Comunión con los hombres.

Mas la luz deja el campo.
Es tarde y nace el frío.
Cerrada está la puerta,
Alumbrando la lámpara.

Por las sendas sombrías
Se duele el viento ahora
Como alma aislada en lucha.
La noche será breve. (286)

Following the affirmation of divine love, as symbolised in the 'cruz sin nadie' of earlier in the poem,[22] the persona looks forward to a new idyllic relationship with others which should follow his being reunited with God. Despite this optimism, there follows the line 'Mas la luz deja el campo', given emphasis by its position as a single bald sentence at the beginning of a stanza. Before he may see the dawn, night must come. Cold reappears and the door is closed: as is so often the case, the persona is confined inside. Then in the final stanza the darkness is reiterated and the wind ominously 'se duele' 'como alma aislada en lucha'. What is more, even although the over-riding sentiment is one of hope with the last line 'La noche será breve', nevertheless it is not yet a reality. In the same way that Cernuda's Magi are physically separated from God, the persona of 'Cordura' can as yet communicate neither with God, nor with other people.

Considering that this quest is to find absolute order in the face of chaos, there has been so far remarkably little evidence of joy, anticipation or excitement at the prospect. Despite all the doom and gloom which surrounds these various poems (and thus prepares us for the failure), Melchor in 'La adoración de los Magos' nonetheless does register some genuine personal excitement at the prospect of meeting with God incarnate, albeit extremely short-lived. This emerges in that very doom-laden section III, when, in the third stanza, the star stops over the 'choza':

Vimos la estrella hacia lo alto
Que estaba inmóvil, pálida como el agua
En la irrupción del día, una respuesta dando
Con su brillo tardío del milagro

---

[22] See above, p. 56.

Sobre la choza. Los muros sin cobijo
Y el dintel roto se abrían hacia el campo,
Desvalidos. Nuestro fervor helado
Se volvió como el viento de aquel páramo.
Dimos el alto. Todos descabalgaron.
Al entrar en la choza, refugiados
Una mujer y un viejo sólo hallamos. (304–05)

At the beginning of the stanza we see the 'miracle' happening before our very eyes. The star has been moving, the Magi have been following it and now it comes to rest. Melchor, who we assume to be the speaker, gratefully imagines his life's dream to be coming true, and he cannot contain his excitement. Admitting to having been discouraged earlier ('fervor helado'), he now joyously puts all his doubts aside and rushes towards the 'choza' to see the Christ-child. There is real joy and hope evident here, but nevertheless what Melchor sees is enough to cause us consternation: 'Los muros sin cobijo', 'el dintel roto', the adjective 'desvalidos', placed in the strong position at the beginning of the line to emphasise how bleak the picture really is. The fact therefore that they only find 'una mujer y un viejo' inside may be a surprise to the Magi, but it is by now precisely what we expect. The joy of anticipation and excitement is sheer delusion.

Melchor now believes and hopes that he is on the threshold of attaining his goal (although the obvious tragedy is that he is in reality on the threshold of disaster). Before we analyse that in detail it is important to note that there are two different ways expressed in *Las nubes* of communicating with God: directly with God the Father and less directly through Christ. It is clearly the way through Christ that is explored in 'La adoración de los Magos', but first it is worthwhile to consider direct communion with God, which appears towards the end of 'Atardecer en la catedral':

El suelo besan quedos unos pasos
Lejanos. Alguna forma, a solas,
Reza caída ante una vasta reja
Donde palpita el ala de una llama amarilla.

Llanto escondido moja el alma,
Sintiendo la presencia de un poder misterioso
Que el consuelo creara para el hombre,
Sombra divina hablando en el silencio.

Aromas, brotes vivos surgen,
Afirmando la vida, tal savia de la tierra

> Que irrumpe en milagrosas formas verdes,
> Secreto entre los muros de este templo, (284)

The scene of the solitary individual at prayer is clearly profoundly moving for the persona, possibly far more so than his own dreams of peace and tranquillity and escape from the trials of the world.[23] The climax of the experience comes at the end of the first stanza quoted, where there is an almost mystical awareness of a 'poder misterioso' and a 'sombra divina'. The genuine faith and meaningful prayers of the stranger have led to direct communion with God, so intimate that even the persona is able to sense it. The closing stanza then enunciates the joyous emotions attendant on such an experience of God: the second line in particular stresses the abundance of life and vitality, the assonance on the 'a'-vowel bringing together and underlining the key words 'afirmando', 'vida', 'savia' and finally 'tierra', which, contrary to other poems, where it can suggest death, here is indicative of the element from which 'formas verdes' will grow. As always with Cernuda's poetry, however, there is a negative side to this as well: the persona is only a spectator, and, while he has been moved, he has not experienced God for himself at first hand.

Direct communion with God in this way is, however, only one possibility. In addition to this, there is a desire for mediation between the divine and human spheres, seeking Christ, 'the one mediator between God and man'.[24] Potentially, the Risen Christ of 'Cordura' can fulfil this rôle and allow 'comunión con los hombres', but that is not the only way in which Christ is portrayed. While, according to the Bible, Christ is the one true mediator precisely because he is also God, in 'La adoración de los Magos', this is the child the Magi find:

> Un niño entre sus brazos la mujer guardaba.
> Esperamos un dios, una presencia
> Radiante e imperiosa, cuya vista es la gracia,
> Y cuya privación idéntica a la noche
> Del amante celoso sin la amada. (305)

This is the *desengaño* in the search for God. The Magi expected to find the divine Christ, the Messiah, the Saviour of the world, who would be imbued with the omnipotence and love of God and who would be able to rescue mankind from its misery. God incarnate is not however present in this

---

[23] See above, pp. 52–54.
[24] I Timothy 2:5.

'choza', and the tragedy of human life separated from God is expressed in the vivid image of a jealous lover abandoned by his beloved. Life without God is typified by an acute solitude combined with an all-consuming longing for what has been missed. They are instead forcibly returned to that entirely human sphere, for the potential mediator whom they find is an ordinary child:

> Hallamos una vida como la nuestra humana,
> Gritando lastimosa, con ojos que miraban
> Dolientes, bajo el peso de su alma
> Sometida al destino de las almas, (305)

The Magi desperately seek the Absolute and in doing so place their hope in the ability of someone to act as a bridge between the earthly and the eternal. For that bridge to be effective, it must be equal with God, but, rather than finding Christ the Saviour, all they encounter is someone in a situation no less pitiable than their own, i.e., he is entirely equal with man. Indeed, Cernuda's Christ child is burdened more than he can stand by people's expectations of him which he cannot fulfil. The Magi then make one final, desperate attempt to realise their dream by presenting their gifts, still longing to find a mediator between God and man, 'tal si la ofrenda rica/Pudiera hacer al dios' (305), but the grim reality is that they are only trying to engender faith from what they now recognise was a vain hope. Thus from direct, actual communion with God in 'Atardecer en la catedral', we shift ground in 'La adoración de los Magos'. This should only be a difference of perspective, for the focus is on Christ, who is also God, but by the end of section III Christ has become exclusively human, and in humanity there is no hope of salvation.

Metaphysical yearnings are not the only content of 'La adoración de los Magos'. Attention has been drawn previously to the hedonism of Gaspar, and this is an integral part of the process of searching in 'La adoración de los Magos'. The temptation to yield to the demands of ordinary life still makes itself felt, as is evident in the second section:

> Amo el jardín, cuando abren las flores serenas del otoño,
> El rumor de los árboles, cuya cima dora la luz toda reposo, (301)

In the midst of the struggle for faith, there is a pull, equally strong, to be side-tracked by physical, sensuous pleasures. When in the same stanza Gaspar says, 'Vivo estoy' (302), this deviation from the chosen path appears at least equally valid. What is surprising is that there are actually hints that Melchor, for all his protestation in the opening stanza that 'Todo lo cansa el tiempo' and 'sólo encuentro en los demás mentira' (298), is not so far away from Gaspar's hedonistic desires as we might expect. In the sixth stanza of that same first section he betrays such feelings:

> Mas tengo sed. Lágrimas de la viña,
> Frescas al labio con frescor ardiente,
> Tal si un rayo de sol atravesara
> La neblina. Delicia de los frutos
> De piel tersa y oscura, como un cuerpo
> Ofrecido en la rama del deseo. (299–300)

In admitting to needs such as thirst he cannot help but realise that satisfying bodily functions can be a source of genuine pleasure: 'Lágrimas de la viña' is surely a (rather over-written) way of referring to wine, which slakes the thirst 'con frescor ardiente'. The thought of grapes then leads him on to 'un cuerpo/Ofrecido en la rama del deseo'. Is this perhaps regret for an actual person he has renounced? He certainly cannot hide the note of wistful longing. Despite the desire for pleasure, however, both Melchor's attitude and indeed Gaspar's are relativised when, in the fourth section, a shepherd remembers their fate:

> Uno muerto al regreso, de su tierra distante;
> Otro, perdido el trono, esclavo fue, o mendigo;
> Otro a solas viviendo, presa de la tristeza. (307)

According to Harris, the fates that the three suffer correspond, respectively, to those of Melchor, Baltasar and Gaspar.[25] If we assume that Gaspar returns to the pursuit of pleasure, then his fate is solitude. Melchor, meanwhile, 'muerto al regreso', evidently did not even see his hedonistic impulses as worth pursuing as a substitute. Thus, while being distracted from the search may appear attractive and even potentially more fulfilling than the search itself, its ultimate result is no less distressing.

The lack of fulfilment in becoming side-tracked in 'La adoración de los Magos' does not however lead to a more single-minded determination to seek the Absolute in the rest of *Las nubes*. The attractions of the world are also visible in Cernuda's arrangement of the poems, for, while the majority in this section of *Las nubes* deal with Cernuda's religious musings, certain poems are interpolated which reiterate a desire to concentrate on other things. The poem 'Jardín antiguo', for example, is an expression of nostalgia

---

[25] Harris, *Luis Cernuda. A Study*, p. 83.

for the hidden garden of *Primeras Poesías* where everything seemed in harmony.[26] All its beauty and tranquillity are recalled, and there is a strong inclination to return:

> Sentir otra vez, como entonces,
> La espina aguda del deseo,
> Mientras la juventud pasada
> Vuelve. Sueño de un dios sin tiempo. (297)

Cernuda remembers with longing and affection the 'paradise substitute' of his youth. It would give him great pleasure to abandon his search for existential security in the chaos of his present life in favour of that sense of security he once felt away from the temporal world. At the same time, however, he is too honest to pretend that the present is, or could ever be, the same as the past. The poem expresses a dream, not reality, and, however positive the poet may be towards dreams, the speculative 'sentir' as opposed to an affirmative 'siento' makes this unreality clear.[27] It is gone, and again the world seems to have little to offer.

If the attitude towards hedonism and past pleasures is ambivalent, i.e., attractive and yet unfulfilling, the disastrous outcome of the quest is definitive. The search for absolute order becomes merged back into a more general search for order and meaning in life, seeking largely material rather than metaphysical, supra-human order, which may at least enrich the moment. This is of course immediately reminiscent of the side-tracking into sensuality which we have just investigated, but it is not so simple. Rather than mere hedonism or a dream of a hidden refuge, the 'Epitafio' of 'La adoración de los Magos' opens thus:

---

[26] The hidden garden is a refuge, a haven of peace and tranquillity, where the dreaming persona may revel in indolent rest. (See for example poem XXIII of *Primeras Poesías* (122–23), and below, pp. 84–85.)

[27] Such a desire for a 'paradise substitute' is a recurrent feature in Cernuda's poetry, but it is interesting that, in his more mature poetry, this attitude becomes more ambivalent. Bruton points out that 'Elegía Anticipada' recalls a cemetery which 'contains all the elements of Sansueña, Cernuda's paradise on earth' ('The Cemetery Poems of Luis Cernuda', *Anales de la Literatura Española Contemporánea*, 13 (1988), 194, and *Poesía completa*, pp. 358–60), but there is the awareness in the sixth stanza of the poem of 'la conciencia/De que tu vida allí tuvo su cima' (359). The preterite 'tuvo' indicates that this 'cima' is passed and gone. Bruton comments further that in all of Cernuda's cemetery poems there is a 'tension created between the cemetery as *temenos* encapsulating innermost values and the cemetery as unpalatable Death' ('The Cemetery Poems', 202).

> La delicia, el poder, el pensamiento
> Aquí descansan. Ya la fiebre es ida. (308)

For the shepherd of the epitaph, this idyll in nature is a reality. After the defeat of the quest, fulfilment in nature is, at least temporarily, presented as a genuine possibility rather than a vague Romantic dream, and the 'fiebre' of the Magi is gone. It is this quality of peaceful reality which makes it different from the distractions previously noted. Nevertheless, while it would appear to be a reality for the shepherd, it is not reality for the Magi. Not only that, while the whole of the quest has illustrated the problems, doubts, setbacks and steady loss of faith at least as much as the signs of progress towards the goal, it is not until the conclusion of the quest is reached that the despair of the final loss of faith acquires its greatest tragic intensity.

The Result of the Search

The loss of faith is by now apparent. We should however focus briefly on a discussion of the way in which this failure is expressed. It was seen earlier how, in section III of 'La adoración de los Magos', the discovery of the feeble child is anticipated by the atmosphere of doom and foreboding. The perspective in section IV then shifts to that of an old shepherd recalling the coming of the Magi when he was a young man. He is able to afford further insights into the disastrous outcome of the Magi's quest, in particular building upon the aura of tragic inevitability so apparent in section III:

> Tiempo atrás, siendo joven, divisé una mañana
> Cruzar por la llanura un extraño cortejo:
> Jinetes en camellos, cubiertos de ropajes
> Cenicientos, que daban un destello de oro. (306)

There are certain unsettling elements evident in the appearance of the Magi. First, he refers to them as an 'extraño cortejo': he is obviously baffled by their presence, and the overtones of 'cortejo fúnebre' lend an ominous ring. Second, they are '*jinetes* en camellos': 'horsemen on camels'. There is something incongruous, even false about them. Third, and most serious of all, they are 'cubiertos de ropajes/*Cenicientos*' which only 'daban un destello de oro'. 'Ashen' is a very odd adjective to use for robes, and it is not satisfactorily explained by the likelihood of dust from the desert adhering to them. It is as if ashes have been deliberately used to give the appearance of gold. All of these elements suggest that they are rather unimpressive 'Magi-substitutes' rather than exuding the Eastern exotic regal nature of the true Magi. The seventh and eighth stanzas then undermine them and their quest even more:

> Eran reyes que el ocio y poder enloquecieron,
> En la noche siguiendo el rumbo de una estrella,
> Heraldo de otro reino más rico que los suyos.
> Pero vieron la estrella pararse en este llano,
>
> Sobre la choza vieja, albergue de pastores.
> Entonces fue refugio dulce entre los caminos
> De una mujer y un hombre sin hogar ni dineros:
> Un hijo blanco y débil les dio la madrugada. (307)

Far from being prompted by a prophetic vision, the Magi according to the shepherd were driven mad by 'ocio y poder': they are petty tyrants with little better to do and no deductive power to appreciate the pointlessness of their behaviour. What is more, the fact that the star is depicted as 'heraldo de otro reino más rico que los suyos' suggests that the pursuit of earthly wealth (rather than true spiritual wealth) may well have been a motivating factor. Then, finally, after all this building up of gloom and foreboding, which illustrates the sheer folly of the Magi, the finding of the child is again described. Unlike in section III, however, when Melchor describes his enthusiasm at witnessing a miracle, i.e., the stopping of the star, the shepherd is rather less awe-struck. This is because, rather than a 'reino más rico', it has been revealed as a refuge of a poverty-stricken, homeless couple with a weak child. The shepherd knows of no miracle to describe, and has no reason to pretend.

All the signs of imminent failure have been made quite unmistakable, but the Magi fail to perceive them until they see the child for themselves. By the same token, while we already know of the failure in section III from Melchor's account, it is not until this stage that we have full access to all of those signs either, because the Magi held them back. The disastrous climax is reached at the end of the fourth section:

> Y al entrar en la choza descubrieron los reyes
> La miseria del hombre, de que antes no sabían.
>
> Luego, como quien huye, el regreso emprendieron.
> También los caminantes pasaron a otras tierras
> Con su niño en los brazos. Nada supe de ellos.
> Soles y lunas hubo. Joven fui. Viejo soy.

> Gentes en el mercado hablaron de los reyes:
> Uno muerto al regreso, de su tierra distante;
> Otro, perdido el trono, esclavo fue, o mendigo;
> Otro a solas viviendo, presa de la tristeza.
>
> Buscaban un dios nuevo, y dicen que le hallaron.
> Yo apenas vi a los hombres; jamás he visto dioses. (307–08)

The Magi sought divine grace, the one mediator between God and man, the miracle of salvation, but all they found was 'la miseria del hombre'. The extent of the *desengaño* is such that they are actually in a worse situation than before: previously they did not know of this misery. All that had once been the driving force of existence has been identified as worthless, rendering their lives far more meaningless than ever before. This is highlighted by the fact that they leave 'como quien huye': they cannot bear to remain any longer in the sight of the source of all despair. The unexceptional nature of Cernuda's Christ is emphasised by the way in which the family also leave and go on their way, to return to a normal, mundane existence. The opening line of the final stanza quoted is however curious, for it claims, 'dicen que le hallaron'. Why should this be, given the acute sense of failure? There is a similar sentiment in the epitaph, viz., 'Buscaron la verdad, pero al hallarla/No creyeron en ella' (308). There is thus a tension between finding there is nothing in which to believe, and finding genuine faith but consciously rejecting it. The shepherd who narrates this confirms that he too has never seen any gods. The most likely interpretation is this: they *did* find truth, but what was true was that man was only faced with misery and no prospect of salvation. Their claim to have seen 'un dios nuevo' must therefore have been little more than the last feeble protestation that their life and quest had not been in vain.

One of the principal motivating factors for undertaking the search for absolute order was to find solace from existential isolation in the midst of a chaotic, meaningless world. It is easy to see that the 'verdad' the Magi in this poem find has returned them to that situation. Thus the Magi would have been better off had they never tried to find God. We are reminded of just how acute this abandonment of man to his own destiny is in the much later poem 'Nochebuena cincuenta y una' from *Con las horas contadas*, which is a bitter reflection on the loss of faith:

> Amor, dios oscuro,
> Que a nosotros viene
> Otra vez, probando
> Su esperanza siempre. (467)

'Amor', stressed as it is by being placed at the very beginning of the poem, is a key concept in the poem as a whole, being mentioned again in the third and fifth stanzas. (As a five-stanza poem, the symmetrical arrangement is clear and underscores the importance of 'amor'.) Crucial as it is to the poem, it is important to recognise that it is a Christian or spiritual love to which it assuredly refers rather than an erotic form of love. The poem thus seems to start on a positive note, but this is immediately negated by the following phrase 'dios oscuro': in the first place the refusal to capitalise 'dios' clearly robs the word of some of its importance,[28] while the adjective 'oscuro' points towards distance, indifference, concealment. The latter part of the stanza then, through the use of 'probando', indicates that there is little point in trying to pretend that 'amor' can have any effect upon this world. The most cynical part of the poem is the second stanza:

> Ha nacido. El frío,
> La sombra, la muerte,
> Todo el desamparo
> Humano es su suerte. (467)

This stanza has a clever construction. The first bald sentence 'Ha nacido' ostensibly means 'He (i.e., Christ) is born'. While grammatically 'El frío', 'La sombra', 'la muerte' and 'Todo el desamparo/Humano' are all in apposition to each other as the subject of 'es', the juxtaposition of 'Ha nacido' with 'El frío', together with a verb postponed for three lines, can equally suggest the meaning 'El frío ha nacido', especially if the poem is read aloud. The anniversary of the birth of Christ is, for the persona, no more than a painful reminder of man's isolation, and his Christ is no more than a helpless heir to all of human misery and suffering.

The basic stance of the poem has now been articulated, and the remaining three stanzas reflect upon it. It is interesting that, having mentioned 'dios' in the opening line of the poem, it never recurs. Not only that, it is really only the title, 'Nochebuena cincuenta y una', which tells us that the poem is about Christ, for the name is never mentioned at all. This can only devalue the status of both God and Christ in the poem, which must be intended to reflect the lack of relevance of the Deity in Cernuda's world. Such cynicism forms the core of the closing part of the poem:

> Desamparo humano
> Que el amor no puede

---

[28] Cernuda does frequently capitalise it. See for example 'La visita de Dios' (274–77).

Ayudar. ¿Podría
Él, cuando tan débil

Contra nuestro engaño
Su fuerza se vuelve,
Siendo sólo aliento
De bestia inocente?

Velad pues, pastores;
Adorad pues, reyes,
Su sueño amoroso
Que el mundo escarnece. (467)

The degree of human misery and helplessness ('Desamparo humano') is coupled with the inability of this Christ to help in these circumstances: 'Que el amor no puede/Ayudar'. Not only that, he is 'tan débil/Contra nuestro engaño': the persona includes himself among a vast body of disbelieving humanity and sees no prospect of divine intervention. It is however the final stanza which is particularly interesting, for, after the despair and cynical lack of faith of the rest of the poem, there is an injunction to the shepherds to 'velar' and to the Magi to 'adorar'. Surely this does not advocate a return to faith after all that has been done to express its failure? On the contrary, the object of 'valer' and 'adorar' is subtly changed from 'el amor' to the '*sueño amoroso*'. It is only the dream of love which is left in the world as far as the persona is concerned (which is why there is no explicit reference to Christ) and that is the only thing in which hope can be placed. The tragic devaluation of God could not be more definitive.

We must bear in mind the devaluation of God's relevance if we are to grasp the full meaning of 'Las ruinas' from *Como quien espera el alba*, which deals explicitly with the loss of faith in God. (The 'tú' here is God Himself):

Mas tú no existes. Eres tan sólo el nombre
Que da el hombre a su miedo y su impotencia,
Y la vida sin ti es esto que parecen
Estas mismas ruinas bellas en su abandono:
Delirio de la luz ya sereno a la noche,
Delirio acaso hermoso cuando es corto y es leve. (325)

Man for Cernuda is alone in the universe because Gos is only a projection of man's 'miedo y impotencia'. We observed in 'La adoración de los Magos' the way in which the old shepherd lives a peaceful, idyllic existence in harmony with the natural environment.[29] Such a stance is reflected in 'Las ruinas'. The phrase 'Delirio de la luz' reiterates the feeling of disorientation, but there is a crucial change: it is 'ya sereno' and 'acaso hermoso'. There is a tentative suggestion that there is something in the natural world that is worth seeking for its own sake, something to give order in the world of chaos which is not absolute but may nevertheless be meaningful:

> Todo lo que es hermoso tiene su instante, y pasa.
> Importa como eterno gozar de nuestro instante.
> Yo no te envidio, Dios; déjame a solas
> Con mis obras humanas que no duran:
> El afán de llenar lo que es efímero
> De eternidad, vale tu omnipotencia. (325)

Any concept of absolute order is here rejected. While the search originally appeared to have the potential to find transcendental order, the reality is failure. The persona now seeks a permanence within the temporal sphere as opposed to a permanent force which has authority and power over the temporal sphere. It is an expression of independence, of a desire to go forward on his own, for he can see a relevance and significance in individual moments and thus focus on the details of life rather than have to grapple with the major questions of universal import. There is indeed a solipsistic arrogance in these lines which revalues the persona's own individuality to the exclusion of all else. There is a desire to ignore death, to seize the day and recognise beauty for what it is. It sounds almost heroic, but is there a new order to come, or is chaos still looming on the horizon? The very fact that this is phrased as a question suggests a lack of total certainty. Just how precarious such a stance proves to be will quickly become apparent.

---

[29] See above, p. 71.

CHAPTER FOUR

SEARCH FOR ORDER IN THE MATERIAL WORLD I:
'LOVE'

The Sexual Awakening

'Love'[1] and eroticism form one of the most frequently recurring themes in *La realidad y el deseo*. While it should not be accorded undue emphasis (*La realidad y el deseo* as a whole is far from being a book of erotic poetry), nevertheless it plays a major rôle. Many poems are devoted to various aspects of eroticism, while in still more poems an erotic situation can be used as a springboard for considering matters of more general or even universal concern.[2] It is useful to subdivide the poetry dealing with 'love' into that which is concerned with adolescent erotic experiences on the one hand[3] and that which is concerned with experiences in maturity on the other, since much of what happens in adolescence is a preparation for the later events.

Even although the world of adolescence only receives limited attention, there is no reason to assume that the poetry relating to that period is all exactly the same. On the contrary, the poetry of adolescence can be further subdivided into that which focusses on a world of innocence, and that which focusses on the awareness of awakening sexual inclinations. The world of innocence is very positive, even idyllic: this has already been witnessed in the

---

[1] The general term 'love' has been chosen for reasons of convenience rather than for its semantic accuracy. In more specific terms it covers a wide range of emotions which form part of the human experience whereby one person feels attraction for another. Thus while 'love' in its most common meaning of mutual attraction and emotional involvement between two people is certainly one aspect of this discussion, it also involves the related emotions of desire, passion, erotic impulses and instincts, physical infatuation and so on.

[2] See above, pp. 8–15.

[3] While *Primeras Poesías* does not mention the specific age of the persona, it can be deduced as referring to adolescence by the presence of, and subsequent fall from, the world of innocence. See also Harris, *Luis Cernuda. A Study*, pp. 20–33, for a detailed study of the poetry of adolescence. Hughes meanwhile rightly stresses that *Primeras Poesías* is poetry 'with an adolescent protagonist' as opposed to 'mere adolescent outpourings' ('Cernuda and the Poetic Imagination: *Primeras Poesías* as Metaphysical Poetry', *Anales de Literatura Española*, 1 (1982), 322).

opening poem of *Primeras Poesías*, where there is a tranquil picture of an harmonious natural world, upon which the persona can gaze in optimism.[4] That poem is probably the most positive one in the collection. From then on there is a disillusionment which steadily encroaches upon the life of the persona. One poem where the joy of innocence is still central is number V. Like the first poem of the collection, this poem is witness to the harmony of nature:

> Ninguna nube inútil,
> Ni la fuga de un pájaro,
> Estremece tu ardiente
> Resplandor azulado.
>
> Así sobre la tierra
> Cantas y ríes, cielo,
> Como un impetuoso
> Y sagrado aleteo.
>
> ...
>
> Y el acorde total
> Da al universo calma:
> Árboles a la orilla
> Soñolienta del agua.
>
> Sobre la tierra estoy;
> Déjame estar. Sonrío
> A todo el orbe; extraño
> No le soy porque vivo. (110)

This poem concentrates on the splendour of a clear blue sky, and all of nature works together to ensure that this scene is quite perfect. The harmony and unity are underlined by the sound of the very first line: the alliteration of the 'n' sound, together with the assonance of the 'i' and 'u' vowels, closely binds the three words together, stressing that there is no cloud, no negative feature, to interrupt the beauty of the sky. Not only that, the sky is an essential part of this world. It is not separate or distant from it at all, but 'laughs and sings' in the joy of existence. All of this is then summed up in the phrase 'el acorde total': everything in the universe is both vital and plays an integral rôle in this idyll.[5] The persona then finally appears in the closing stanza, and

---

[4] See above, pp. 23–25.
[5] See also Harris, p. 23.

he too is incorporated into this universe, assuming the rôle of the sky 'sobre la tierra'. There is obviously nothing to detract from this. This is the joy of innocence in all its wonder and excitement. Despite this, the very fact that he is 'sobre la tierra' indicates that he is dreaming. He may claim to be alive but that sort of reverie is no more than a half-life, and the world proper has not yet been encountered. Some of the subtlest hints of that initial encounter do appear in poem XIV:

> Ingrávido presente.
> Las ramas abren trémulas.
> Cándidamente escapan
> Estas horas sin fuerza.
>
> ...
>
> Olvidarán mis días
> Su abanico de humo
> Y un ángel lo abrirá
> Una noche ya mustio.
>
> Una noche que finja
> Lo distante inmediato.
> Y bajará la luna
> A posarse ¿en qué mano? (116–17)

This poem opens in a manner strongly reminiscent of poems I and V, with the same sense of joy and harmony, but the closing two stanzas are slightly different. In the first place, the phrasing is rather enigmatic: what is the 'abanico de humo'? What is the rôle of the 'ángel' and the 'luna'? Any interpretation of these lines must be somewhat speculative, but the fact that the 'abanico de humo' will not be opened again until it is 'ya mustio' lends an ominous ring. In addition, the fact that the poem ends with a question, with the persona only wondering into whose hands the 'moon' will be placed, suggests uncertainty. It seems at least plausible that these future events are symbolic of an interaction with the world, whatever it might be, which has yet to take place. What matters most is that the persona seems to register feelings of disquiet and uncertainty when he faces the future.

If these feelings of disquiet and uncertainty, however muted, are indeed present in poem XIV, then it is with good reason that the persona experiences them. That is because, when definite indications of erotic impulses do emerge, they are swiftly attended by negative emotions. This can be seen explicitly in poem VII:

Existo, bien lo sé,
Porque le transparenta
El mundo a mis sentidos
Su amorosa presencia.

Mas no quiero estos muros,
Aire infiel a sí mismo,
Ni esas ramas que cantan
En el aire dormido.

Quiero como horizonte
Para mi muda gloria
Tus brazos, que ciñendo
Mi vida la deshojan.

Vivo un solo deseo,
Un afán claro, unánime;
Afán de amor y olvido.
Yo no sé si alguien cae. (111–12)

The amorous experience here is far removed from genuine involvement. We argued above that the opening stanza does suggest a degree of happiness and fulfilment, inasmuch as the 'amorosa presencia' confirms the persona's existence, but that the second stanza highlights feelings of frustration.[6] As far as the first stanza is concerned, it is little more than the awareness of the presence of passion which is the confirmation that he is alive, for the persona himself is clearly alone:[7] there exists the physical barrier of the walls between the persona and the 'brazos' of the beloved.[8] What is more, the use of

---

[6] See above, pp. 11–12.

[7] While Manuel Ulacia acknowledges the isolation (*Luis Cernuda: Escritura, cuerpo y deseo* (Barcelona: Laia, 1986), p. 120), he nevertheless overstates the degree of happiness in the first stanza when he claims that the poet is 'en extática comunión con el mundo' and there is 'un momento de plenitud' (p. 117).

[8] As Soufas comments, Cernuda 'defines himself as an incompleteness or absence' ('Ideologizing Form: Anti-Mimetic Language Theories in the Early Poetry of Jorge Guillén and Luis Cernuda', *Anales de la Literatura Española Contemporánea*, 16 (1991), 111). Francisco Romero ignores this aspect of the wall imagery in *Primeras Poesías*, arguing that the wall represents the protection which the persona's room offers, although he concedes that the wall does later come to represent a 'cárcel' ('El muro y la ventana: La "otredad" de Luis Cernuda', *Cuadernos Hispanoamericanos*, No. 396 (1983), 551 & 559). Begoña Ibáñez Avendaño meanwhile differentiates between 'muro' and 'pared', arguing that, 'Las paredes protegen la fragilidad del mundo infantil, el muro, sin embargo,

the verb 'existir' rather than 'vivir' (as for example in poem V) suggests that the persona's life is not particularly vibrant or dynamic. The third and fourth stanzas then emphasise the eroticism, with the persona gripped by a powerful desire for the loved one.[9] Despite this, the desire is curiously one-sided: the only explicit reference to the beloved (or imagined beloved) is 'Tus brazos'.[10] The preoccupation may be at least as much with a largely impersonal infatuation as with a specific human being. The sensuous side of 'love' as the important one at this stage is emphasised by the line 'Quiero como *horizonte*'. The word 'horizonte' suggests that it is with the beloved's arms that 'love' begins and ends, that there is nothing of significance beyond.[11] Nonetheless, the overall picture is ambivalent, and it is clear that the persona has had more than a glimpse of chaos.

From feelings of isolation and frustration it is but a short step to despair in the face of a sterile, pointless existence, where fruitful interaction with others is denied. That sort of sentiment lies at the heart of poem XXI. Like poems V and XIV, XXI opens with the persona observing the landscape, but this time the light of day is disappearing, making way for 'la noche desierta' (121), and the persona is confined inside, in a room lit by feeble artificial lamp-light. The atmosphere of gloom intensifies substantially from the third stanza onwards:

> Sólo el azul relámpago,
> Que vierte la ventana
> Hacia fuera, en el tiempo
> Misterioso resbala.

presagia la muerte y el olvido' (*El símbolo en «La realidad y el deseo» de Luis Cernuda. El aire, el agua, el muro y el acorde como génesis literaria* (Kassel: Reichenberger, 1994), p. 36, n. 147). She is right to stress both sides of the wall imagery, but it is difficult to reconcile the 'muro/pared' split with poem XXIII of *Primeras Poesías* (122–23 and below, pp. 84–85), which depicts an idyllic garden 'Escondido *en los muros*'.

[9] Harris is correct up to a point when he says, 'Here is the emphatic proclamation of love's dream as the sole aim and purpose of his existence' (*Luis Cernuda. A Study*, p. 26), certainly in the context of poem VII. The generalisation which this statement implies is however an exaggeration.

[10] The reference to 'olvido' is also significant, a state frequently suggesting, as Newman comments, a means of 'evasión de la soledad' ('«Primeras Poesías». 1924–27', *La Caña Gris*, Nos. 6–8 (Otoño de 1962), 94). This emphasises the fact that the desire is very one-sided: such a state of 'olvido' has little need of another person.

[11] Harris observes that 'este horizonte se revela como el recinto cerrado por los brazos de un amante, y, por lo tanto, es otra forma de encarcelamiento' ('La preocupación existencial y su expresión poética en *La realidad y el deseo*', in *Actas del primer congreso internacional sobre Luis Cernuda (1902–1963)*, ed. J. Cortines (Sevilla: Universidad de Sevilla, 1990), p. 111). This underlines the frustration felt by the persona.

> Cuán vanamente atónita
> Resucita de nuevo
> La soledad. ¿Soñar?
> Soñaremos que sueño.
>
> Es la paz necesaria.
> No se sabe; se olvida.
> Otra noche acunando
> Esta dicha vacía. (121–22)

The third stanza, describing the thunderstorm, creates an aura of eerie desolation, emphasising the persona's sadness and loneliness. This is reiterated when 'soledad' is said to 'resucitar', as if it were an animate being capable of deliberately tormenting the persona. The apparent antidote to this solitude is subsequently suggested in the form of dreaming, but, whereas in poem V the dream is something vital and exciting, here there is an impression of tedium and even disgust: the verb is repeated monotonously in three different forms, with a steady movement in scope from the generalised, unconjugated 'soñar', through the more specific first person plural (which could suggest interaction), and finishing with the first person singular, as a painful reminder that the persona is quite alone. The closing stanza is then the bleakest of the whole poem. He has no inclination to dream, but has no other option, and reluctantly resigns himself to 'esta dicha vacía', an empty, sterile, pointless activity (almost certainly an erotic, even masturbatory, reverie) which is only a source of 'dicha' because the alternative ('soledad') is still worse. Just how much worse that alternative is shines through in poem VI:

> ¿Dónde huir? Tibio vacío,
> Ingrávida somnolencia
> Retiene aquí mi presencia,
> Toda moroso albedrío,
> En este salón tan frío,
> Reino del tiempo tirano.
> ¿De qué nos sirvió el verano,
> Oh ruiseñor en la nieve,
> Si sólo un mundo tan breve
> Ciñe al soñador en vano? (111)

The fact that the persona is a 'soñador' suggests again a sterile, indolent, awakening eroticism, reminiscent of the 'dicha vacía' of poem XXI. The picture of sterility and confinement is here however considerably more intense. Cernuda encapsulates his misery in the question, '¿Dónde huir?'. The persona does not know to where he can flee, and of course the answer is painfully apparent: there is nowhere. The images of emptiness are then piled up in claustrophobic intensity, and everything that surrounds and affects the persona is a source of frustration. Even the room is cold, freewill is 'moroso' and time is 'tirano'. Summer too is perceived as pointless, with the powerful image of the 'ruiseñor', normally a positive element of a vibrant nature, sadly 'en la nieve'. The pain of trapped, isolated adolescence is all too apparent.

Adolescent encounters with the world are therefore painful and chaotic. Nevertheless, just as there is a desire to rediscover a sense of cosmic order in the midst of metaphysical chaos, so too there is registered a yearning for order in this world. How then is the need for order expressed in the poetry of adolescence? We know already how much Cernuda's adolescent persona is given to erotic dreams, and yet at the same time in poem XXI he undermines their value so conclusively: they are a 'dicha vacía'. Why he clings to them in spite of their sterile pointlessness is explained in poem XIII:

> Se goza en sueño encantado,
> Tras espacio infranqueable,
> Su belleza irreparable
> El Narciso enamorado.
> Ya diamante azogado
> O agua helada, allá desata
> Humanas rosas, dilata
> Tanto inmóvil paroxismo.
> Mas queda sólo en su abismo
> Fugaz memoria de plata. (115–16)

The eroticism is obvious, but what is more significant is that, for all its fleetingness, the dream is 'encantado' and thus a vision of genuine beauty. The Narcissism is admittedly rather disconcerting, for it locks the persona ever more securely into a sterile, egocentric environment with ever less hope of escape, and the fact that the 'memoria de plata' 'queda sólo en su *abismo*' could well indicate that the persona is pushed further and further into a void. There are therefore two sides to the story: pleasure is to be derived from the experience (the 'paroxismo' may well point to a masturbatory climax), but, if this is a finding of order, it is achieved all too close to the margins of an abyss of emotional chaos.

A much more successful quest for order is realised when the persona uses nature as a source of refuge for his tortured existence. This takes the form of an evasive flight from reality into an ordered, tranquil world of an enclosed hidden garden, as can be seen in poem XXIII:

> Escondido en los muros
> Este jardín me brinda
> Sus ramas y sus aguas
> De secreta delicia.
>
> Qué silencio. ¿Es así
> El mundo? Cruza el cielo
> Desfilando paisajes,
> Risueño hacia lo lejos. (122–23)

The garden is the focus of an evasive strategy (similar to the dream in poem V), a place of order and harmony to which the persona can flee and hide from the source of desolation. Unlike poem V, however, the garden itself is real, not imagined, and 'escondido', an isolated microcosm. Not only that, however, this very separation from the world actually makes it easier for the persona to enjoy the experience, for such a microcosm is apparently not so subject to the world's decay.[12] (It is only in this situation, when walls are protective of the microcosm, that they appear as genuinely positive.) Consequently the 'ramas' and 'aguas' afford a '*secreta* delicia' which is only possible in the enclosed microcosm and known only to itself and the persona. The question in the second stanza then reiterates the fact of separation from the world: the persona has to ask if the world 'es así', because his experiences have too often taught him that it is not. Particularly striking about this garden is the 'silencio', which is reiterated onomatopoetically in the language of the second stanza, with the predominance of soft 's' and 'c' sounds. The latter part of the poem then expands upon the significance of the garden for the persona and its relationship to the outside world:

---

[12] This sense of decay is visible in poem XII:
> Siento huir bajo el otoño
> Pálidas aguas sin fuerza,
> Mientras se olvidan los árboles
> De las hojas que desertan.
>
> ...
>
> Cuán lejano todo. Muertas
> Las rosas que ayer abrieran, (115)

Tierra indolente. En vano
Resplandece el destino.
Junto a las aguas quietas
Sueño y pienso que vivo.

Mas el tiempo ya tasa
El poder de esta hora;
Madura su medida
Escapa entre sus rosas.

Y el aire fresco vuelve
Con la noche cercana,
Su tersura olvidando
Las ramas y las aguas. (123)

Once again the peace and tranquillity are made plain, and the line 'Sueño y pienso que vivo' suggests a sense of romanticised fulfilment. The transient nature of the experience is however painfully apparent in the opening two lines of the penultimate stanza: the ordered world is limited by time. The word 'hora', relating to the time spent in the garden, emphasises its shortness, especially in comparison with the much more vague concept of 'tiempo', which is the time which both signals that the day is drawing to a close and which pulls the persona back to reality. While he is able to enjoy the 'aire fresco' of night-time, the 'ramas' and 'aguas', the visible features of the garden, are being forgotten in the darkness, and the persona must return to the confines of his room.[13]

A more successful response to the awakening chaos is possibly to be found in the writing of poetry. From a biographical point of view, Cernuda's own desire to mould his personal experiences into poetry is illustrated by the existence of the collection itself, but the process of writing *per se* is also mentioned explicitly in *Primeras Poesías*. It is explored in detail in poem VIII. It is not insignificant that Cernuda chooses the sonnet form for this poem, where strict form and order play such a major rôle, requiring a particularly careful attention to details of construction. However chaotic the poet's life and experiences may be, in writing a sonnet he is forced to exercise constraint and actually fashion order out of the chaos. The opening of

---

[13] Juan Alfredo Bellón Cazabán observes that the walls of the garden not only protect it, but also 'impiden una vez más la salida' (*La poesía de Luis Cernuda. Estudio cuantitativo del léxico de* La realidad y el deseo (Granada: Universidad de Granada, 1973), p. 21). Even here the persona is a prisoner.

the poem establishes an atmosphere of considerable gloom, with both nature and the persona's emotions close to chaos:

> Vidrio de agua en mano del hastío.
> Ya retornan las nubes en bandadas
> Por el cielo, con luces embozadas
> Huyendo al asfaltado en desvarío.
>
> Y la fuga hacia dentro. Ciñe el frío,
> Lento reptil, sus furias congeladas;
> La soledad, tras las puertas cerradas,
> Abre la luz sobre el papel vacío. (112)

The persona's alienation in the opening quatrain is obvious, stressed by 'hastío' and 'desvarío', both in strong positions at the end of the first and fourth lines and linked phonologically by the '-ío' assonance. Not only that, the two words refer, respectively, to the persona's emotions on the one hand and to the chaos of nature on the other. (This is of course a pathetic fallacy, suggesting that the natural world suffers from an apparent delirium and thus reflects the emotions of the persona.) Hence there is no possibility of interaction, either with nature or with another person. The second quatrain then makes explicit that the only option is to retreat from reality to the inner world of the imagination, but rather than reveries, the poet here concentrates on poetic creation as a potential means of alleviating his sadness. The attempt, however, causes the problems to multiply: with words of coldness and loneliness abounding, we see the light shining on 'el papel vacío'. The attempt to give poetic form to adolescent experiences is failing also, and the desire to channel the as yet undirected eroticism is thwarted by artistic sterility. This is in turn emphasised by the use again of the '-ío' assonance: just as it brings together the persona's misery and the apparent chaos of nature, so too now it brings together the 'frío' which surrounds the persona and the 'vacío' which is the evidence of the artistic 'coldness' of non-creation. The disaster is short-lived, however:

> Las palabras que velan el secreto
> Placer, y el labio virgen no lo sabe;
> El sueño, embelesado e indolente,
>
> Entre sus propias nieblas va sujeto,
> Negándose a morir. Y sólo cabe
> La belleza fugaz bajo la frente. (112)

The persona perseveres with the creative act, and is able to use the adolescent erotic reverie as the formless raw material for the poem: 'El sueño, embelesado e indolente,/Entre sus propias nieblas va sujeto'. We are witness to the creation of order from the chaos, and eventually the 'papel vacío' is replaced by 'la belleza fugaz' of the finished poem.

Just as the worlds of the dream or of the hidden garden do not represent a definitive finding of order, so too the flight into poetic creation, successful as it is in poem VIII, is far from the panacea for all of the persona's problems. The persona's misery reaches new depths when he finds himself quite unable to create poetry, as is the case in poem XXII:

> En soledad. No se siente
> El mundo, que un muro sella;
> La lámpara abre su huella
> Sobre el diván indolente.
> Acogida está la frente
> Al regazo del hastío.
> ¿Qué ausencia, qué desvarío
> A la belleza hizo ajena?
> Tu juventud nula, en pena
> De un blanco papel vacío. (122)

The situation of this poem is very similar to that of poem VIII, and indeed even much of the vocabulary is similar: 'hastío', 'desvarío', 'papel vacío'. Such lexical similarities certainly serve to underline both the misery of the persona and his hermetic isolation, but they also highlight the differences: whereas in poem VIII the world outside is threatening but at least still visible, here there is only a brief reference to 'El mundo, que un muro sella'. Worst of all, this time there is no 'belleza fugaz' to satisfy the persona: the poem ends with the blank page and the bitter comment 'Tu juventud nula'. He has locked himself away from the world to write poetry and fails in that very ambition. The irony is of course that what we are reading *is* a finished poem, testimony to the poet's, even if not the persona's, ultimate triumph. This tension between the poet's achievement of order and the persona's failure is perhaps in turn representative of the more general tension between order and chaos in the poetry of the sexual awakening. The joy of innocence versus the pain of unfulfilled erotic impulses, the excitement of dreams versus the sterility and frustration of no more than vicarious experiences, the escape from the world into a garden which is yet limited by time, the escape into artistic creation versus the despair of artistic sterility. The desire for order followed by the finding of chaos and the experience of chaos necessitating the search for order: the poetry of adolescence is a rehearsal for the poetry of sexual maturity.

The Experience of 'Love'

Cernuda's departure from his native Seville in 1928 marks a turning-point in his poetry. While *Égloga, Elegía, Oda*, completed in Seville in 1928, continues (albeit less successfully) in the vein of *Primeras Poesías*, combining indolent dreams with formal elegance, the two following collections display a marked influence of Surrealism. From a biographical point of view, the two collections are also probably influenced by the first real experiences of sexual maturity.[14] The proximity of such real experiences is mirrored in many poems in intense emotion, which becomes muted in the subsequent collection, *Donde habite el olvido*. There is also a second major experience of love, which took the form of an affair while in Mexico and inspired the late poem cycle 'Poemas para un cuerpo', which forms the later part of *Con las horas contadas*. The two experiences are markedly different, however, because in the later one Cernuda had a rare moment of contentment. It is therefore appropriate to discuss the earlier poetry first, analysing the ways in which the adolescent expectations of desire are developed, fulfilled and then frustrated, before exploring the later cycle.

The most recurrent features of *Primeras Poesías* are innocence and joy on the one hand and alienation and frustration leading to dreams and evasive strategies on the other. From *Un río, un amor* onwards, alienation and frustration all but supplant the innocence and joy. The persona himself can only lament the loss of innocence, and it is now other adolescents who inhabit that world of innocence. What is more, the essentially sensual, erotic nature of 'love', already visible in *Primeras Poesías*, is now much more strongly to the fore. The interaction of the greater sexual awareness and the ability to recognise adolescent innocence in others means that the persona can enjoy a one-sided sensuous voyeuristic excitement. This is what happens in 'Sombras blancas' from *Un río, un amor*:

> Sombras frágiles, blancas, dormidas en la playa,
> Dormidas en su amor, en su flor de universo,

---

[14] Harris, *Luis Cernuda. A Study*, p. 34, 'Both these books are concerned in part with what seems to have been an experience of unrequited love, or at least of a failed dream of love.' Emilio Barón Palma speaks further of 'varios amores' between 1928 and 1936 (*Luis Cernuda: vida y obra* (Sevilla: Editoriales Andaluzas Unidas, 1990), p. 76). Whatever the specific circumstances, the poems themselves do suggest an actual love affair on the part of the persona(e).

> El ardiente color de la vida ignorando
> Sobre un lecho de arena y de azar abolido. (144)

According to Silver, the 'sombras' are 'boys playing on the beach',[15] and they clearly inhabit a state of innocence before the sexual awakening. (The adjective 'frágiles' suggests the precarious nature of this state, as the persona knows all too well.[16]) Innocent love is crucial to the poem. The 'flor' of the second line is, I believe, not so much 'the preferred synecdoche for adolescent boys', as Silver claims,[17] but rather the love they have for each other: the juxtaposition of 'en su amor, en su flor de universo' is enough to suggest this.[18] Moreover, this love is uncorrupted and therefore one which the persona is able to enjoy as a kind of vicarious experience. The boys' love and the persona's enjoyment are then explored further in the second and third stanzas:

> Libremente los besos desde sus labios caen
> En el mar indomable como perlas inútiles;
> Perlas grises o acaso cenicientas estrellas
> Ascendiendo hacia el cielo con luz desvanecida.
>
> Bajo la noche el mundo silencioso naufraga;
> Bajo la noche rostros fijos, muertos, se pierden.
> Sólo esas sombras blancas, oh blancas, sí, tan blancas.
> La luz también da sombras, pero sombras azules. (144)

The innocent love of the boys is symbolised by the word 'besos' in line one, which in turn emphasises the degree of idealisation of this scene: the per-

---

[15] Silver, *Et in Arcadia Ego*, p. 65.

[16] Apparently the title refers to the title of a film 'White Shadows in the South Seas'. Soufas suggests, from knowledge of the film, that the white shadows are 'the white men who destroy the Paradise of the natives' ('Agents of Power', p. 71, note 25), arguing for 'the sterility of the adolescent ideal' (p. 71) and 'the adolescent's impotence to affirm a viable form of love' (Soufas, *Conflict of Light and Wind: The Spanish Generation of 1927 and the Ideology of Poetic Form* (Middletown, Connecticut: Wesleyan University Press, 1989), p. 145). If this were to be the case (although I am not at all convinced that the shadows are 'men', since they are 'el ardiente color de la vida *ignorando*', strongly suggesting a state of innocence), then it would confirm Cernuda's awareness that the pleasure is purely transient. It is however debatable how much such an obscure allusion can really tell us about the poem itself.

[17] Silver, *Et in Arcadia Ego*, p. 66.

[18] The word 'flor' is also used elsewhere in the poetry of this time for 'love', for example 'Daytona': 'Alguien cortó la piedra en flor' (154). See also Harris, *Luis Cernuda. A Study*, p. 37.

sona's voyeurism and imaginative dreams are closely intertwined. The simile in line two, comparing the 'besos' with 'perlas inútiles', at first sight is rather discordant with the idealism, but it does in fact enhance it further. The kisses are 'inútiles' because the boys, in their innocence, are not using them to consummate an actual erotic encounter. They are therefore not tainted by the problems of 'love' which is the fundamental difficulty which lies at the heart of *Un río, un amor*. In the following stanza the scene (or vision) then begins to disappear as night falls, which is where 'el mundo silencioso naufraga'. This does not cause the persona undue concern, however, for the last two lines suggest that he is able to carry this idyllic vision with him in his mind: shadows cast by light are 'sombras azules', and thus lost when darkness falls, but these shadows, as he is at such pains to tell us with the thrice use of the adjective, are *white*. Therefore it would appear that they are not obscured by night. It is consequently because this sort of vicarious experience is an idyllic antidote to the pain of direct encounters that it is so valuable.

The tone of 'Sombras blancas' is joyful and optimistic, but positive emotions tend to be the exception rather than the rule in *La realidad y el deseo*. An expression of the tragic confrontation with 'love' and the consequent definitive loss of innocence is to be found in 'Esperaba solo' from *Los placeres prohibidos*:

> Esperaba algo, no sabía qué. Esperaba al anochecer, los sábados. Unos me daban limosna, otros me miraban, otros pasaban de largo sin verme.
>
> Tenía en la mano una flor; no recuerdo qué flor era. Pasó un adolescente que, sin mirar, la rozó con su sombra. Yo tenía la mano tendida.
>
> Al caer, la flor se convirtió en un monte. Detrás se ponía un sol; no recuerdo si era negro.
>
> Mi mano quedó vacía. En su palma apareció una gota de sangre.
> (181)

The first sentence establishes the persona's innocence, even naïveté: he did not know what was going to happen when he became involved with another person. The second two sentences are however strange: why should the persona be akin to a beggar in the streets? The key is 'esperar': in his naïveté he sees himself as only able to wait for what will happen, and his rôle is entirely passive as the receiver of the lover's affections. (This conveniently also absolves him from any guilt when things go wrong.) The second paragraph then describes the first actual encounter, with the 'flor' again referring to 'love'. The persona innocently shares his love for the beloved to do with it what he will. This is what seems to happen in the third paragraph, when the persona is, in terms of the poem, quite literally 'deflowered' (is the 'monte' phallic?), leaving only the tragedy of emptiness and pain at the end of the poem suffered by the lover. Furthermore, if 'su palma' means 'his palm', rather than 'its (my hand's) palm', then the pain must be suffered by the beloved also, thus making the tragedy complete.

In addition to the emptiness and pain, these direct encounters illustrate also the captivating, consuming nature of passion. This aspect is clearest in poem IV of *Donde habite el olvido*, where Cernuda has greater detachment from the actual experience, allowing him a more detailed analysis:

> Yo fui.
>
> Columna ardiente, luna de primavera,
> Mar dorado, ojos grandes.
>
> Busqué lo que pensaba;
> Pensé, como al amanecer en sueño lánguido,
> Lo que pinta el deseo en días adolescentes.
>
> Canté, subí,
> Fui luz un día
> Arrastrado en la llama.
>
> Como un golpe de viento
> Que deshace la sombra,
> Caí en lo negro,
> En el mundo insaciable.
>
> He sido. (203–04)

The first line gives succinct expression to the sheer disaster which has attended the transition from adolescence to maturity. The second stanza then uses only noun phrases to provide a very intense, visual description of the encounter. The 'columna ardiente' in particular has definite phallic overtones, while the 'ojos grandes' and their evident seductive power are all we need to know about the beloved. The third and fourth stanzas then tell more explicitly of the loss of innocence. The line 'Arrastrado en la llama' is especially vivid: passion is a violent, consuming, destructive force which grips the lover and takes over his whole existence. The change is underlined by the words 'luz' in the second line of the fourth stanza and 'llama' in the following line: the calm light of adolescent sexual awakening has become a flame which engulfs and destroys. The desire is 'insaciable', and the malevolent force of passion is so strong that it does not merely grip him, it flings him into 'lo negro', which must be the very depths of chaos.[19]

It is there, in the depths of chaos, that we should see the major part of *Un río, un amor* and *Los placeres prohibidos* as being situated. The persona has let himself be swept away by the captivating power of love, and the effect has been disastrous. It is crucial that we bear in mind that the persona *lets* himself be swept away, since his rôle, as Cernuda portrays it, is predominantly passive. He is the victim when things go wrong. It is precisely this attitude of victimisation which lies at the heart of 'Unos cuerpos son como flores' from *Los placeres prohibidos*, although the opening is relatively optimistic:

> Unos cuerpos son como flores,
> Otros como puñales,
> Otros como cintas de agua;
> Pero todos, temprano o tarde,
> Serán quemaduras que en otro cuerpo se agranden,
> Convirtiendo por virtud del fuego a una piedra en un hombre.
>
> Pero el hombre se agita en todas direcciones,
> Sueña con libertades, compite con el viento,
> Hasta que un día la quemadura se borra,
> Volviendo a ser piedra en el camino de nadie. (180)

Surrealist expression, with its apparently disordered, chaotic nature, could not be more suited to the chaotic nature of Cernuda's emotions at this time. The initial lines of this poem are a good example of this apparently 'chaotic' style, with a breathless succession of similes which are not immediately comprehensible. That chaos is however more apparent than actual: 'flores' (and probably also 'cintas de agua') provide an obvious link with beauty, and 'puñales' with pain, while the 'quemaduras' of line five are strongly reminiscent of the violent consuming nature of passion so prominent a fea-

---

[19] Curry analyses this poem in detail, concentrating on the word 'Caí'. He sees the need to 'recurrir al contexto genético creado por todos aquellos textos de la poesía cernudiana en que aparece una referencia a «caída»' in order to 'entender la totalidad del significado de «caída»' (*En torno a la poesía de Luis Cernuda* (Madrid: Pliegos, 1985), p. 126). This lets him assert that there are two 'falls': one refers to birth, and one to the fall from innocence (p. 141). The 'fall' in poem IV of *Donde habite el olvido*, he therefore argues, is the *second* fall. This is interesting, but the argument is dependent on evidence which is external to the poem itself, which must be treated with caution.

ture of poem IV of *Donde habite el olvido*. The second stanza then reasserts the chaotic nature of the amatory experience before speaking of its inevitable failure. Like all flames, the flame of passion burns out, leaving the lover devastated:

> Yo, que no soy piedra, sino camino
> Que cruzan al pasar los pies desnudos,
> Muerto de amor por todos ellos;
> Les doy mi cuerpo para que lo pisen,
> Aunque les lleve a una ambición o a una nube, (181)

It is here that the persona is most plainly cast as the victim. He is the 'camino' upon which 'los pies desnudos' walk, an ingenious image which neatly combines the eroticism of 'desnudo' with the victimisation of being walked upon.[20] There is also simultaneously the rather arrogant assumption that, if he is a 'camino', then to be associated with him must 'lead' the other person to a goal, presumably of ecstasy and fulfilment. It is the victimisation which dominates: 'love' is captivating and the persona cannot resist, only to find himself emotionally ruined by the experience. Despite some of the imagery, this however is not one of Cernuda's finest poems. The insistence that the persona is so totally guiltless suggests more in the way of petulance than reasoned attitude, and this, combined with the use of the first person singular, limits the poem much more to Cernuda in the 1930s.

A rather more successful poem which deals powerfully with the sheer chaos of emotional catastrophe is 'Cuerpo en pena' from *Un río, un amor*, where the persona is imagined as a drowned man (rather than the more personalised 'yo' of 'Unos cuerpos son como flores'). This image of a 'life in death' conveys vividly the isolation and alienation which failed love has caused:

> Lentamente el ahogado recorre sus dominios
> Donde el silencio quita su apariencia a la vida.
> Transparentes llanuras inmóviles le ofrecen   .
> Árboles sin colores y pájaros callados. (144)

Life has lost all meaning for the persona. He can only roam about in a world which is like a desolate wilderness, portrayed succinctly in the image of the 'colourless trees and silent birds'. One striking contrast with *Primeras*

---

[20] See also Consuelo García-Devesa, who stresses both the eroticism and the victimisation ('Cuatro poemas de amor o un poema de Luis Cernuda a la luz de Bécquer, Rosalía y A. Machado', *Romance Notes*, 33 (1992–93), 203).

Poesías is the fact that, while in adolescence the persona could take refuge in an enclosed garden, there is now no such place where the world of nature still offers its vitality: he is surrounded by a sense of emptiness and emotional extinction.[21] This idea of extinction intensifies in the next two stanzas:

> Las sombras indecisas alargándose tiemblan,
> Mas el viento no mueve sus alas irisadas;
> Si el ahogado sacude sus lívidos recuerdos,
> Halla un golpe de luz, la memoria del aire.
>
> Un vidrio denso tiembla delante de las cosas,
> Un vidrio que despierta formas color de olvido;
> Olvidos de tristeza, de un amor, de la vida,
> Ahogados como un cuerpo sin luz, sin aire, muerto. (145)

The chaotic nature of what has happened is evident from the 'sombras indecisas', which are no longer the positive visionary shadows of 'Sombras blancas', but vague, imprecise memories of past events which are already 'alargándose'. We might expect this gradual distancing from such painful events to be something positive, but even a memory is a 'golpe de luz' when confronted with the 'vidrio denso' of present existence. The glass of course immediately suggests a window, an image so resonant of confinement and frustration, while at the same time also describing the water which is now the new prison. What is more, this new prison is much more suffocating than the bedroom of adolescence.

For all the emotional chaos of the experience in 'Cuerpo en pena', the images we have discussed thus far have been remarkably straightforward to interpret for a poem supposedly influenced by Surrealism. This alleged influence becomes even more surprising when we consider that, far from free verse, it is written in elegant Alexandrines. Rather than creating chaos to match the chaos, what Cernuda does here is create order out of the chaos.[22] The elegance and comprehensibility continue throughout the poem, and particularly striking is stanza seven:

> Desdobla sus espejos la prisión delicada;
> Claridad sinuosa, errantes perspectivas.
> Perspectivas que rompe con su dolor ya muerto
> Ese pálido rostro que solemne aparece. (145)

---

[21] See also Harris, *Luis Cernuda. A Study*, p. 39.
[22] See also below, p. 121.

The seventh stanza builds on the 'vidrio' of stanza three, emphasising first that it represents a prison, before describing the 'errantes perspectivas' caused by the distortion of light through the shimmering surface of the water. Again it is chaos which underlies this image; not emotional chaos this time as much as the loss of ordered mental faculties. On a structural level however it is clear that the ideas of drowning, water and glass are being closely tied together throughout the poem. The imagery is then neatly drawn together in the last two stanzas:

> En plena mar al fin, sin rumbo, a toda vela;[23]
> Hacia lo lejos, más, hacia la flor sin nombre.
> Atravesar ligero como pájaro herido
> Ese cristal confuso, esas luces extrañas.
>
> Pálido entre las ondas cada vez más opacas
> El ahogado ligero se pierde ciegamente
> En el fondo nocturno como un astro apagado.
> Hacia lo lejos, sí, hacia el aire sin nombre. (146)

The images of water and glass again pervade the penultimate stanza, while the last stanza, redolent with light imagery, suggests loss of personality, individuality, identity as a human being. The erotic experience has not just denied him satisfaction, it has robbed him of his existence. The phrase 'se pierde ciegamente/En el fondo nocturno' reinforces the ideas of wandering lost in a labyrinth of despair where there is no hope of light, while the only light that is left is not the 'golpe de luz' of stanza two but the bewildering 'luces extrañas'. More crucial than this is the way the comparison is made with 'un astro apagado': a star which has been 'apagado', i.e., one which has lost its light source, is not so much 'lost' as extinguished forever. It has effectively lost *its very being*. The persona's loss of humanity is then reinforced by the repetition of the second line of the previous stanza, but with one important change, i.e., 'la flor' has been replaced by 'el aire'. Whereas 'la flor' presumably again stands for 'love' and is therefore a hold on life, however tenuous, 'el aire' is much more imprecise and not in itself animate.

---

[23] This line bears a remarkable similarity to two lines from the first tercet of poem number 133 from Petrarch's *Canzoniere*, 'S'amor non è, che dunque è quel ch'io sento?', although it is difficult to establish any clear line of influence:
> Fra sí contrari vènti in frale barca
> mi trovo in alto mar senza governo,
(Francesco Petrarca, *Canzoniere*, ed. Roberto Antonelli, Gianfranco Contini and Daniele Ponchiroli (Torino: Einaudi, 1992), p. 184).

The lover is thus forced from elemental passion merely to communion with two of the elements, air and water. The persona of 'Cuerpo en pena' is lost amongst the 'ondas cada vez más opacas', haunted by a hopeless desire which causes him to carry on 'hacia el aire sin nombre'.

If 'Cuerpo en pena' vividly conveys the chaos resulting from the disastrous amatory encounter, it is positively light-hearted when it is compared with the acutely depressing prose poem 'En medio de la multitud' from *Los placeres prohibidos*. It represents the culmination in extreme form of the themes of chaos, isolation and non-being:

> En medio de la multitud le vi pasar, con sus ojos tan rubios como la cabellera. Marchaba abriendo el aire y los cuerpos; una mujer se arrodilló a su paso. Yo sentí cómo la sangre desertaba mis venas gota a gota.
>
> Vacío, anduve sin rumbo por la ciudad. Gentes extrañas pasaban a mi lado sin verme. Un cuerpo se derritió con leve susurro al tropezarme. Anduve más y más.
>
> No sentía mis pies. Quise cogerlos en mi mano, y no hallé mis manos; quise gritar, y no hallé mi voz. La niebla me envolvía.
>
> Me pesaba la vida como un remordimiento; quise arrojarla de mí. Mas era imposible, porque estaba muerto y andaba entre los muertos. (176–77)

This is a powerful expression of emotional catastrophe.[24] The mental turmoil is such that the persona's entire being disintegrates. The sight of the beloved at the beginning of the poem, who, we note, is particularly beautiful, is enough to cause the blood, symbol of life itself, to drain from the persona's veins. As in 'Cuerpo en pena', the persona's life has no direction, no purpose, no *life* whatsoever: his existence is no longer tangible to other people or even to himself.[25] The parts of his body become a collection of lifeless objects with which he cannot make contact; his voice, the principal physical means of interpersonal communication, remains silent. The gloomy atmos-

---

[24] See also Valender, '*Los placeres prohibidos*: An Analysis of the Prose Poems', in *The Word and the Mirror*, ed. Jiménez-Fajardo, p. 84.

[25] The idea of an 'hombre vacío' was present also, for example, in Rafael Alberti's *Sobre los ángeles* and T. S. Eliot's *The Hollow Men*. See Francisco Ruiz Soriano, 'Ejemplos coincidentes de los tópicos de "la ciudad estéril" y "los hombres vacíos" en T. S. Eliot, Luis Cernuda y Rafael Alberti', *Anales de la Literatura Española Contemporánea*, 18 (1993), 298 and 303–04. In addition, as Ruiz Soriano comments in another article, not specifically on 'En medio de la multitud', the setting of the city was also a popular image, as 'un espacio donde se reflejan sus angustias y crisis personales' ('Eliot, Cernuda y Alberti: la ciudad vacía', *Cuadernos Hispanoamericanos*, Nos. 539–40 (1995), 53).

phere is enhanced by the mist, which tends to be associated with an eerie quiet, reinforcing his own inability to speak. The poem is then concluded with the despairing comment that the persona is condemned to carry on living this non-life. The atmosphere of death in the last part is also emphasised by the alliteration of the 'm' sound: 'me' is linked phonologically with 'remordimiento', the negative conjunction 'mas', 'imposible' and, finally, 'muerto', repeated in the strong position as the last word of the poem. The chaos is echoed further in the form of the poem. Structurally, with two longer verse paragraphs followed by two shorter verse paragraphs, this, and other prose poems in *Los placeres prohibidos*, are like 'deformed sonnets':[26] it is almost as if the chaos of the experience cannot be contained in a conventional metrical form.[27] The indictment of 'love' as a means of losing identity could therefore not be more serious: 'love' is foregrounded as one of the major ontological problems.

Egocentrism in a 'love' relationship is another central issue, far removed as it is from genuine love. Rather than exhibiting genuine loving human concern, individuals in *La realidad y el deseo* lock themselves, intentionally or unintentionally, ever more definitively into their tragic isolation by reacting to partners with selfishness and disregard. This, inevitably, leads to disaster. Precisely this sort of situation is seen to arise in 'Telarañas cuelgan de la razón' from *Los placeres prohibidos*. The poem begins with a statement of love's passing:

> Telarañas cuelgan de la razón
> En un paisaje de ceniza absorta;
> Ha pasado el huracán de amor,
> Ya ningún pájaro queda. (175)

This is not an easy poem to interpret, but the last two lines of this stanza are clear: the violence of love is past, leaving emptiness and desolation. This clarifies the second line, which evokes an image of sadness and death. 'Ceniza' may suggest the consequence of the 'fire' of passion (as it is expressed in poem IV of *Donde habite el olvido* and 'Unos cuerpos son como flores'), that is, the dead ashes after the flames have died away (although with a Surrealist mixture of images 'amor' in this poem is an 'huracán').

---

[26] I am indebted to Professor D. G. Walters for this suggestion.

[27] This obviously contrasts with the formal elegance and regularity of 'Cuerpo en pena', where order is created from the chaos. In addition to these two extremes, there are other poems in *Un río, un amor* and *Los placeres prohibidos* which are often 'almost' regular with a series of regular stanzas followed by a single line. See for example 'Duerme, muchacho' (162).

This only leaves the title/opening line, which seems to have genuine Surrealist disregard for logic. Perhaps this line is suggesting something of the physicality of the affair and the lack of spirituality. Since 'cobwebs' are normally associated with staleness, mustiness and sterility, perhaps this is an indication of an eroticism on which reason has had no effect. Whatever the imagery behind this line, the general tone of the poem becomes clear as it continues later in the second stanza:

> Porque alguien, cruel como un día de sol en primavera,
> Con su sola presencia ha dividido en dos un cuerpo. (175)

This reveals the reason why the 'huracán de amor' has passed. The two lovers had become united as one body, but the selfish nature of one caused the joy of union to turn to tragedy. It is not clear whether the 'alguien' is the beloved himself or a third party who took the beloved away, but in either case the love was not strong enough, not selfless enough to be faithful and enduring. This idea is stated even more explicitly in 'Estaba tendido', also from the same collection:

> Estaba tendido y tenía entre mis brazos un cuerpo como seda. Lo besé en los labios, porque el río pasaba por debajo. Entonces se burló de mi amor. (179)

This opening description of love-making is brought to an abrupt close by the stark comment 'se burló de mi amor': the love-making has turned into crass physicality and an excuse for a bitter taunt of the persona. There is also no reason given for this taunting. It is merely stated as a fact. Is there in fact no reason, or at least none which the persona can comprehend? The rest of the poem then speaks of pain and rejection. It is part of the tragedy of 'love', such as it is, in a world of chaos, and a tragedy in which Cernuda and his personae are, once again, the victims.

Cernuda's attitudes towards the experience of 'love' go through various stages of development after this. This has been analysed thoroughly by Harris,[28] and there is therefore little reason to analyse these points in excessive detail. They should nevertheless not be ignored, in order that we might proceed to a thorough understanding of the 'love' poetry as a whole. The first stage of development follows logically from the disastrous experience of 'love'. The result is a desire for evasion, so prominent in the poetry of adolescence. In 'Soliloquio del farero', from *Invocaciones*, it takes

---

[28] Harris, *Luis Cernuda. A Study*, especially chapters II and V.

the form of an attempt to abandon amatory commitment altogether in order to avoid the pain and misery of rejection. The choice of a lighthouse-keeper as an isolated figure, if perhaps a little unimaginative, is a convenient one in which to extol the virtues of an entirely hermetic existence:

> Cómo llenarte, soledad,
> Sino contigo misma.
>
> De niño, entre las pobres guaridas de la tierra,
> Quieto en ángulo oscuro,
> Buscaba en ti, encendida guirnalda,
> Mis auroras futuras y furtivos nocturnos,
> Y en ti los vislumbraba, (223)

This poem forms something of a hymn in praise of being alone. Solitude is identified as the source of peace and harmony while the persona was a child: we are once again returned to that world of pre-adolescent innocence, as the time before the reality of eroticism shattered that harmony. Much of the poem is written in an elegiac tone which laments the persona's problems. The penultimate stanza is central to the poem's significance:

> Tú, verdad solitaria,
> Transparente pasión, mi soledad de siempre,
> Eres inmenso abrazo;
> El sol, el mar,
> La oscuridad, la estepa,
> El hombre y su deseo,
> La airada muchedumbre,
> ¿Qué son sino tú misma? (225)

Passion and desire seem now to have been subsumed under the heading of 'soledad': in solitude, the trials caused by failed desire disappear and life is blissfully peaceful. This is very similar to the longing for a limbo-like existence in 'Atardecer en la catedral',[29] although the motives for seeking it are different. Here it is prompted by a chaotic experience of love which causes the destruction of his personality and identity, while in the later poem there is a much greater religious concern. That similarity at the same time illustrates again the overlap between erotic and existential themes.

---

[29] See above, pp. 52–54.

The desire for solitude quickly develops into a narcissistic, egocentric hedonism, where there is a concern with a kind of sterile desire which does not reach out to make contact with another but continually returns to its own obsessive self-interest. One of the finest examples of this is '*Dans ma péniche*', also in *Invocaciones*:

> Quiero vivir cuando el amor muere;
> Muere, muere pronto, amor mío.
> Abre como una cola la victoria purpúrea del deseo,
> Aunque el amante se crea sepultado en un súbito otoño,
> Aunque grite:
> «Vivir así es cosa de muerte». (234)

While the interest in interpersonal love resulted in disaster, solitude *per se* is not an answer either, for Cernuda continues to believe that his sensual inclinations cannot be without value. The result is a reappraisal, and the identification of two different concepts: 'deseo' and 'amor'. 'Amor', i.e., love *between* people, is exhorted to perish itself, because it is now implicated as the cause of the earlier distress, while 'deseo' is now seen as an elemental force in its own right and thus not subject to the problems of 'amor'.[30] (The two words are however only sometimes used so exclusively: 'amor' can be used for the love force as well as 'deseo'.) The persona finds this attitude extraordinarily liberating, at least for a time, and it enables him to pour scorn on the foolishness of those who persist with interpersonal erotic relationships rather than enjoying this hedonistic dream-world of 'deseo', whatever it might be. (It is difficult to envisage without entering Cernuda's own world. This is of course impossible, and therefore could be seen as a defect in the poem, but it is in any case so egocentric that the poet probably does not care.[31]) The scorn of other people reaches a peak in stanza four:

> Pobres amantes,
> ¿De qué os sirvieron las infantiles arras que cruzasteis,
> Cartas, rizos de luz recién cortada, seda cobriza o negra ala?
> Los atardeceres de manos furtivas,

---

[30] See Harris, *Luis Cernuda. A Study,* pp. 50–51.

[31] There is no satisfactory solution to this sort of interpretative problem. From a theoretical point of view, it can be argued that it is always impossible to know exactly what a poet intended. In a situation like this, however, this means that we either declare interpretative impossibility or interpret it in whatever way we choose. While the first solution tells us nothing, the second will probably tell us more about ourselves than the poem. Hence we are more or less excluded from the most intimate areas of the poem.

> El trémulo palpitar, los labios que suspiran,
> La adoración rendida a un leve sexo vanidoso,
> Los ay mi vida y los ay muerte mía,
> Todo, todo,
> Amarillea y cae y huye con el aire que no vuelve. (235)

The persona presumably includes himself when he was a younger man amongst those 'pobres amantes' who fail to see the pointlessness and emptiness of all the various rituals which they perform. Letters, locks of hair, 'manos furtivas', romantic sighs of 'ay mi vida' are all held up to ridicule. There is no point to any of this sort of romantic behaviour because it is always transient ('huye') and subject to decay ('amarillea y cae'). The following stanza is then again more serious in tone, as it makes the final scornful address to 'amantes', and there is more in the way of bitterness, with references to 'crueldad' and 'la tumba de los sueños'. The last part of the poem is the climax however, for it is there that the nature of the persona's hedonistic egocentric dreams is made more explicit:

> Cuánto vale una noche como ésta, indecisa entre la primavera última
>   y el estío primero,
> Este instante en que oigo los leves chasquidos del bosque nocturno,
> Conforme conmigo mismo y con la indiferencia de los otros,
> Solo yo con mi vida,
> Con mi parte en el mundo.
>
> Jóvenes sátiros
> Que vivís en la selva, labios risueños ante el exangüe dios cristiano,
> A quien el comerciante adora para mejor cobrar su mercancía,
> Pies de jóvenes sátiros,
> Danzad más presto cuando el amante llora,
>   ...
> Y el deseo girará locamente en pos de los hermosos cuerpos
> Que vivifican el mundo un solo instante. (236)

There is a sense of exhilaration in the enjoyment of sensual pleasure for its own sake, and this focus on 'deseo' does indeed seem to lead to 'communion with the natural world'.[32] The persona is very defiant and confident of his own importance and of the insignificance of other people for his satisfaction, suggested by 'Conforme conmigo mismo y con la indiferencia

---

[32] Harris, *Luis Cernuda. A Study*, p. 122.

de los otros,/Solo yo con mi vida'. This is an entirely egocentric erotic involvement, for no-one else matters, not even the reader: it is extremely
difficult for us to visualise the dream of the 'jóvenes sátiros'. Nonetheless
this reference to the 'jóvenes sátiros' demands attention. The 'satyrs' were
'attendants of the god Dionysus, boisterous creatures of the woods and
hills'.[33] Their affinity with the natural world is brought out in the physical
setting, while Dionysus was the 'god of wine and of ecstasy'[34] and as such
the ideal focus for a hedonistic poem glorifying pagan sensuality. Such a focus is totally opposed to restraint and control. This primeval passion is then
juxtaposed with its opposite, i.e., civilisation, represented by 'mercancía'
and the blasphemous 'el exangüe dios cristiano'. The choice of the word
'exangüe' strikes at the very heart of Christian symbolism, based on the
blood sacrifice for eternal salvation. Here the indication seems to be that the
spilling of Christ's blood only resulted in a loss of vitality. In addition, the
primeval passion, opposed as it is to restraint and control, finds this lack of
restraint reflected in the form of the poem. If the chaotic imagery of Surrealism is useful for expressing the chaos of a meaningless existence, so too
chaotic form can mirror chaotically unrestrained hedonism. This is deliberate
and effective up to a point: the considerable variation in line and stanza
lengths conveys an impression of almost breathless excitement and the description of the dream almost as it occurred. There are however times in the
poem when the poet loses control and there is not enough reflection: the line
'Que cuando el hombre no tiene ligados sus miembros por las encantadoras
mallas del amor' (235), for example, while certainly clear in its exposition of
theme, is also quite stunningly unmemorable. In the midst of all this hedonistic lack of restraint, there is however a note of doubt sounded in the last
two lines about the value of this experience: 'desire' will seek 'los hermosos
cuerpos', which in itself suggests the risk of the hopelessness of interpersonal relationships. It is however the final line which makes it clear that it is
'wishful thinking',[35] because the bodies only have an effect for 'un solo
instante'. The poem expresses a surrender to 'deseo', but it is a joy which
cannot last.[36]

[33] Howatson and Chilvers, p. 483.
[34] Howatson and Chilvers, p. 183.
[35] Harris, *Luis Cernuda. A Study*, p. 123.
[36] A similar poem is 'El joven marino' (236–42), in which the sailor desires a hedonistic
union, not with another person, but with the elemental force of the sea. Such a union is
still no substitute for a mutually satisfying interpersonal relationship, for it only results in
the drowning of the sailor. As Bruton comments, 'His relationship to the sea is that of a
slave to his master, a passive attitude which cannot satisfy the sailor's yearning for a
close, physical embrace' ('"El joven marino": a Landmark in Cernuda's Poetic Development', *Quinquereme*, 4, No. 1, (1981), 89).

The fact that *'Dans ma péniche'* fails to reach a definitive conclusion, instead ending with a degree of doubt and uncertainty, means that further changes of attitude are more or less inevitable. Furthermore, since *'Dans ma péniche'* is based on a dream rather than an interpersonal encounter, it is not surprising that, in the later poetry between *Invocaciones* and *Con las horas contadas*, the rôle of direct experiences diminishes still further. Not only that, the intense eroticism of *'Dans ma péniche'* also diminishes. There is however one further facet to the experience of 'love' in the earlier poetry which provides something of a bridge between the earlier poetry and the 'Poemas para un cuerpo' cycle of *Con las horas contadas*. There is evidence of an ideal for 'love' in the form of a Romantic 'Liebestod' or 'love-death'. Typical of Wagnerian opera, the 'Liebestod' is the ultimate consummation of the lovers' union in their simultaneous deaths. This sort of idea is evoked in the short poem 'Te quiero' from *Los placeres prohibidos*, much of which is a simple, sincere declaration of love:

> Te lo he dicho con el viento,
> Jugueteando como animalillo en la arena
> O iracundo como órgano tempestuoso; (191)

Five of the seven stanzas focus on a feature of the natural world, using each of them as a metaphor for the range and intensity of feelings. Here the wind symbolises playfulness and innocent joy, but also violent, elemental passion. The poem culminates at the end:

> Te lo he dicho con el miedo,
> Te lo he dicho con la alegría,
> Con el hastío, con las terribles palabras.
>
> Pero así no me basta:
> Más allá de la vida,
> Quiero decírtelo con la muerte;
> Más allá del amor,
> Quiero decírtelo con el olvido. (192)

The closing stanza articulates the desire to give ultimate expression to love by seeking to achieve a permanent, eternal, ultimate consummation. It bears much in common with a Romantic 'Liebestod', but is 'Te quiero' the expression of a true Romantic apotheosis? There are two things which challenge this interpretation: first, it is expressed as 'Quiero decírtelo'. This conveys desire, certainly, and intention, possibly, but not actuality: it is the way the persona would *like* things to be. Second, the penultimate stanza speaks of 'alegría' (presumably the persona's when he was in love), but also of 'miedo', 'hastío' and 'terribles palabras'. Given the context of *Los placeres prohibidos*, these emotions must relate to the pain of rejection and disappointment. This lends a poignancy to the desire of the final stanza, given the sad reality that, if the persona were to die, it would never be the consummation of love, but an appreciation of its disaster. The poem thus moves swiftly from ideal to tragedy.

The persona of 'Te quiero' reaches towards an ideal but fails. The persona of the later 'Poemas para un cuerpo' however comes much closer to an ideal, not in the attainment of freedom outwith the natural world, but in the enjoyment of a pleasurable experience in actual lived reality. 'Contigo', poem X of the cycle, is typical:

> ¿Mi tierra?
> Mi tierra eres tú.
>
> ¿Mi gente?
> Mi gente eres tú.
>
> El destierro y la muerte
> Para mí están adonde
> No estés tú.
>
> ¿Y mi vida?
> Dime, mi vida,
> ¿Qué es, si no eres tú? (478)[37]

The poem is an expression of unadulterated happiness, of an amatory encounter as it ought to be, although the concepts here are somewhat trite and unoriginal, and there is little profundity. The sentiment is nevertheless entirely sincere, and a good example of the difference between this love affair and the earlier disaster. This poem cycle would thus seem to be a final

---

[37] The poem is also strongly reminiscent of Bécquer's 'Rima' XXI (Gustavo Adolfo Bécquer, *Rimas*, ed. José Luis Cano (Madrid: Cátedra, 1983), p. 61):

> ¿Qué es poesía? dices mientras clavas
> en mi pupila tu pupila azul.
> ¿Qué es poesía? ¿Y tú me lo preguntas?
> Poesía... eres tú!

It is interesting that 'tierra', 'gente' and 'vida' all take the place of 'poesía' in Cernuda's poem. Is Cernuda deliberately rewriting Bécquer's poem, or does the concept of 'poesía' echo intertextually in 'Contigo' as well? This is pure speculation, but nonetheless poetry does provide a climactic and immortalising response to this lived experience.

refutation of the earlier poetry, where the experience of 'love' leads to chaos.[38] Even in 'Poemas para un cuerpo' there are however a few discordant notes sounded. The eighth poem, 'Viviendo sueños', is ostensibly written from the same perspective of joyous fulfilment as 'Contigo':

> Tantos años que pasaron
> Con mis soledades solo
> Y hoy tú duermes a mi lado.
>
> ...
>
> Mas ahora en fin llegaste
> De su mano, y aún no creo,
> Despierto en el sueño, hallarte. (476)

The persona looks back over all the problems of his life and is unable to believe that he is now able to find such joy. At the same time, however, there is a degree of ambiguity created by the title 'Viviendo sueños' and the line 'Despierto en el sueño'. Is this really a genuine experience or are we back in the vicarious world of dreams? This doubt becomes stronger in the closing stanza:

> Lo raro es que al mismo tiempo
> Conozco que tú no existes
> Fuera de mi pensamiento. (477)

Where do the boundaries of dream and reality lie? We know that the love affair which inspired 'Poemas para un cuerpo' is an historical fact, and yet the poet casts doubt on it. Is it that he has become so given to fantasising that reality immediately becomes absorbed inextricably into it? Or has reality finally corresponded to the dream? Whichever is the correct interpretation, we cannot help but wonder if the dream has come to dominate, and that reality can never be positive unless it conforms to the dream.

More disconcerting within the context of this happy love affair is the twelfth poem of the cycle, entitled 'La vida', where the beloved is compared to the sun. The poem opens very positively: just as the sun heats the earth and fills it with 'risas verdes' (480), so too the presence of the beloved

---

[38] Valender comments further that Cernuda is once again using 'yo' for himself rather than 'tú', as in poems such as 'El intruso' (see above, pp. 36–38), demonstrating that he is 'más seguro de quién [es]' ('Cernuda y sus "Poemas para un cuerpo"', *Revista de la Universidad de México*, 38, No. 15 (1982), 37).

brings warmth and joy. The tone however changes sharply in the final stanza:

> Pero también tú te pones
> Lo mismo que el sol, y crecen
> En torno mío las sombras
> De soledad, vejez, muerte. (481)

The experience of love has been joyful, it is true, but it is still subject to the passing of time, and it must come to an end. Once it is over (if it is not over already), sadness and loneliness will once again be part of the persona's existence: there is still a threat, if not the actual presence, of the resurgence of chaos and catastrophe. Even at its best, the experience of 'love' can always lead to chaos.

The Purpose of 'Love'

The emotional torment in *Un río, un amor* and *Los placeres prohibidos* is very intense. It is above all an account of that emotion which predominates. In the long term, however, Cernuda is not content with merely recording emotional responses. 'Soliloquio del farero' and *'Dans ma péniche'* from *Invocaciones* both illustrate the importance of the inner life and the need to seek solutions to the problems caused by 'love', either in terms of total evasion or in a visionary reconstruction of the erotic experience. These however form only one part of the story. The inner life is so important that, in addition to dreams, meditation and analysis of 'love' play a major rôle. Cernuda's personae want to discover, not only what went wrong and why, but also what *ought* to happen, i.e., what purpose 'love' ought to fulfil.

We have already discussed the question of ideals for 'love': 'Te quiero' from *Los placeres prohibidos* expresses a failed desire for Romantic apotheosis, while 'Poemas para un cuerpo' speaks mostly of simple joy and pleasure, albeit temporally limited. It is that straightforward desire for pleasure which provides the link between the experience of 'love' and its purpose. While 'Te quiero' is concerned primarily with the consummation of love outwith the natural world, and 'Poemas para un cuerpo' are relatively straightforward and unreflective, 'Qué más da', from *Los placeres prohibidos*, provides greater insight into the potential effects of a pleasurable experience on actual lived reality:

> Qué más da el sol que se pone o el sol que se levanta,
> La luna que nace o la luna que muere.

Mucho tiempo, toda mi vida, esperé verte surgir entre las nieblas
  monótonas,
Luz inextinguible, prodigio rubio como la llama;
Ahora que te he visto sufro, porque igual que aquéllos
No has sido para mí menos brillante,
Menos efímero o menos inaccesible que el sol y la luna alternados.
(188)

The nonchalance of the title and opening lines belie the depth of sentiment. What the experience of 'love' should be is stated succinctly in these initial stanzas, i.e., equivalent to the brightness and intensity of the sun or the moon. In the second stanza, the beloved himself is a 'luz inextinguible', as bright as the sun. But there is a problem. This goal of joyous fulfilment is sought, inevitably, in direct amorous encounters, which, as we know only too well, are in *Un río, un amor* and *Los placeres prohibidos* doomed to failure: joyous union is impossible, because the beloved is not merely 'brillante', he is also just as 'efímero' and 'inaccesible' as the sun and moon. Despite this, the poem is still able to end relatively optimistically:

Tu recuerdo, como el de ambos astros,
Basta para iluminar, tú ausente, toda esta niebla que me envuelve.
(188)

The faculty of memory means that the persona can retreat into his inner world and dream of what was (or might have been). Even if there is no direct physical involvement, there still exists, at least in theory, the possibility of spiritual enrichment and an end to emotional extinction. At this stage in Cernuda's poetic development, this is admittedly a vain hope. The poem is nonetheless significant for the stress it places on the persona's ability, even in the midst of such torment, to reflect on his situation.

By the time of *Donde habite el olvido*, a notable distance has been achieved from the erotic experience. This allows the persona, first, to reiterate that the disastrous experience of 'love' is far removed from the goal, second, to assert that the goal is not to be abandoned as a result of the disaster, and third, to redefine that goal. This subsequent redefinition substantially develops the emphasis on the inner life: the importance of erotic fulfilment diminishes and the importance of spiritual enrichment increases considerably. 'Love' explicitly becomes conceptualised anew as a search for order. It is remarkable in fact how much it bears in common with a search for an Absolute, as can be ascertained from poem X of this fifth collection.[39] The poem has an elegiac tone, and focusses initially on what man has lost through the experience of 'love':

> Bajo el anochecer inmenso,
> Bajo la lluvia desatada, iba
> Como un ángel que arrojan
> De aquel edén nativo. (208)

These lines remind us of the disaster which resulted from the loss of innocence. We are once again in the gloomy world where the persona is doomed to an empty, meaningless non-existence. While the reference is to 'edén', it should be stressed that there is no genuine Judeo-Christian significance, but rather a pagan one, with clear Platonic echoes:

> Lo que en la luz fue impulso, las alas,
> Antes candor erguido,
> A la espalda pesaban sordamente. (208)

According to Plato, 'The soul before birth ... was acquainted with the world of Ideas'.[40] This is echoed in the phrase 'Lo que en la luz fue impulso'.[41] While God, or any kind of deity, is admittedly absent from this picture, the goal is still quite explicitly to regain an understanding of transcendent order. It is evident however that such a goal could not be further removed from reality. This is expressed vividly in the image of the wings which 'A la espalda pesaban sordamente.' There is no hope of celestial transport, for the wings are dull and lifeless. This world is presented, not so much as an imperfect copy of the eternal realms, but rather as a realm where such reflection of the eternal cannot even survive. The fourth and fifth stanzas of the poem then analyse further the nature of 'love' in the world:

---

[39] The title *Donde habite el olvido* is a line taken from poem LXVI of Bécquer's *Rimas* (p. 85):

> En donde esté una piedra solitaria
> sin inscripción alguna,
> donde habite el olvido,
> allí estará mi tumba.

It is precisely this sense of desolation and non-existence which sets the mood for this stage of Cernuda's poetry.

[40] Howatson and Chilvers, p. 429.

[41] See also Curry, 'Between Platonism and Modernity', p. 125.

Entre precipitadas formas vagas,
Vasta estela de luto sin retorno,
Arrastraba dos lentas soledades,
Su soledad de nuevo, la del amor caído.

Ellas fueron sus alas en tiempos de alegría,
Esas que por el fango derribadas
Burla y respuesta dan al afán que interroga,
Al deseo de unos labios. (208–09)

The image of the 'vasta estela de luto sin retorno' evokes a striking picture of death and decay. Everything is following relentlessly after death with no hope of escape or return to the divine sphere. Tragically, 'amor' is 'caído' and equated with 'soledad'. It is therefore inextricably linked to this empty, fallen world. The parallel between 'amor caído' and the angel thrown from 'edén' implies that *true* love is the perfect means of attaining genuine transcendence of this world, but now that possibility has gone. Hence the persona is only able to lament this modern situation, and there is a very strong suggestion that in the action of kissing ('Al deseo de unos labios'), there can only be seen the very last feeble remnants of that former transcendent power, to which the only response is a 'burla'. It is therefore curious that, by the end of the poem, the goal of transcendent order reappears as if it were still some kind of a possibility:

Fuerza joven quisieras para alzar nuevamente,
Con fango, lágrimas, odio, injusticia,
La imagen del amor hasta el cielo,
La imagen del amor en la luz pura. (209)

While the emphasis is on the importance of regaining the sense of order, the phrase 'Fuerza joven', which should be the principal means to achieve that end, is ambiguous. Considering the reference at the beginning of the poem to the 'edén nativo', this could refer to a regaining of the state of sexual innocence. There is however another possibility, in line with Platonic theory, whereby the true Platonic lover progresses from a love of beautiful people to an understanding of the Idea of Beauty:[42] the 'Fuerza joven' is therefore not his own self rejuvenated but the young life of another, and the love which

[42] 'This is the right way of approaching or being initiated into the mysteries of love, to begin with examples of beauty in this world, and using them as steps to ascend continually with that absolute beauty as one's aim' (Plato, *The Symposium*, trans. Walter Hamilton (Harmondsworth: Penguin, 1951), p. 94).

the persona would feel would then guide him once more to a sense of order and harmony. Considering how debased and ineffectual 'amor' has been shown to be, however, this continued clinging to the goal can be nothing other than an impossible dream.

It is however inadequate to understand this search for order purely in terms of a desire for spiritual fulfilment frustrated by the shortcomings of 'love' in the fallen world. That understanding suggests a straightforward binary opposition between flesh and spirit. Poem II of *Donde habite el olvido* however interweaves the two realms of spiritual fulfilment and erotic desire in a much more complex fashion. The first of the poem's two stanzas concentrates once more on the transcendent aim for 'love':

> Como una vela sobre el mar
> Resume ese azulado afán que se levanta
> Hasta las estrellas futuras,
> Hecho escala de olas
> Por donde pies divinos descienden al abismo,
> También tu forma misma,
> Ángel, demonio, sueño de un amor soñado,
> Resumen en mí un afán que en otro tiempo levantaba
> Hasta las nubes sus olas melancólicas. (202)

This is a difficult poem. The most important aspect is established in line two, namely 'ese azulado afán', foregrounding the concept of elemental desire as opposed to personal love, as identified in the later poem '*Dans ma péniche*'.[43] The choice of 'azulado' to describe 'afán' is not obvious; this links it with the 'mar' of line one and the 'olas' of line four, and the coldness frequently associated with the colour blue may well reinforce the sense of desolation. Blue however is also the colour of the sky, and so the 'afán' is not only linked back to the 'mar' but also forward to the realms of the 'estrellas' of the following line, thus in the first four lines binding closely together the two regions of heaven and earth, with which the second part of the stanza then deals in greater detail. These lines are also reminiscent of Platonic philosophy, with 'escala' and 'estrellas futuras' suggesting the continual progression upwards of the true Platonic lover. The following lines however also indicate something of an opposite process, that is, of the descent of the gods to the earthly realms. This relates to the fact that Eros in Platonic doctrine was a 'daimon', a being which was 'half-god and half-

---

[43] See above, pp. 100–02.

man'.[44] As Soufas comments, 'Acting in the capacity of an intermediary and not as a god in the Platonic system, love thus facilitates access by mortals to a more intense, almost divine reality.'[45] The reference to 'Ángel, demonio' in this stanza clearly alludes to this dual, 'daimonic' character of 'love', and the yearning, therefore, represents the desire for 'love' to help reveal a vision of eternal order. This is now spiritual enrichment to the point of metaphysical revelation. On the other hand, Eros' approach to this modern fallen world could imply contact with destructive 'amor'. Not only that, this philosophy does not apply now: '... afán que en *otro tiempo* levantaba/Hasta las nubes'. While this, on a biographical level, could refer to the fact that the love affair is over, the imagery of the poem suggests that the transcendent aim for 'love' is one to which modern man no longer has access. To sum up, within this very complex stanza, there is suggested the following: first, the possibility of the attainment of the highest spiritual order; second, the action of Eros as an intermediary; third, the risk of destructive 'amor'; and fourth, the irrelevance of Platonic philosophy in the modern world.

The risk of destructive 'amor' is only the first hint of the continuing importance of worldly, carnal, erotic impulses as opposed to transcendent spiritual fulfilment. This more mundane side to 'love' is brought firmly into the foreground of the second stanza:

> Sintiendo todavía los pulsos de ese afán,
> Yo, el más enamorado,
> En las orillas del amor,
> Sin que una luz me vea
> Definitivamente muerto o vivo,
> Contemplo sus olas y quisiera anegarme,
> Deseando perdidamente
> Descender, como los ángeles aquellos por la escala de espuma,
> Hasta el fondo del mismo amor que ningún hombre ha visto. (202)

Where in the first stanza there is an 'escala de olas' and the 'olas' of the 'afán' are supposed to rise 'hasta las nubes', now the poet wishes to 'anegar[se]' and 'descender ... hasta el fondo del mismo amor'. In a previous Platonic age of order and harmony man could rise to the heights of spiritual fulfilment, but now the persona is much more concerned with indulging himself in sensual desire. While this puts us in mind of the Romantic 'Liebestod' of 'Te quiero',[46] there is here not so much a desire for an ulti-

---

[44] Plato, p. 81.
[45] Soufas, 'Cernuda and Daimonic Power', *Hispania*, 66 (1983), 168.
[46] See above, pp. 103–04.

mate consummation but an interest rather in the 'amor' *per se*. The goal therefore cannot be entirely metaphysical or transcendental, but also intermingled with a desire for erotic fulfilment which, considering how catastrophic it has proved, does appear rather unrealistic. Nonetheless, the ambivalence is plain.

Since *Donde habite el olvido* was written in response to a disastrous experience of 'love', it is clear from the beginning that the quest for order in 'love' has been a failure. The poetry is primarily concerned with the way in which 'love' went wrong and the resulting anguish. 'Love' is ineffectual. Indeed true Platonic love does not exist: it is thwarted by the interference of an overwhelming erotic experience, preventing any possibility of rising above the purely physical. It should however be stressed that there is no single poem where the reasons for failure are definitively presented. As we have seen many times already, *La realidad y el deseo* provides no single unified vision, but selects different aspects of the experience. As we know, poem IV is an expression of the violence of passion.[47] A calmer evaluation of what goes wrong is to be seen in poem III:

> Esperé un dios en mis días
> Para crear mi vida a su imagen,
> Mas el amor, como un agua,
> Arrastra afanes al paso.
>
> Me he olvidado a mí mismo en sus ondas;
> Vacío el cuerpo, doy contra las luces;
> Vivo y no vivo, muerto y no muerto;
> Ni tierra ni cielo, ni cuerpo ni espíritu.
>
> Soy eco de algo; (202–03)

The first two lines of this poem are a reiteration of the potential transcendental power of 'love'. It is however perhaps this very identification of 'love' as 'un dios' in itself that is the persona's mistake: 'love', at least when the persona encounters it, is not a god but that powerful, malevolent force which 'arrastra afanes al paso'. The persona of this poem is however tragically aware of the chaos which underlies the love force. Thus, while he is emotionally destroyed by the experience, here he does not accept that escapist limbo, but rather confronts the fact that he is condemned to the

[47] See above, pp. 91–92.

half-life of 'Vivo y no vivo, muerto y no muerto'.[48] (Ultimately, however, we must wonder if the difference between the two states – escapist limbo and empty half-life – can really be very large.) What matters most however is the sense of sheer emotional emptiness.

The interplay of spirit and flesh is reiterated in the evaluation of what goes wrong. Just as a desire for erotic fulfilment parallels a desire for spiritual fulfilment, so too the emotional disaster of poem III parallels a metaphysical catastrophe in poem VIII. 'Love' becomes another absurdity in an absurd world:

> Ya no es vida ni muerte
> El tormento sin nombre,
> Es un mundo caído
> Donde silba la ira.
>
> Es un mar delirante,
> Clamor de todo espacio,
> Voz que de sí levanta
> Las alas de un dios póstumo. (207)

This poem works on two levels. On the one hand, the world has lost contact with the Absolute and lacks all direction.[49] On the other, 'love' has completely failed, and the persona is defeated. The fact that this life is 'ni vida ni muerte' is strongly reminiscent of the attitude of poem III. The closing line above is in fact a tragic ironic comment on the Platonic-type ideal for 'love': the wings of the soul are now powerless, as they are in poem III, and the god is 'póstumo'. Like poem III however, the attitude of this poem is much more radically despairing than that of poem X, where there is an indication that a 'fuerza joven' could signify a redemptive power. Here there is no hope.

The very fact that poems of *Donde habite el olvido* are contradictory, with some hopeful and others not, means that it is not surprising that this tragedy proves not to be the definitive statement of the purpose of 'love'. When Cernuda comes to write the later poetry of *Como quien espera el alba*, the earlier disaster can be viewed much more calmly, and he experiences a new freedom to meditate upon 'love'. The result is poetry which gives a new expression to the search for order which develops beyond what

---

[48] This line is very reminiscent of San Juan de la Cruz's poem 'Vivo sin vivir en mí' (pp. 20–21). The comparison with the mystic poet however only underlines Cernuda's failure to rise above the purely physical world.

[49] See above, pp. 29–31.

appears to be a definitive failure in some poems of *Donde habite el olvido*.
A particularly interesting poem from this eighth collection is 'Urania':

> Es el bosque de plátanos, los troncos altos, lisos,
> Como columnas blancas pautando el horizonte
> Que el sol de mediodía asiste y dora,
> Al pie del agua clara, a cuyo margen
> Alientan dulcemente violetas esquivas.
>
> Ella está inmóvil. Cubre aéreo
> El ropaje azulado su hermosura virgen;
> La estrella diamantina allá en la frente
> Arisca tal la nieve, y en los ojos
> La luz que no conoce sombra alguna. (328)

All is peace and calm in this idyllic landscape, and there is a sense of harmony and order. Urania, one of the nine Muses of Greek mythology, is 'inmóvil', which links her figure to the 'troncos altos' of the first stanza and thus conveys to the reader how she is integrated into this landscape. (This sense of integration contrasts with *Primeras Poesías*, where the persona was separate from life. Moreover, the time when the persona felt most 'at home' in a natural environment was in the enclosed atmosphere of the hidden garden, not in an open landscape.) Another striking feature of Urania is the reference to her 'hermosura virgen'. Collections III, IV and V of *La realidad y el deseo* are laden with references to the devastating effects of physical 'love', whereas now the stress is on a wholly spiritual, Platonic dimension. In addition, the name Urania was the 'title of the goddess Aphrodite, describing her as "heavenly"'.[50] This is confirmed by the description of her in the latter part of the second stanza, especially in the way the light in her eyes 'no conoce sombra alguna'. This is in stark contrast to the dark, gloomy scene so common in the earlier poetry. The poem abounds with images of order, mirrored in turn by the regular structure of five-line stanzas. Nothing in the modern world is allowed to taint that peace and order:

> La mano embelesada que alza un dedo
> Atenta a la armonía de los astros,
> El silencio restaura sobre el mundo

---

[50] Howatson and Chilvers, p. 560. See also Silver, *Et in Arcadia Ego*, p. 123, and p. 126, note 25.

> Domando el corazón, y la tormenta
> No turba el cielo augusto de su frente.

> Musa la más divina de las nueve,
> Del orden bello virgen creadora,
> Radiante inspiradora de los números, (328)

The second line of the first stanza above is an allusion to the Platonic world view, whereby the spheres of the planets interlock harmoniously.[51] What is particularly striking is the fact that 'el corazón' is now being 'domado'. Passion can be held in check and controlled. It does not have to be the violent force which 'arrastra afanes al paso' (202). The disparity between all of this and the strain of modern life is summed up in the way that 'la tormenta/No turba el cielo augusto de su frente': modern life is still a 'tormenta', and we should not blind ourselves to this, but that does not mean that the *vision* has to be subject to the same blight. The poem then culminates with the appearance of the persona in the final stanza:

> Si en otros días di curso enajenado
> A la pasión inútil, su llanto largo y fiebre,
> Hoy busco tu sagrado, tu amor, (329)

The goal of order through 'love' appears finally to have been achieved. Passion and lust are now recognised as 'inútil', replaced by the heavenly order and transcendence of the Greek mythological world. Temporally separate from 'pasión inútil', the persona is now able to meditate in such a way that he can attain what appeared to be more or less irrevocably lost. It must however be emphasised that order is still only a reality within meditation. Urania is not physically present.

The successful meditative search for order is developed further, in the closing poem of *Como quien espera el alba*, 'Vereda del cuco'. The opening stanzas of this long poem are an examination of Cernuda's 'relationship with desire since the time of his adolescence'.[52] We could perhaps make the charge that this poem suffers a little from verbosity, above all in the early part of the poem, for there is a substantial shift in pace and vigour as it

---

[51] Ruiz Silva similarly speaks of the 'música de las esferas' ('La música en la obra de Luis Cernuda', *Revista de Literatura*, 39 (1978), 74), while Carmelo Gariano ('Aspectos clásicos de la poesía de Luis Cernuda', *Hispania*, 48 (1965), 241) argues that the 'números' in the third line of the fourth stanza 'representan la misteriosa esencia del arte clásico formado de ritmo y medida'.
[52] Harris, *Luis Cernuda. A Study*, p. 125.

comes to a climax. The first stanzas do little more than introduce the central image of the 'fuente' of 'love' (the 'cuco' of the title is only allowed a brief mention in stanza four and merely associates the 'vereda' and the 'fuente' with the natural world) and point out that adolescence was the time of his first encounter with the 'fuente'. There is rather more substance to stanza three:

> Vencido el niño, el hombre que ya eras
> Fue al venero, cuyo fondo insidioso
> Recela la agonía,
> La lucha con la sombra profunda de la tierra
> Para alcanzar la luz, y bebiste del agua,
> Tornándose tu sed luego más viva,
> Que la abstinencia supo
> Darle fuerza mayor a aquel sosiego
> Líquido, concordante
> De tu sed, tan herido
> De ella como del agua misma,
> Y entonces no pudiste
> Desertar la vereda
> Oscura de la fuente. (376)

What is most striking about this poem when compared with 'Urania' is that, whereas the former poem depicts a vision of a mythical figure, this poem, and especially this stanza, directly confronts the poet's own past experiences. There is this time no creation of another world. He is fully aware of the chaos, the 'sombra profunda de la tierra', which was apparently always intended as a means of finding order ('Para alcanzar la luz').[53] Not only that, for all its pain, it has never been possible to avoid 'love', and 'abstinencia' can only make the attraction all the stronger. All of this is then summed up in the phrase 'la vereda oscura de la fuente'. The 'fuente' represents 'love', the adjective 'oscura' all the problems associated with contact with the 'vereda', while the 'vereda' itself is more complex: it not only suggests the ongoing development of his life, but also the fundamental understanding that 'love' is not pure experience. It has a goal towards which he must travel, be that goal order or chaos.

We have already contrasted the basic realism of 'Vereda del cuco', i.e., its confrontation with the poet's own life, with the visionary unreality of

---

[53] This is assuredly a perspective only gained with hindsight. There is little indication in the earlier poetry that 'la lucha con la sombra' is anything other than a source of chaos.

'Urania'. As 'Vereda del cuco' proceeds, it becomes clear that this realism is possible because the physical experience of 'love' is now to be accepted as a valuable stage in the process of attaining this new-found order. It is however the love *force* which is paramount and not individual experiences, as becomes apparent in the fourth stanza:

> Y al invocar la hondura
> Una imagen distinta respondía,
> Evasiva a la mente,
> Ofreciendo, escondiendo
> La expresión inmutable
> La compañía fiel en cuerpos sucesivos,
> Que el amor es lo eterno y no lo amado. (377)

This part of the fourth stanza, in describing the turning-point in the poet's attitude towards 'love', marks the turning-point in the poem. The poet recalls how he came to perceive 'la expresión inmutable', which is the realisation that the love force 'es lo eterno y no lo amado'. This is expressed in '*Dans ma péniche*' as a distinction between 'deseo' and 'amor',[54] but here the fact that the word 'amor' is used means that 'amor' is now much more similar to 'deseo'. It is not exactly the same: the explicit physicality of the 'cuerpos' of the penultimate line is not present in the definition of 'deseo', but at the same time the reference to 'cuerpos *sucesivos*' means that the understanding of 'amor' is far broader. It is physicality as part of the eternal cycle which the love force engenders and not purely crass destructive eroticism. Bearing this in mind, let us consider the poem's vigorous and triumphant climax in the fifth stanza:

> Es el amor fuente de todo;
> Hay júbilo en la luz porque brilla esa fuente,
> Encierra al dios la espiga porque mana esa fuente,
> Voz pura es la palabra porque suena esa fuente,
> Y la muerte es de ella el fondo codiciable.
> Extático en su orilla,
> Oh tormento divino,
> Oh divino deleite,
> Bebías de tu sed y de la fuente a un tiempo,
> Sabiendo a eternidad tu sed y el agua. (377)

---

[54] See above, p. 100.

According to Harris, 'The concept of love ... has become again a means of attaining that mystic state of the *acorde* where the visible and invisible realities are fused'.[55] This mystic element is certainly underlined by the exultant exclamations which echo the language of San Juan de la Cruz,[56] and order has been found and experienced. As far as the *experience* of 'love' is concerned, we should however be careful not to be misled by Harris' reading: it is a calm acceptance of the value of having experienced 'love' despite its chaos. This poem is *not* an indication that the persona has found order at *first* hand in erotic experiences *per se*, but in contemplation of them at *second* hand. We can thus revise Harris' reading slightly and say that Cernuda may be able to use the word 'amor', but, as already discussed, this sort of 'amor' has much in common with 'deseo' as it is defined in *'Dans ma péniche'*, although experiences do have a certain part to play now.[57] This does not necessarily mean that a physical erotic encounter would now be better than it was before. It may (or may not, there is no way of knowing[58]) require detachment and meditation just the same. The value of 'love' is then developed in the following stanza:

> Que si el cuerpo de un día
> Es ceniza de siempre,
> Sin ceniza no hay llama,
> Ni sin muerte es el cuerpo

[55] Harris, *Luis Cernuda. A Study,* p. 127.

[56] See Harris, *Luis Cernuda. A Study,* p. 127, Silver, *Et in Arcadia Ego,* p. 115, and Jiménez-Fajardo, *Luis Cernuda,* p. 94.

[57] Harris does admit that this is 'purely theoretical', but still insists that love and desire are separate concepts: 'love, and not merely desire, is "la realidad profunda"' (*Luis Cernuda. A Study,* p. 127).

[58] As it happens, the next and last major experience which is given poetic form is 'Poemas para un cuerpo'. Whether its joy was because of the new-found attitude of 'Vereda del cuco' or because the love affair was more genuinely enjoyable is something only Cernuda could know. Personally, I suspect the latter.

Harris argues that the new 'attitude to love ... is put to a practical test by what appears to have been a new experience of love, expressed in the series "Cuatro poemas a una sombra" which begins *Vivir sin estar viviendo'*, although he admits the love 'possibly existed only on Cernuda's part' (*Luis Cernuda. A Study,* p. 128). There is in fact precious little evidence of 'practical test', for any lived interpersonal experience is far removed from the poems themselves, written in what Harris concedes is a 'detached, philosophical tone' and redolent with images of distance and separation. The first poem is ominously entitled 'La ventana' (383–86), while the second speaks of 'recordando/Lo pasado' (386), and the fourth revealingly ends 'Creando otro deseo, dando asombro a la vida,/Sueño de alguno donde tú no sabes' (391). This last quotation stresses not only the separation from a 'practical' experience, but also the fact that 'amor' and 'deseo' do now have much in common.

> Testigo del amor, fe del amor eterno,
> Razón del mundo que rige las estrellas. (378)

It is now explicitly stated that the chaotic experience of 'love' was necessary so that this new vision might be attained. 'Love' is identified as the necessary death before the 'rebirth' into a new perception and understanding of it. 'Love' has thus been transformed by the persona's meditation from the source of chaos into the source of order, and the life of the persona has consequently been transformed by it. Nevertheless, let us not forget that this is a *meditative* experience. While 'el cuerpo' is 'testigo del amor', it is also 'fe del amor *eterno*'. Just as we saw with the 'cuerpos sucesivos' in stanza four, where physicality is part of an eternal cycle, so too here this 'amor eterno' must be a cyclical love force. This is then reiterated in the following stanza, when the persona sees the cyclical love force played out by 'formas juveniles': 'dudas si no eres/Su sed hoy nueva, si no es tu amor el suyo,/En ellos redivivo' (378). This is a graphic illustration of the difference in definition of 'amor'. If this were 'amor' as it is understood in the earlier poetry, then, if it were repeating itself, the 'formas juveniles' would be writhing in agony and wandering lost in mist. 'Amor' is now viewed from a much more detached perspective. The degree of detachment is emphasised by the way in which the persona addresses himself as 'tú', and holds both past and present at arm's length. This is the culmination of a steady process of internalisation, begun in 'Qué más da', where the persona moves further and further away from the reality, and above all the immediacy, of lived experience. But we should not stop here. 'Vereda del cuco' is not exclusively about 'order'. It finds order, certainly, but this involves an understanding of *all the chaos* which has gone before. The poem is therefore an interweaving of the basic dichotomy of order and chaos.

The joy of the insight of 'Vereda del cuco' does not however last, perhaps for the very reason that it was successful, namely because it is contemplation and not life itself. The poem 'El retraído', from *Vivir sin estar viviendo*, deals, not specifically with love, but rather with memories and the value of the inner life as opposed to external reality. The greater part of the poem adopts a positive stance towards memories,[59] but the closing stanza contradicts this apparent idyll:

> Si morir fuera esto,
> Un recordar tranquilo de la vida,
> Un contemplar sereno de las cosas,

---

[59] See Silver, *Et in Arcadia Ego*, p. 74.

Cuán dichosa la muerte,
Rescatando el pasado
Para soñarlo a solas cuando libre,
Para pensarlo tal presente eterno,
Como si un pensamiento valiese más que el mundo. (400)

The opening lines of this stanza certainly convey an idealised vision of the values of contemplation. The validity of this is however thrown into question by the final line 'Como si un pensamiento valiese más que el mundo'. Silver remarkably suggests that this line supports the stance of the rest of the poem, but in so doing he is ignoring the grammar of it, namely the subjunctive after 'como si'.[60] The persona here is aware that this is wishful thinking, and that reality does not conform to this ideal. Thus while the poetry of this later period is certainly much more serene than the earlier poetry and the greater interest in inner reality has helped the persona to remain rather closer to order than to chaos, nevertheless it is evident that such a solution is an evasion and not definitive.[61]

This degree of ambivalence is very important in Cernuda's love poetry. The critical literature has tended to concentrate on the contrast between the chaos of the experience of 'love' in the earlier poems and the order of the later meditation on 'love'. In spite of this, as already mentioned, even in 'Vereda del cuco' there is an interweaving of both order and chaos. This idea of interweaving of order and chaos encourages us to re-evaluate such a firm distinction. 'Dans ma péniche', for example, represents the most important step towards the profoundly meditative poetry of Como quien espera el alba, since it depicts the persona's withdrawal into himself and his

---

[60] 'Supreme among the attributes of memory is that of experiencing any fragment of the past as eternal present, possible because a thought ... *is* worth more than the world.' (My emphasis) (Silver, *Et in Arcadia Ego*, p. 75.)

Attitudes towards inner contemplation show subtle variations. In 'Qué más da', memory of the beloved 'Basta para iluminar ... toda esta niebla' (188). In 'Río vespertino' in *Como quien espera el alba* however a similar idea to that in 'El retraído' is expressed in the form of a real condition, but in the midst of the question, '¿... Si sólo un pensamiento vale el mundo?' (372). The reappraisal in 'El retraído' is surely very significant, although again not definitive. In 'Viviendo sueños', the persona acknowledges 'Conozco que tú no existes/Fuera de mi pensamiento' (477). There is therefore a subtle shifting back and forth in the evaluation of thoughts and memories which hints that there is a longing for the persona's inner life to conform to, and be as valuable as, the real world.

[61] Bruton comments on 'El fuego', from *Vivir sin estar viviendo* (389–91), that 'Cernuda is unable to maintain his faith in reality and must make do with its metamorphosis into memory' ('Luis Cernuda and the Poetics of Desire', *Ibero-Romania*, 27 (1988), 75). The phrase 'make do' further suggests that memories are not entirely positive.

complete divorcing of himself from the external world and its chaos. This is established as early as the first line, 'Quiero vivir cuando el amor muere' (234), and runs as a thread throughout the poem. There is a deep-rooted desire for order *and* an active search for it. The fact on the other hand that the erotic hedonism of the dream, together with its transitoriness, is so close to chaos is in itself illustrative of the *coexistence* of order and chaos.

What about 'Cuerpo en pena'? The presence of order is less obvious, but the first line of the fifth stanza is 'Flores de luz tranquila despiertan a lo lejos,' (145): even here, in the depths of despair, there seems to be something positive. It is far away, no more than 'awaking', but it is still there. The persona's commitment to it is reiterated in the penultimate stanza, in the phrase 'hacia la flor sin nombre' (146). What is more, the poem is written in regular Alexandrines, which reflects a desire for poetic order even in the midst of existential chaos. All around is chaotic, and yet still the poem hints that the persona has to seek order, has to try to unite the two poles. Similarly, 'Esperaba solo' juxtaposes the persona's hopeful innocence with the pain of amatory involvement (181), while 'Unos cuerpos son como flores' speaks of a joyous goal frustrated (180–81). 'Telarañas cuelgan de la razón' likewise asserts that 'hace falta recoger los trozos de prudencia' (175), while 'Estaba tendido' juxtaposes the beloved's beauty and selfishness (179).[62]

Let us return now to the later poetry, where order is predominant. We have already seen the presence of order and chaos together in 'Vereda del cuco'. 'Urania' is however about as close to an ideal of order that is conceivable in Cernuda's poetry, and yet even here there are discordant notes. We saw above that 'la tormenta' of the modern world does not affect Urania. In addition, in the penultimate stanza, the power of this experience of order is said to work 'Sobre el dolor informe de la vida,/Sosegando el espíritu a su acento' (328–29). This experience is *exclusively* a spiritual one which has an *effect* on day-to-day reality. It still contrasts with that day-to-day reality. Thus what a careful reading shows us is the extent to which, time after time, chaos meets order and order meets chaos. They stand side by side as a constant dichotomy. One particularly striking illustration of the way in which this dichotomy is expressed is the fourth poem of 'Poemas para un cuerpo', entitled 'Sombra de mí'. Written as a result of the happy love affair in Mexico, it is not surprising that spiritual, emotional and physical fulfilment all have a part to play in the poem, but pain and sorrow are subtly interwoven as well:

[62] One poem where admittedly there is no sign of order at all is 'En medio de la multitud' (176–77).

> Bien sé yo que esta imagen
> Fija siempre en la mente
> No eres tú, sino sombra
> Del amor que en mí existe
> Antes que el tiempo acabe.
>
> Mi amor así visible me pareces,
> Por mí dotado de esa gracia misma
> Que me hace sufrir, llorar, desesperarme
> De todo a veces, (472)

The central image of the 'sombra' is a Platonic one: the presence of the beloved allows the lover to recall his soul's knowledge of perfect love in the heavens and permits him to glimpse that celestial perfection. (Unlike *Donde habite el olvido*, this time the 'flight of the soul' is successful.) Genuine love thus allows the persona fulfilment to the point of contact with a totally ordered and harmonious universe. But that is only part of the story. He speaks also of 'sufrir, llorar, desesperarme/De todo'. This is a total lived experience, not a dream, and there is no attempt to conceal the painful 'chaotic' side. Instead, it appears as an integral part. The Platonic analogies are then pushed further in the third stanza:

> Y aunque conozco eso, luego pienso
> Que sin ti, sin el raro
> Pretexto que me diste,
> Mi amor, que afuera está con su ternura,
> Allá dentro de mí hoy seguiría
> Dormido todavía (472–73)

This memory of celestial glory is not something of which the persona is automatically aware. It requires the presence of a beloved to 'waken' it from its dormant state. The fact that the beloved has done so emphasises the attainment of order, but he still acknowledges that, without the beloved, this awareness 'seguiría dormido'. While order is predominant, the poem still has enough ambivalence to ask 'what if ...?' And if 'amor' had not been awoken, what would have happened? Isolation? Evasive dreams and vicarious experiences? Once again chaos is on the fringes of order. In general terms, then, in the midst of chaos there is the search for order, in the apparent finding of order there is an awareness of chaos. It is a continual awareness of the meeting of the two poles in Cernuda's own existence, which results in a perpetual striving to bring those two poles together into the final order which is the individual poems. The ultimate goal is to make *that* order look,

Janus-like, in two different directions at once, and it is perhaps there that the search for order in 'love' is most successful.

CHAPTER FIVE

SEARCH FOR ORDER IN THE MATERIAL WORLD II: ART

A. The Theory of Art

After love and eroticism, art is one of the most important themes in *La realidad y el deseo*.[1] It is understandably close to Cernuda's heart, and, while he often makes direct reference to real historical figures, such as Goethe, Lorca, Larra and Mozart, we frequently have the feeling that we are learning more about the poet's own ideas than we are about the ostensible subject of the poem. Incidentally, while 'Romantic' is often too restrictive a term to apply to Cernuda's poetry, it must be admitted that it is in some of his attitudes towards the nature of art and the artist that Cernuda can be seen to be most overtly Romantic. On the other hand, it will be seen that this very Romanticism has the consequence of bringing the order/chaos dichotomy into particularly sharp focus.

What is the nature of art for Cernuda? We know that his poetry moulds something ordered and permanent out of his chaotic and transient personal experiences. His ideas about the rôle of chaos and order in his poetry are however much more far-reaching than raw material plus poetic form. A brief digression is useful at this stage. Something of a *topos* in Romantic thought was the idea that art is a process whereby form and order are given, not merely to disordered personal experiences, but to the dark, demonic forces of chaos. One of the writers to conceptualise this idea most clearly and succinctly was Nietzsche. In his analysis of Greek tragic art, *Die Geburt der Tragödie* (*The Birth of Tragedy*), he identifies two poles: the Apollonian and the Dionysian. The Dionysian he defines as follows:

> ... das Wesen des *Dionysischen*, das uns am nächsten noch durch die Analogie des *Rausches* gebracht wird ....[2]

---

[1] While the most common artistic genre to appear is poetry, the more general term 'art' has been chosen so that music in particular might not be excluded.

[2] Nietzsche, *Werke*, I, p. 24.

(... the substance of the *Dionysian*, which is brought to us most nearly by means of analogy with *intoxication* ....)

The Dionysian consists of the dark forces of chaos: unbridled passion, violent forces of the natural world, everything which resists control and restraint. As Nicholls comments, 'The Dionysian is the rebirth of the primitive and savage'.[3] This in Nietzschean terms is the nature of artistic inspiration. The problem with the Dionysian force is that, since it engenders a state of 'Rausch' ('intoxication'), it must be controlled or it will lead to decadence. The controlling principle is the Apollonian:

Dies ist die wahre Kunstabsicht des Apollo: in dessen Namen wir alle jene zahllosen Illusionen des schönen Scheins zusammenfassen, ...[4]

(This is Apollo's true artistic intention: it is in his name that we gather together all those innumerable illusions which form beauty in appearance ....)

Art in Nietzschean terms is therefore a union of these two poles. While it is impossible to know whether Cernuda was directly influenced by Nietzschean ideas (he did read some Nietzsche, although exactly what and when is uncertain[5]), the comparison is useful because it bears a striking similarity with the third poem of Bécquer's *Rimas*, with which Cernuda was acquainted:

> locura que el espíritu
> exalta y desfallece;
> embriaguez divina
> del genio creador...
>
> ¡Tal es la inspiración!
>
> Gigante voz que el caos
> ordena en el cerebro,
> y entre las sombras hace
> la luz aparecer;
>
> ...
>
> ¡Tal es nuestra razón!

[3] Roger A. Nicholls, *Nietzsche in the Early Work of Thomas Mann* (Berkeley, Los Angeles: University of North California Press, 1955), p. 85.
[4] Nietzsche, *Werke*, I, p. 133.
[5] See 'Historial de un libro', *Prosa I*, p. 629.

Con ambas siempre en lucha
y de ambas vencedor,
tan sólo al genio es dado
a un yugo atar las dos.[6]

Bécquer's analysis of 'la inspiración' could not be a better example of the Dionysian, accurate even to the phrase *'embriaguez* divina'. 'La razón' meanwhile is characterised by images of order and restraint, and art must be the union of both forces. Incidentally, questions of influence do not really arise here, since Bécquer died in 1870, while *Die Geburt der Tragödie* dates from 1871. What matters is that the comparison between Nietzsche and Bécquer helps to crystallise, first, the fundamental importance of two opposing extremes held together in tension, and second, the currency of such ideas at that time.

Cernuda proves to be heir to these ideas. Indeed, he treats ideas of order and chaos in art in a thoroughly Romantic fashion, so Romantic in fact that it feels a little uneasy in 'A un poeta muerto (F.G.L.)' from *Las nubes*:

Triste sino nacer
Con algún don ilustre
Aquí, donde los hombres
En su miseria sólo saben
El insulto, la mofa, el recelo profundo
Ante aquel que ilumina las palabras opacas
Por el oculto fuego originario. (255)

'Chaotic' poetic inspiration is formulated here as the 'oculto fuego originario'. (This is conveyed even more explicitly as '[el] Caos primero' (530) in 'Desolación de la Quimera'.[7]) This seems anachronistic in a poem from 1937. Cernuda seems to be nostalgic for a past age, which echoes the very Romantic phase of *Invocaciones* and persists in his attitude to art, although less so towards other matters, throughout his poetic career. Art, as far as Cernuda is concerned, consists of the dark forces of chaos which are then 'illuminated' by the poet.[8] What is more, the poet emerges as a

---

[6] Bécquer, pp. 46–48.

[7] See below, pp. 134–36.

[8] Silver interprets 'oculto fuego originario' purely as referring to 'love' (*Et in Arcadia Ego*, p. 109). Assuming it does refer to love as well as 'chaotic inspiration', this form of 'love' suggests a complex set of ideas. The word 'oculto' especially is similar to Lorca's phrase 'amor oscuro' in his *Sonetos del amor oscuro*. The following is the octet of the

'chosen' figure (it is a 'sino' to be born with the 'don ilustre' of poetry) whom the unthinking masses cannot understand. Cernuda has regressed to a quite remarkable extent towards conventional Romanticism.

The life of the artist, and the impact of art on his life, is at least as important, and possibly more so, than what actually constitutes art. In 'A un poeta muerto', the argument quickly progresses from art *per se* to what existence is like for those born with this particular 'don ilustre'. The poet's life involves more than alienation from an uncomprehending society, as is illustrated in the third last stanza, which speaks much more of the effects of the poetic 'gift':

> Para el poeta la muerte es la victoria;
> Un viento demoníaco le impulsa por la vida,
> Y si una fuerza ciega
> Sin comprensión de amor
> Transforma por un crimen
> A ti, cantor, en héroe,
> Contempla en cambio, hermano,
> Cómo entre la tristeza y el desdén
> Un poder más magnánimo permite a tus amigos
> En un rincón pudrirse libremente. (257)

ninth sonnet of the series (Federico García Lorca, *Poesía*, Vol. I of *Obras completas*, ed. Miguel García-Posada (Barcelona: Galaxia Gutenberg, 1996–97), p. 632):

> ¡Ay voz secreta del amor oscuro!
> ¡ay balido sin lanas! ¡ay herida!
> ¡ay aguja de hiel, camelia hundida!
> ¡ay corriente sin mar, ciudad sin muro!
>
> ¡Ay noche inmensa de perfil seguro,
> montaña celestial de angustia erguida!
> ¡Ay perro en corazón, voz perseguida,
> silencio sin confín, lirio maduro!

In its most general sense, 'amor oscuro' is homosexual love, suggested by the fact that the 'voz secreta del amor oscuro' is also a 'voz perseguida'. It is obviously also a source of pain in this sonnet. (See further Andrew A. Anderson, *Lorca's Late Poetry: A Critical Study* (Leeds: Francis Cairns, 1990), p. 376.) Anderson additionally argues that the 'amor oscuro' in general terms 'is dark in that it has to do with the darker, murkier, Dionysian, side of the passions' (p. 306). Given Cernuda's friendship with Lorca and the fact that this poem is dedicated to him, it is perfectly possible that the 'oculto fuego originario' is a reading of Lorca's phrase, for the 'murkiness' and pain of love, together with homosexuality, have very obvious parallels in *La realidad y el deseo*. C.f. also Cernuda's poem 'Amor oculto', from *Las nubes* (308–09), which speaks of '[el] otro amor' which 'el mundo bajo insulta'.

The 'true' poet is portrayed in very grandiose terms: he is a romantic, heroic, almost superhuman figure. The 'viento demoníaco' refers to a kind of supernatural power which only the poet has. It is in fact a little confusing in Cernuda's poetry. On the one hand there is the sense of something 'devilish',[9] which in turn links up with the ideas of Dionysian chaos in stanza three. On the other hand, this supernatural power bears much in common with the power of the Greek 'daimon', which, like Eros,[10] can act as an intermediary between humanity and the gods.[11] There is a hint of this in the way that Lorca's death is not a disaster but a culmination, as he is transformed 'en héroe'. Hence the poet is simultaneously dragged downwards to destruction and transported upwards to the celestial heights. The poet's life therefore runs parallel to the nature of art itself, as a union of both order and chaos. Moreover, the poet as a result can never be at home in the world. In being simultaneously destroyed and uplifted he has no place amongst ordinary human beings. It is that understanding of the effect of art on the life of the artist that leads Cernuda to his bizarre re-evaluation of Lorca's murder: since the true artist is an outsider, then total escape from the world (i.e., death) is the most appropriate course of action. Lorca's murder can then be re-interpreted as an agent in a weird cosmic plan to save him from the world's misery.[12] This 'salvation' is thus preferable to the condemnation the persona has to endure of carrying on 'pudriéndose en un rincón'. Again, this idea is thoroughly Romantic, while conveniently side-stepping the logical consequence that a dead poet cannot write anything. The most serious issue, however, is the way that the poet's existence is defined as a mixture of order and chaos.

'A un poeta muerto' is not the definitive expression of Cernuda's understanding of the life of the artist. In 'A Larra con unas violetas', from *Las*

---

[9] I agree with Hughes when he says (*Luis Cernuda and the Modern English Poets*, p. 27) that these ideas are 'childish and outmoded'.

[10] See above, pp. 110–11.

[11] Cernuda seeks to explain this in 'Palabras antes de una lectura'. On the one hand 'ciertos poetas ... [se ven] arrastrados a la destrucción' (*Prosa I*, p. 605). On the other, when 'la poesía fija a la belleza efímera', 'lo sobrenatural y lo humano se unen en bodas espirituales, engendrando celestes criaturas' (*Prosa I*, p. 604). See further Soufas, 'Cernuda and Daimonic Power', 170, Coleman, pp. 106 and 154, and Juan García Ponce, 'El camino del poeta: Luis Cernuda', in *Luis Cernuda ante la crítica mexicana*, ed. Valender (México: Fondo de Cultura Económica, 1990), p. 82.

[12] We should also remember the more convincing reason that the poet is not at home in this world because society is quite simply hostile to him. See also Juan Gil Albert, 'Realidad y deseo en Luis Cernuda. Visión de un contemporáneo', in Jaime Gil de Biedma, Juan Gil Albert and Luis Antonio de Villena, *3 Luis Cernuda* (Sevilla: Universidad de Sevilla, 1977), p. 58.

nubes, there is a much greater stress on the power of artistic creation to guide its creator upwards, even towards absolute order. It is not insignificant that Cernuda has chosen a Romantic to whom he wishes to dedicate such a poem, for again these sorts of idea are indebted to Romanticism. The poem is elegiac in tone, and there is some space devoted to the poet's alienation from society, together with a caustic comment about the literary sterility of Spain.[13] The fifth stanza is the most succinct expression of the poet's alienation:

> La tierra ha sido medida por los hombres,
> Con sus casas estrechas y matrimonios sórdidos,
> Su venenosa opinión pública y sus revoluciones
> Más crueles e injustas que las leyes,
> Como inmenso bostezo demoníaco;
> No hay sitio en ella para el hombre solo,
> Hijo desnudo y deslumbrante del divino pensamiento. (267)

It is curious that the element of chaos has shifted from the 'viento demoníaco' of Dionysian inspiration to the 'bostezo demoníaco' of the world and society from which the poet is best advised to flee. It is remarkable that both 'A un poeta muerto' and 'A Larra con unas violetas' were written in 1937, for the obvious similarity of the two phrases serves only to highlight the substantial difference in meaning between 'viento' and 'bostezo'. Has Cernuda merely changed his mind and is no longer driven by a 'viento demoníaco'? It is worth considering that, while the 'viento' is an active, deliberate force, a 'bostezo' is no more than an expression of weariness or disinterest. We could possibly argue that the misery of the world is like the bored pastime of the underworld, whereas the poet of 'A un poeta muerto' is gifted with strange, inexplicable powers. Whatever the explanation of the 'bostezo demoníaco', there can be no question that the world and society can never be home for the poet. His life is given over to poetic creation, the power of which is revealed in the closing lines of the poem:

> Es breve la palabra como el canto de un pájaro,
> Mas un claro jirón puede prenderse en ella
> De embriaguez, pasión, belleza fugitivas,
> Y subir, ángel vigía que atestigua del hombre,
> Allá hasta la región celeste e impasible. (267)

[13] 'Escribir en España no es llorar, es morir' (267).

The poet now does not have contact with the underworld as in 'A un poeta muerto'. On the contrary, poetic creation is perceived as having a religious, almost mystical power.[14] What is more, the very fact that 'la región celeste' is said also to be 'impasible' is a further indication of man's need to find transcendence. If he has failed to find it in religion proper, then it is not surprising that art is considered as a new religion. The only disquieting words in these lines are 'embriaguez' and 'pasión'. It is not the case however that the poet is 'intoxicated' in the Nietzschean sense of succumbing to the power of the Dionysian, but rather that 'embriaguez', 'pasión' and 'belleza' all form part of the inspiration for the poem which can then soar to the heights of celestial glory.

Inconsistencies are now beginning to emerge. Is the artist caught between two poles, as in 'A un poeta muerto', or progressing steadily towards 'la región celeste', as in 'A Larra con unas violetas'? While some of the inconsistency is accounted for by the fact that both poems are odes to different poets, nonetheless they do have equal status in La realidad y el deseo as a whole. What is more, there are still more ideas in La realidad y el deseo which create an even more complex picture. There is an image of the artist figure as a 'man of synthesis', i.e., a man in whom order and chaos, and, indeed, all the conflicts and tensions of existence, are held together. The prime example of this is 'El poeta y la bestia' from Desolación de la Quimera. This is Cernuda's picture of German Neo-Classical poet Johann Wolfgang von Goethe. The poem opens with a meditation on 'el hombre medio', which is contrasted with the figure of Goethe in the second stanza:

> El poder, el saber y la pendiente favorable
> Que, para afortunados, del destino es regalo
> (El poder y el saber, sin ella, son inoperantes
> En medio indiferente o enemigo),
> En pocos hombres como en Goethe vemos
> Coincidir y actuar dichosamente
> Ayudados, y ayudándoles él, por tantas dotes
> Que ilustra y equilibra un desarrollo
> Tan vario como sabio y armonioso. A eso llama el hombre,
> Sin conocer razón de así llamarlo: genio. (518–19)

Cernuda concentrates primarily, not on Goethe's writings, but on the man himself. Goethe's art is great because Goethe himself is a genius. The most

---

[14] See further Coleman, p. 17, and Bruton, 'Symbolical Reference and Internal Rhythm: Luis Cernuda's Debt to Hölderlin', Revue de Littérature Comparée, 58 (1984), 44.

crucial phrases in the description are 'Ayudados, y ayudándoles él' and 'ilustra y equilibra'. The first phrase demonstrates the fruitful interaction between man and world which is a sign of greatness (contrasting with the 'Triste sino' of being born a poet, according to 'A un poeta muerto', where total escape from the world is the only viable course). In the second phrase, the verb 'ilustrar' denotes the artist's power of creation, while 'equilibrar' points towards the 'man of synthesis', whose very life is an achievement of order. As mentioned, however, this seems to be in conflict with the 'triste sino' of the poet expressed in earlier poetry. In 'El poeta y la bestia', Cernuda is talking about someone he considered greater than himself.[15] The first person plural 'vemos' in the fifth line quoted is a clear reminder that he is meditating on an entirely different person. Cernuda in this poem does not think he is like Goethe. Goethe is rather a figure to be admired. The rest of the poem continues in similar terms, stressing also the fact that Goethe was far greater than the society around him ('la bestia'). This problem of society's prejudicial influence on the artist is of great concern to Cernuda, and it is voiced particularly strongly in the third stanza:

> Mas genio y circunstancias favorables,
> Maravillosa coincidencia, una vez realizada
> Entre tantas fallida, aún está sujeta
> A la posible intervención de fuerzas brutas
> De las que algún patán tiene la iniciativa
> Con un impulso ciego que va precipitándole.
> Lo mismo que la flor, su perfección abierta
> Y erguida entre las hojas al borde de un sendero,
> Puede verse deshecha por el casco o pezuña
> De animal trashumante que ignora cómo daña. (519)

Cernuda's understanding of the artist is fundamentally elitist. Once the artist has been bestowed with the gift of creation, he is immediately vastly superior to all those around him. For someone who expressed sympathy with the Communist cause in the Civil War, it is remarkable that Cernuda should use a term as pejorative as 'patán' to refer to those people who cannot appreciate art. There are admittedly times when his reverence of artistic genius can be every bit as blind as the society's incomprehension which he so vehemently censures. Nonetheless we should not trivialise his fear of how art, fragile as a perfect flower, can become so easily destroyed, although again the scorn visible in the comparison of society both with 'la bestia' and the

---

[15] See also Harris, *Luis Cernuda. A Study*, p. 174.

'casco o pezuña/De animal trashumante' is rather disconcerting. Further-more, the closing section, when Cernuda meditates on Goethe's admiration of Napoleon, is rather weak. The poem as a whole is nevertheless significant for Cernuda's feelings about the greatness of the ideal artist.

While in 'El poeta y la bestia' there is an impression that the artist's life *ought* to be like Goethe's, it is hinted that Cernuda's own life as an artist is somewhat different. Furthermore, there is a considerable degree of conflict with, and rejection by, the rest of society. While a poet as great as Goethe is able to survive 'la bestia', it has a prejudicial effect on poets like Cernuda. As far as he is concerned, the negative side of the life of the artist stems, in one respect, from that relationship (or more accurately the lack of it) with society. In his later poetry especially, Cernuda is very bitter about society's treatment of the artist. 'Limbo' (460–62), for example, from *Con las horas contadas,* is, amongst other things, an extremely sarcastic poem about 'dilettante' members of society who think they appreciate art, but do so very superficially.[16] '*Birds in the Night*' (495–97) on the other hand, from *Desolación de la Quimera,* expresses horror at society's deliberate 'misreading' of Rimbaud and Verlaine to make them more 'respectable' and acceptable to traditional values.[17] Another poem which is a long and in-volved indictment of the artist's relationship with society is the very Romantic 'La gloria del poeta' from *Invocaciones.* In this poem, unlike 'El poeta y la bestia', it is not the order which the genius can impose on life which matters, but rather the rôle which chaos has to play in the poet's existence, as well as his art, before that art can be created. There are two sides to this chaos: society on the one hand and the 'demonio' on the other. The rôle of the 'demonio' in 'La gloria del poeta' is however more complex than in 'A un poeta muerto':

> Demonio hermano mío, mi semejante,
> Te vi palidecer, colgado como la luna matinal,
> Oculto en una nube por el cielo,
> Entre las horribles montañas,
> Una llama a guisa de flor tras la menuda oreja tentadora,
> Blasfemando lleno de dicha ignorante,

---

[16] See also above, pp. 38–40.

[17] I am not convinced that Cernuda ever wanted to reform society through his poetry, as Maximino Cacheiro seems to suggest, asserting that, 'Cernuda ... se presenta como un sujeto portador de valores revelándolos a toda la sociedad para que cambie de rumbo' ('La problemática del escrito en "La realidad y el deseo"', *Cuadernos Hispanoamericanos,* No. 316 (1976), 56). He criticised society certainly, but I am not convinced he attempted to do very much more.

Igual que un niño cuando entona su plegaria,
Y burlándote cruelmente al contemplar mi cansancio de la tierra.
(230)

In 'A un poeta muerto', the 'viento demoníaco' is a fundamental aspect of poetic inspiration and the power of poetic expression. In this poem, Cernuda is much less concerned (until the last stanza) with creation and much more concerned with the poet's own life. Not only that, the 'demonio' here is not so much a force as a kind of 'alter ego', a living entity with whom the poet can interact and who is part autonomous and yet also inseparable from the poet. It is intimately linked to devilish spirits: it is 'oculto en una nube', it emits 'una llama', it is 'blasfemando' and it scoffs at and ridicules the persona. This 'demonio' is an ally of Beelzebub, an integral part of the darkest forces of chaos. (It is also frankly rather difficult to believe that this should have anything whatsoever to do with poetry.) This then gives way to the long and at times petulant complaints about society, the other side of the poet's chaos. A good example is the eighth stanza:

Ésos son, hermano mío,
Los seres con quienes muero a solas,
Fantasmas que harán brotar un día
El solemne erudito, oráculo de estas palabras mías ante alumnos
     extraños,
Obteniendo por ello renombre,
Más una pequeña casa de campo en la angustiosa sierra inmediata a
     la capital;
En tanto tú, tras irisada niebla,
Acaricias los rizos de tu cabellera
Y contemplas con gesto distraído desde la altura
Esta sucia tierra donde el poeta se ahoga. (232–33)

The artist is persecuted more by society than by his 'demonio'. Life in society is no more than a death sentence because of its shallowness and lack of understanding of 'abnormal' people and because of its trite, boring, glib academics who may read and teach poetry but who do not 'live' it as the poet does. The world is 'esta sucia tierra', corrupt, vile, debased, and the poet can only 'ahogarse', a verb which immediately recalls 'el ahogado', the protagonist of 'Cuerpo en pena', whose life could not be more desperate. In addition, the fact that all this evil and misery is looked upon by the 'demonio' 'con gesto distraído' reminds us of the 'bostezo demoníaco' of 'A Larra con unas violetas'. The evil in the world for which the 'demonio' is responsible is but a bored pastime compared with the more serious business of tormenting the poet.[18]

It is against the background of double torment in 'La gloria del poeta' that the poet is required to engage in his writing. He could not be much further removed from the Goethean man of synthesis. But we have not yet sunk to the nadir:

> Es hora ya, es más que tiempo
> De que tus manos cedan a mi vida
> El amargo puñal codiciado del poeta;
> De que lo hundas, con sólo un golpe limpio,
> En este pecho sonoro y vibrante, idéntico a un laúd,
> Donde la muerte únicamente,
> La muerte únicamente,
> Puede hacer resonar la melodía prometida. (233)

Superficially it could be argued that this stanza is expressing essentially the same ideas as 'A un poeta muerto', i.e., that the poet is better to die because his home can never be in this world. This could certainly account for the desire for death, but the logical inconsistency noted in the Lorca poem, namely that a dead poet is unproductive, is more complex here. It is not purely escape the poet wants, but a death at the hands of his 'demonio' so as to 'hacer resonar la melodía prometida', i.e., so as to realise the finished poem. It is therefore not literal death but metaphorical death. The poet cannot write to the best of his ability unless he endure the very worst that chaos can offer. Poetry may have to be a union of chaos and order, and Goethe may be able to unite the two in his life, but Cernuda's life can *only* be chaos. We are left to wonder what the source of order will be.

The poet's life as a life of chaos is explored further in 'Desolación de la Quimera'.[19] The poem presents the chimæra, not simply as a strange mythological creature, but as a kind of poetic Muse, in whom mankind no longer believes. The poem again takes a very Romantic view of art, stressing

---

[18] In 'Noche del hombre y su demonio' (366–70), the 'demonio' torments the 'hombre' (clearly Cernuda himself), for forgetting 'de estar vivo' (367), because of his devotion to poetry, but Lorraine Ledford rightly stresses that there the 'demonio' also makes the man 'realize his personal strength', which is his poetry ('Cernuda's *demonio*: Devil or Divinity?', in *Essays in Honor of Jorge Guillén on the Occasion of his 85th Year*, no ed. (Cambridge, Massachusetts: Abedul, 1977), p. 47).

[19] The title of this poem and the collection is apparently derived from T. S. Eliot's *Little Gidding*, specifically the line 'The loud lament of the disconsolate Quimera [*sic*]' (Ortiz, 104).

the importance of the devilish powers and the 'Caos primero' (530). The chimæra itself, a statue, is a pathetic, miserable sight, destroyed by time:

> No hay agua, fronda, matorral ni césped.
> En su lleno esplendor mira la luna
> A la Quimera lamentable, piedra corroída
> En su desierto. Como muñón, deshecha el ala;
> Los pechos y las garras el tiempo ha mutilado; (527)

The sight of the chimæra is every bit as appalling as that of the poet in 'La gloria del poeta'. All around is dryness and sterility, while the 'esplendor' of the moon contrasts pitifully with the ruined statue. If the chimæra is a poetic Muse, why should Cernuda choose to portray it in this way? Is he suggesting that an old statue might be the wrong sort of focus for inspiration, and that the natural world ('la luna') might be a more valid focus? Is this perhaps almost a tentative admission that Cernuda's attitude towards poetry is somewhat *passé*? Or is it purely that, like the gods of 'A las estatuas de los dioses',[20] the chimæra needs people to believe in it before it can survive? I suspect it is the third possibility which Cernuda intends, but the other two questions are raised, and the poem does not really make any attempt to find a satisfactory solution to them. It is the following, however, from the sixth stanza, which deals with the character of the modern poet himself, which is of greatest import. (The chimæra itself is speaking):

> »Flacos o fláccidos, sin cabellos, con lentes,
> Desdentados. Ésa es la parte física
> En mi tardío servidor; y, semejante a ella,
> Su carácter.« (529)

The poet is feeble, pathetic and inadequate. (There is an extent to which Cernuda must be including himself in this.) He is the exact opposite of the Goethe figure, and there would appear to be little indication that he would be able to give order to the 'Caos primero'. Thus the steady ascent which has been documented, from the tension between order and chaos in 'A un poeta muerto', through the ascent to celestial glory in 'A Larra con unas violetas', to the Goethe figure as a man of synthesis, is counterbalanced by a steady descent through the tormented existence in 'La gloria del poeta' to a vision of the poet in 'Desolación de la Quimera' as the man of *disintegration*. His life is no more than a collection of chaotic fragments. How can

---

[20] See above, p. 18.

Cernuda's pictures of the artist differ so radically from each other? There is no satisfactory solution, other than the fact that it is the number of inconsistencies which makes *La realidad y el deseo* such a richly honest poetic expression, boldly creating a picture of disunified fragmentation. Such a process of fragmentation can however go too far: it can create weaknesses when, in individual poems, inconsistencies arise in the central concept.[21] A regrettable example of this is to be found in 'Desolación de la Quimera'. As noted, Cernuda himself must be one of the chimæra's 'tardíos servidores', but in the seventh stanza he expresses considerable loathing of them:

> »¿Es que pueden creer en ser poetas
> Si ya no tienen el poder, la locura
> Para creer en mí y en mi secreto?
> Mejor les va sillón en academia
> Que la aridez, la ruina y la muerte,
> Recompensas que generosa di a mis víctimas, ...« (529)

Cernuda's talent at making enemies shines through in the bitterly sarcastic line 'Mejor les va sillón en academia', a quite unnecessarily offensive side-swipe at poets such as Guillén who managed to have successful academic careers. (It is supremely ironic that Cernuda himself spent most of his life in academic circles as well, although he never achieved any more than minor positions.) We should however take care not to allow Cernuda's petulance to colour his more serious points, which, despite their cloyingly excessive Romanticism, are still firm convictions. As far as Cernuda's persona is concerned, the average 'tardío servidor' of the poetic Muse is not nearly feeble and alienated enough. The commitment to chaos must be total and unstinting. This is consequently a strident reiteration of the sentiment of 'La gloria del poeta', where the 'true' poet's life must suffer the very worst of chaos. It therefore contrasts with the lives of poets such as Guillén, which ironically have too much order: not the regulating, controlling order of Apollonian poetic creation, but a stale, sterile order of 'certeza burguesa' (529). Only misery produces poetry, Cernuda suggests here. As in 'La gloria del poeta', the problem of how someone whose life is so chaotic is able to produce that Apollonian order in his poetry is another question which the poem leaves unanswered. This lack of answer in turn suggests that by this stage in Cernuda's career the influence of Apollo was becoming increasingly sparse.

---

[21] Cf. 'A un poeta muerto', when the exaltation of Lorca's death ignores the consequent inability to continue to create poetry, or 'La gloria del poeta', where the poet's life is so chaotic that the chances of his creating order seem somewhat remote.

There is still more to the 'theory' of art. The more passive appreciation of a work of art rather than its active creation also has a rôle to play. The chaos of daily life is a principal reason for seeking some kind of order in art and the artistic experience. While Cernuda spent most of his life miserable and alienated, by the time of *Desolación de la Quimera*, he was resident predominantly in Mexico, and was rather happier than earlier. Even then, however, he is quite specific that the artistic experience can be sought in response to the chaos which is normal existence. 'Mozart', from *Desolación de la Quimera*, speaks of this, a eulogistic poem written in 1956, the bicentenary of the composer's birth. The opening of the third and final section of the poem tells us the reason for and purpose of the artistic experience:

> En cualquier urbe oscura, donde amortaja el humo
> Al sueño de un vivir urdido en la costumbre
> Y el trabajo no da libertad ni esperanza,
> Aún queda la sala del concierto, aún puede el hombre
> Dejar que su mente humillada se ennoblezca (491)

It is striking how generalised these lines are. There is no single, individual persona here (neither 'yo' nor 'tú') but rather 'el hombre' who is resident in 'cualquier urbe oscura'. The implication is thus that the musical experience is open to everyone. (Incidentally, it seems possible that the 'urbe oscura' is an echo of London in the 1940s, where Cernuda attended concerts of Mozart's music.[22]) The objective is a straightforward one, i.e., 'Dejar que su mente humillada se ennoblezca', in other words, find some kind of order in the chaos. It is striking that we have moved away again in the portrayal of art from darkness and chaos: it is the city which is 'oscura', while the music is equated with nobility. It is entirely positive. There is nothing discordant about the music whatsoever.

Much of 'Mozart' is eulogistic in tone. Paramount are the virtues of harmony and order. It is surely no accident that in this poem Cernuda should have chosen a Neo-Classical composer whose music is not only supremely melodious, but also, like the poetry of his contemporary Goethe, very regular and ordered in its composition. (This contrasts with the choice of Wagner in 'Luis de Baviera escucha *Lohengrin*', 513–17, but this is only in part a poem about a musical experience. It is at least as much a poem of a sensuous erotic dream with homosexual overtones, although the beneficial effect of this on King Ludwig II after the tedium of everyday life has ob-

---

[22] See 'Historial de un libro', *Prosa I*, p. 649. See also José Carlos Ruiz Silva, 'En torno a un poema de Luis Cernuda: "Mozart"', *Cuadernos Hispanoamericanos*, No. 316 (1976), 61–62, for further details of those concerts.

vious parallels with 'Mozart'.) The second, appropriately enough middle, stanza of section I is the most profound part of that section, and sets Mozart's music in a long and illustrious tradition:

> Desde la tierra mítica de Grecia
> Llegó hasta el norte el soplo que la anima
> Y en el norte halló eco, entre las voces
> De poetas, filósofos y músicos: ciencia
> Del ver, ciencia del saber, ciencia del oír. Mozart
> Es la gloria de Europa, el ejemplo más alto
> De la gloria del mundo, porque Europa es el mundo. (489)

Mozart is not just a brilliant composer in his own right, he is also a link in a long chain of 'poetas, filósofos y músicos'. What is more, it is a chain that is entirely unified. There is no fragmentation or disharmony. On the contrary, his art is said to recall the art of Antiquity. It is almost as if there is only one Art, a single, unified entity into whose ordered structure true, great artists' work fits perfectly. To suggest however that all of this knowledge and creation is 'ciencia' might seem rather peculiar, since art and science tend to be viewed less as complementary as they are opposites, but this highlights once again the order and sheer clarity of perspective which they all offer. Mozart is then crowned as the 'gloria de Europa', although there is something disconcerting about the clause 'porque Europa es el mundo'. I suspect there is more than a tinge of personal bitterness on Cernuda's part here, for, now in Mexico, he has largely rejected, and been rejected by, the European literary establishment.[23]

In the last stanza of section I, there is some criticism of Mozart's society for its failure to appreciate his genius. The second section then goes on to explore the effect of Mozart's music on the listener:

> Toda razón su obra, pero sirviendo toda
> Imaginación, en sí gracia y majestad une,
> Ironía y pasión, hondura y ligereza.
> Su arquitectura deshelada,[24] formas líquidas
> Da de esplendor inexplicable, (490)

---

[23] Barón Palma conversely interprets this purely as 'eurocentrismo' (p. 172).

[24] There would appear to be echoes in this phrase of Goethe's idea that 'die Baukunst' is 'eine erstarrte Musik' ('architecture is a kind of frozen music') (Johann Peter Eckermann, *Gespräche mit Goethe in den letzten Jahren seines Lebens*, ed. Fritz Bergmann (Frankfurt am Main: Insel, 1981), I, p. 307).

These lines are situated at the centre of the poem, which, appropriately, has a very regular structure, consisting of three sections of three stanzas each. It is fitting that the music should be in the centre. Of especial significance here is the series of contrasts which are united in Mozart's music. Again it is the creation of order which is paramount. Furthermore, the music serves 'toda imaginación': it has a profound effect on each individual listener. That effect is then explored in more detail in the second stanza of the third section:

> Si de manos de Dios informe salió el mundo,
> Trastornado su orden, su injusticia terrible;
> Si la vida es abyecta y ruin el hombre,
> Da esta música al mundo forma, orden, justicia,
> Nobleza y hermosura. Su salvador entonces,
> ¿Quién es? Su redentor, ¿quién es entonces?
> Ningún pecado en él, ni martirio, ni sangre. (491)

These lines evoke the effect of Mozart's music on the listener.[25] It is blasphemously postulated that listening to music can repair the chaos of God's imperfect creation and redeem mankind.[26] In addition, all the attributes of this experience are specifically related to order and harmony, contrasting with all that is wrong with the real world. There is an explicit possibility of attaining the Absolute itself. We should not however be blind to the fact that the opening of this final section makes it plain that the individual has to escape from the world to hear this music: 'Aún queda la sala del concierto' (491). Cernuda is aware that it is temporary,[27] removed from the outside world, and not life itself.[28] The artistic experience is sought in response to the chaos, but the end of the experience signifies the beginning of chaos.

---

[25] Silver argues that these lines 'confer a transcendental importance upon the *creators* of art' (my emphasis) (*Et in Arcadia Ego*, p. 180), but the stress is on the music: 'Da esta *música* ...'.

[26] Jiménez-Fajardo is not wrong to speak of 'the potential to discover one's lasting essence', but this does obscure the religious overtones (*Luis Cernuda*, p. 139). Schärer makes the interesting point that 'la obra de arte se encuentra siempre *al margen de* la divinidad' ('Luis Cernuda y el reflejo', in *Luis Cernuda*, ed. Harris, p. 323), although I am inclined to think that the stress is rather more on music as the medium rather than on where it might lie in some 'cosmic scheme'. See also Mario E. Ruiz, 'La angustia como origen de *la realidad* y manifestación *del deseo* en Luis Cernuda', *Revista de Estudios Hispánicos*, 5 (1971), 356.

[27] I believe Octavio Paz largely overlooks this transient nature of the artistic experience ('La palabra edificante', in *Cuadrivio*, 2nd ed. (México: Editorial Joaquín Mortiz, 1969), p. 201).

[28] The fact that music is only temporary is reiterated in 'Luis de Baviera escucha *Lohengrin*', which speaks of music as a means to self-affirmation. The last sentence reads 'Y

In general terms, then, Cernuda's understanding of the 'theory' of art is a very complex, even fragmentary one. While artistic creation itself is a production of order from chaos, even dark, demonic chaos, and the artistic experience is a way, albeit transient, of finding order in life, the life of the artist is a confused and confusing jumble of different pictures: artistic creation is of benefit to the alienated, chaotic existence of the artist, and can even lead him to an appreciation of the divine. The artist is therefore a glorious figure, a man of synthesis in whom order and chaos are held together. He is however also alienated from society, a stranger in the world, a weak, feeble individual unfit for life, so involved with the dark forces of chaos that his being entirely disintegrates. Such conflicting views of art and the artist are largely irreconcilable, but, just as *La realidad y el deseo* makes no attempt to reconcile them, neither should we. If the love poetry is continually looking in the two directions of order and chaos simultaneously, the poetry dealing with art and artists looks in a multitude of directions, a fragmented mosaic where the lack of unity does not so much bespeak a failure of poetic expression as it does a conceptual impossibility. A single coherent picture no longer exists. So as we move towards a more specific analysis of Cernuda's poetic expression, we see that order is beginning to disintegrate.

B: The Practice of Art

The Disintegration of Meaning: The Advent of Literary Chaos?

It was remarked at the outset that all acts of reading are today inevitably set against a background of 'crisis of interpretation', whereby stress must be laid on the problems inherent in the process of communication.[29] It was Jacques Derrida in particular who engendered, willingly or unwillingly, vast quantities of Post-Structuralist literary theory and criticism focussing on such problems of communication. Derrida argues that words could only be deemed to be inherently 'meaningful' at a time when meaning was 'guaranteed' by what he calls 'an invariable presence ... transcendentality, consciousness, God, man, and so forth'. Modern society has however lost this 'center or origin', and this extends 'the domain and the play of signification infinitely',[30] whereby there becomes an '*overabundance* of the

---

para siempre en la música vive' (517), with the clear implication that this self-affirmation will end along with the last dying chords.

[29] See above, p. 7.

[30] Jacques Derrida, 'Structure, Sign and Play in the Discourse of the Human Sciences', trans. Alan Bass, in *Modern Criticism and Theory: A Reader*, ed. David Lodge (London: Longman, 1988), p. 110.

signifier'.[31] As George Steiner, himself not an adherent of Post-Structuralist theory, remarks, 'signs are made recognizable and significant by sole virtue of their differences ... from other signs'.[32] Signifiers become laden with a whole range of intertextual resonances which are dependent on the literary, social and cultural contexts of both author and reader. The lack of precision and control in meaning are therefore paramount. There is however a complication in this, for there is a split between Derrida's philosophy and the way it has been 'appropriated' by literary theoreticians. Derrida advocates a response of 'Nietzschean *affirmation*, that is the joyous affirmation of the play of the world',[33] whereby this lack of precision is a liberation. The more pessimistic literary theoreticians on the other hand take the not illogical step that, if meaning is fluid to the point of infinitude, then there is no sure meaning and effectively no meaning at all. As J. Hillis Miller comments, the literary work 'has at least two apparent grounds, centers, foci, or *logoi*, and is therefore incapable of being encompassed in any single coherent or homogeneous interpretation. Any reading can be shown to be a misreading.'[34] It is therefore impossible to rely on any single reading of a word at all.

How does this apply to Cernuda's poetry? We have stressed throughout this study the fact that *La realidad y el deseo* can unquestionably *not* be 'encompassed in any single coherent or homogeneous interpretation.' This has been illustrated most clearly in the fragmented picture of art and artists discussed above. Not only that, one of the first things which we sought to establish is the degree to which erotic and existential concerns interweave and intermingle, with the result that both themes can be presented simultaneously in a single poem. Any choice between the two as to which is more important will inevitably be placed in the hands of the reader, which entails a loosening of authorial control. The love poetry, meanwhile, seeks, not to present a definitive picture of a life of chaos or of a finding of order, but rather a Janus-like double perspective where order and chaos are both continually present. The poet refuses to allow himself to be bound irrevocably to one stance or another, and there is therefore always a degree of ambivalence present.

More ambivalent still is the poetry concerned with the search for the Absolute. There, as with art and artists, we find a multitude of conflicting perspectives revealing doubt and faith, God's saving grace and indifference

---

[31] Derrida, in Lodge, p. 120.

[32] George Steiner, *Real Presences. Is There Anything in What We Say?* (London: Faber and Faber, 1989), p. 122.

[33] Derrida, in Lodge, p. 121.

[34] J. Hillis Miller, 'Stevens' Rock and Criticism as Cure, II', in *Theory Now and Then* (Hemel Hempstead: Harvester Wheatsheaf, 1991), p. 120.

and passivity, the potential for finding God and the tragedy of finding nothing. It does violence to the poetry to attempt to single out certain poems as
being more definitively representative of Cernuda's standpoint than others
(although the general thrust of a loss of faith cannot be denied). What matters is that, at the time of *Las nubes* in particular, all of these various
thoughts and attitudes were present together. When we consider them together we have the same image of a fragmentary mosaic as we have with art
and artists. It therefore makes no sense to attempt to build up a single, coherent, univocal pattern.

It is however inaccurate to imagine that the degree of fragmentation in
the overall picture presented by *La realidad y el deseo* is a direct concomitant of the problematic nature of language and meaning. While we have been
aware of uncertainties in our interpretations of poems, nevertheless we have
had little cause to postulate the Post-Structuralist perspective that all reading is misreading and that every word is open to an infinite range of
significations. So why have we explicitly suggested the 'disintegration of
meaning' and the 'advent of literary chaos'? In formal terms, we have
stressed before the good use Cernuda makes of Surrealist 'chaos' to mirror
the chaos of his emotions in various poems of *Un río, un amor* and *Los
placeres prohibidos*.[35] Chaos is indeed central to Surrealist technique.
Morris has demonstrated convincingly the considerable extent to which the
ideas of the French Surrealists, the pioneers in the movement, were current
in Spain in the 1920s.[36] There is however no space for an in-depth analysis
of Surrealism. What is crucial is that Freud's analysis of the sub-conscious
was very influential in Surrealist circles,[37] and that Surrealist poetry sought
to give literary expression to that subconscious.[38] André Breton, one of the
most prominent French Surrealists, defined Surrealism in the following manner:

> SURRÉALISME, n.m. Automatisme psychique pur par lequel on se
> propose d'exprimer, soit verbalement, soit par écrit, soit de toute
> autre manière, le fonctionnement réel de la pensée. Dictée de la

---

[35] See for example 'Unos cuerpos son como flores' (180–81), discussed above (pp.
92–93). Incidentally, I can see little justification in Capote Benot's insistence that *Donde
habite el olvido* is a collection of Surrealist poetry (pp. 197–233).
[36] Morris, *Surrealism and Spain 1920–1936* (Cambridge: Cambridge University Press,
1972), *passim*. See also Delgado, pp. 121–51.
[37] Morris, *Surrealism*, p. 36.
[38] See for example Real Ramos, *Luis Cernuda y la "Generación del 27"* (Salamanca:
Ediciones Universidad de Salamanca, 1983), p. 37.

pensée, en l'absence de tout contrôle exercé pour la raison, en dehors de toute préoccupation esthétique ou morale.[39]

This formulation is a clear definition of the Surrealist technique of 'automatic writing' in particular, which was concerned with writing down thoughts and emotions as 'spontaneously' as possible.[40] Characteristic of Surrealist poetry therefore is a collection of elements which seem to have little organising logic and structure. Spain's Surrealists were however rarely as extreme in their approach as their French counterparts. Despite this, Cernuda does make use of genuine Surrealist techniques in his poetry, especially in *Un río, un amor*, and certainly he exploits it enough to make his poetry obscure and hard to follow. A good example of this is to be found in 'Estoy cansado' from *Un río, un amor*, the opening two stanzas of which have all the trappings of a capricious and incoherent jumble of ideas:

> Estar cansado tiene plumas,
> Tiene plumas graciosas como un loro,
> Plumas que desde luego nunca vuelan,
> Mas balbucean igual que loro.
>
> Estoy cansado de las casas,
> Prontamente en ruinas sin un gesto;
> Estoy cansado de las cosas,
> Con un latir de seda vueltas luego de espaldas. (152)

The spirit of tedium and *ennui* which pervades this poem is obvious, but that is really all that is obvious. What relationship does 'estar cansado' have to 'plumas'? Why should the feathers be 'graciosas como un loro'? Why is it that the feathers themselves 'balbucean'? The choice of images seems completely arbitrary. Indeed, the only reason for the presence of the parrot at all would appear to be by association with the mention of feathers. It certainly adds precious little to the poem. Similarly in the second stanza the only logic in the first and third lines would appear to be the phonological similarity of 'cansado', 'casas' and 'cosas', and there is minimal evidence of significance behind the 'latir de seda'. The closing stanza is then rather clearer, especially with its first line 'Estoy cansado de estar vivo' (152), but the overriding

---

[39] André Breton, 'Premier Manifeste du Surréalisme', in *Les Manifestes du Surréalisme* suivis de *Prolégomènes à un troisième Manifeste du Surréalisme ou non* (Paris: Éditions de Sagittaire, 1946), p. 45.

[40] See also Ruiz Silva, *Arte, amor y otras soledades en Luis Cernuda* (Madrid: De la Torre, 1979), p. 31.

impression is of a poem where obscurity has triumphed over lucidity. This then marks one stage towards literary chaos.

To understand Cernuda's Surrealist poetry purely in terms of the 'chaos' of obscure imagery and lack of coherence is however thoroughly inadequate. The degree to which Cernuda was not an exponent of true French Surrealism cannot be underestimated.[41] Where his understanding of literary chaos departs most profoundly from mere outpourings of the subconscious is in the extent to which he had a certain anxiety about the nature of language and meaning themselves, as he reveals in his short theoretical lecture 'Palabras antes de una lectura':

> ¿cómo expresar con palabras cosas que son inexpresables? Las palabras están vivas, y por lo tanto traicionan; lo que expresan hoy como verdadero y puro, mañana es falso y está muerto. Hay que usarlas contando con su limitación,[42]

This bears a certain amount in common with Romanticism. Bécquer, for example, in his introduction to *Rimas*, complains that 'entre el mundo de la idea y el de la forma existe un abismo que sólo puede salvar la palabra; y la palabra, tímida y perezosa, se niega a secundar sus esfuerzos'.[43] For all the similarity, however, what Cernuda has to say is more than a mere restatement of what was by this time the cliché that language is inadequate to express exactly what we feel, although at the same time it is assuredly not as extreme as what Miller calls an 'uncanny'[44] Post-Structuralist's empty void of meaninglessness. Cernuda certainly recalls Romantic anxieties, but he goes beyond them. What is at issue is a sense that the poet is unable to exercise absolute and final control over the language that he uses. Nothing can ensure that the words on a page will have exactly the signification that the poet would impart to them. 'Palabras antes de una lectura' was written by Cernuda in 1935. By this time he was writing *Invocaciones* and had already effectively abandoned Surrealism altogether. A critique of language and meaning was however already present, perhaps even more radically so, in his

---

[41] As Carlos Marcial de Onís comments, 'sólo tomó del surrealismo aquello que mejor pudiera servir a sus necesidades expresivas' (*El surrealismo y cuatro poetas de la generación del 27* (Madrid: José Porrúa Turanzas, 1974), p. 213). Cernuda himself was fairly reticent in the way he expressed his affiliation to Surrealism: in 'Historial de un libro', he says that Surrealism was 'una corriente ... ante la cual yo no pude, ni quise, permanecer indiferente', while the first three poems of *Un río, un amor* were 'dictados por un impulso *similar* al que animaba a los superrealistas' (my emphasis) (*Prosa I*, p. 634).

[42] *Prosa I*, p. 605.

[43] Bécquer, p. 40.

[44] Miller, p. 121.

Surrealist poetry, especially in *Un río, un amor*. It may well be that such a critique proves to be of rather more benefit to an analysis of *that* collection than of his later poetry.[45]

How does Cernuda express his critique of language and meaning in *Un río, un amor*? As is so often the case in *La realidad y el deseo* in general, it does not appear in any single straightforward manner. Instead there is a range of standpoints, which vary from direct censure of words themselves to much more subtle and veiled analyses of meaning. One of the poems which is most direct in its approach is 'Durango'. On a superficial level the influence of Surrealism is immediately discernible, with above all the very irregular stanza structure, varying from four to seven lines in no predetermined pattern, visibly apparent on the page. The poem opens with an obscure and hard to interpret assertion about 'guerreros', but the importance of words themselves is also highlighted:

> Las palabras quisieran expresar los guerreros,
> Bellos guerreros impasibles,
> Con el mañana gris abrazado, como un amante,
> Sin dejarles partir hacia las olas.
>
> Por la ventana abierta
> Muestra el destino su silencio;
> Sólo nubes con nubes, siempre nubes
> Más allá de otras nubes semejantes,
> Sin palabras, sin voces,
> Sin decir, sin saber;
> Últimas soledades que no aguardan mañana. (153)

We could speculate that, since the love theme runs, overtly or covertly, throughout *Un río, un amor*, 'guerreros' refers to lovers, especially since they are 'bellos', with their similarity to warriors pointing towards the violence and pain of erotic involvement. On the other hand there is little obvious reason why they should be 'impasibles', let alone why they are 'Con el mañana gris abrazado'. What matters more is the fact that they 'quisieran expresar las palabras'. The use of the imperfect subjunctive 'quisieran' illus-

---

[45] Cernuda had already made a similar statement about language in 1929 about Éluard's poetry, asserting that, 'esas palabras son ya ciertamente muy distintas, bien que, ... como todas las palabras, traicionen también' ('Paul Éluard', in *Prosa II*, p. 16). Quoted also by Juan Alberto Fernández Bañuls, 'Bécquer y la creación poética del 27: el caso de Cernuda', *Archivo Hispalense*, 54, No. 165 (1971), 50, who speaks of 'la lengua como muralla en el camino de la comunicación'.

trates their failure to communicate. (It is actually impossible to tell from the syntax that 'guerreros' is the subject and 'palabras' the object, and a case could be made for saying that the opposite is true, with the words themselves failing to express anything. Either way, it is still the lack of communication which is paramount.) This lack of communication is then reiterated in the second stanza with the word 'silencio'. It is subsequently underscored by the monotonous repetition of 'nubes' – there is no speech, only clouds and more clouds – and underlined even more forcefully by the 'sin palabras, sin voces,/Sin decir, sin saber'. We have therefore been told nothing except that no-one has anything to say to anyone. Admittedly the latter part of the poem is more explicit, with references to 'juventud sangrienta' and 'Raza estéril en flor, tristeza, lágrimas' (154) providing a strong indication that failed love is indeed the basic theme, but nevertheless what the first two stanzas prove is the inability to use language effectively.

The inability to use language effectively is however only a starting-point. The fluid and imprecise nature of meaning can be seen very well in 'Vieja ribera', which is primarily about 'la nostalgia por la pérdida de la niñez'.[46] The first stanza looks back to that world of childhood:

> Tanto ha llovido desde entonces,
> Entonces, cuando los dientes no eran carne, sino días
> Pequeños como un río ignorante
> A sus padres llamando porque siente sueño, (165)

The somewhat elegiac first line sets the mood for the whole poem, while the comparison of 'dientes' to 'carne' and 'días pequeños' has much in common with Surrealist arbitrariness and illogicality. The second stanza is however worthy of consideration in greater detail:

> Unos dicen que sí, otros dicen que no;
> Mas sí y no son dos alas pequeñas,
> Equilibrio de un cielo dentro de otro cielo,
> Como un amor está dentro de otro,
> Como el olvido está dentro del olvido. (165)

The misery and meaninglessness of the persona's present existence (contrasting with childhood) are obvious. The second line does however suggest a further significance. The 'alas pequeñas' seem to offer no link either with 'sí y no' or with anything else in the poem. The comparison

---

[46] Capote Benot, p. 133.

seems completely arbitrary, but this, I suggest, is not so much a result of the chaotic outpourings of a tortured mind as a deliberate ploy:[47] the comparison is arbitrary because the words in themselves mean so little. Furthermore, the fact that such meaningless words are spoken ('Unos dicen que sí') demonstrates the absence of communication. The following three lines then reflect this idea: 'cielo', 'amor' and 'olvido' are each said to be inside themselves. Each element is thus enclosed within its own tight hermetic circle. Where boundaries between entities cannot be crossed, there can be no communication.[48] The closing stanza then rounds off the poem with the persona bitterly wanting to 'apuñalar la vida' and 'sonreír ... a la derrota' (165), but at the same time tragically locked into a death-like state. This is not true 'automatic writing', but a much more deliberate and careful strategy to demonstrate that certain words seem to mean more or less nothing.[49] Have we entered a state of total literary chaos, where words are totally devoid of signification?

If meaning is no longer guaranteed by an 'invariable presence', then this has certain consequences, not just for the meanings of individual words, but also in the way that words, and in particular symbols, are used. In its broadest terms, a symbol may be defined as an entity on to which is projected certain significance, so that it becomes representative of that significance. Symbols in literature can be subdivided into two categories: those which the author invents himself, and those which already exist by way of tradition or convention. The problematic nature of meaning inevitably has an adverse effect on the understanding of symbols. In terms of traditional or conventional symbols, then clearly there is nothing to guarantee any traditional symbolic resonance. If all words are open to the 'infinite play of signification', then a traditional symbolic significance becomes no more than one resonance within that infinite play. As far as symbols the author invents for himself are concerned, then evidently he is very free to construct symbols

---

[47] Bruton argues that the various illogical images spring from an explicitly Surrealist desire to look 'at reality with a new eye' ('The Developing Expression in the Poetry of Luis Cernuda: The Rôle of Image and Symbol', unpublished thesis London 1980, p. 144). This is true up to a point, but does not take account of the way in which the very issues of meaning and of the possibility of meaning also become a theme.

[48] Juan Ramón Resina stresses, in 'Si el hombre pudiera decir' from *Los placeres prohibidos*, the inability to speak, arguing that it is an example of 'lenguaje al borde de la insignificación, lenguaje que se problematiza a sí mismo' ('La realidad y el deseo en la poesía de Luis Cernuda', *Hora de Poesía*, 29 (1983), 83). That poem is however semantically much less obscure than 'Vieja ribera', and may contain more a critique of communication than of meaning itself.

[49] Talens' assertion that (p. 82), 'Cernuda nunca llegó a plantearse el problema del lenguaje, de modo explícito' is unsatisfactory.

entirely as he wishes, but that very freedom makes the process of interpretation all the more uncertain. Within the context of *Un río, un amor*, it is an
analysis of traditional symbols, such as they are, that will prove most fruitful.[50] It may seem trivial, but it is worth analysing 'La canción del oeste' in
this light. The 'oeste' of the title is clearly the American 'Wild West', with a
'jinete' (literally any horseman, but presumably specifically a cowboy), ar-
chetypal symbol of that 'Wild West', the protagonist of the poem:

> Jinete sin cabeza,
> Jinete como un niño buscando entre rastrojos
> Llaves recién cortadas,
> Víboras seductoras, desastres suntuosos,
> Navíos para tierra lentamente de carne, (165–66)

This is a complete 'deconstruction' of the concept of the 'jinete'. The
horseman is an absurd non-person: he is 'sin cabeza'. He is compared with
other absurdities: a child looking for 'Llaves recién cortadas' amongst rub-
bish is a nonsensical activity; 'Navíos para tierra' is a nonsensical idea. In
addition, the choice of a somewhat trivial conventional symbol enhances this
absurdity. This prepares the ground for the introduction of the 'love' theme
in stanza two, forcing us to hold it at a distance and consider it critically.
The trivial symbol is thus being used as a kind of clue, a pointer towards the
more 'serious' issue of 'love'. What we have resembles the pieces of a jig-
saw which we have to fit together to form the picture (the meaning) of the
poem. The elements are brought together in the closing stanza:

> Olvidemos pues todo, incluso al mismo oeste;
> Olvidemos que un día las miradas de ahora
> Lucirán a la noche, como tantos amantes,
> Sobre el lejano oeste,
> Sobre amor más lejano. (166)

The concept of 'love' has been stripped of all its conventional imagery and
placed alongside this 'deconstructed' picture of a Western cowboy. This

---

[50] To analyse all the various images in *Un río, un amor* would be a very laborious process
and well beyond the scope of the present argument. Suffice it to say that there is a wide
array of symbols, which range from the straightforward 'el ahogado' of 'Cuerpo en pena',
clearly symbolic, given the abundant evidence in the poem, of someone in a state of extreme emotional torment, to the enigmatic 'lebrel' of 'Habitación de al lado', discussed
immediately below. Common to all such invented symbols is the need to rely heavily on
textual evidence for interpretation.

causes us to equate the absurdity of this cowboy image with 'love' and see 'love' as absurd also. The desire to 'forget' both the 'jinete' and 'amor' is thus logical, given their presentation as something completely meaningless. Thus Cernuda does make use of a traditional symbol, but his use of it is not to illustrate the infinite play of intertextual significations of the signifier 'jinete'. Rather he exploits its conventional symbolic resonance and then completely empties the word of that resonance, so that 'La canción del oeste' has precious little to do with the 'oeste' at all. The signifier has become entirely separated from the signified.

We are now proceeding in *Un río, un amor* towards a total absence of meaning. In certain poems, in fact, meaning seems to disintegrate altogether. An excellent example is 'Habitación de al lado':

> A través de una noche en pleno día
> Vagamente he conocido a la muerte.
> No la acompaña ningún lebrel;
> Vive entre los estanques disecados,
> Fantasmas grises de piedra nebulosa.
>
> ¿Por qué soñando, al deslizarse con miedo,
> Ese miedo imprevisto estremece al durmiente?
> Mirad vencido olvido y miedo a tantas sombras blancas
> Por las pálidas dunas de la vida,
> No redonda ni azul, sino lunática,
> Con sus blancas lagunas, con sus bosques
> En donde el cazador si quiere da caza al terciopelo. (151)

The opening two lines seem fairly sensible. (It is they, together with the last line 'Sin vida está viviendo solo profundamente' (151), which provide the only clue to the significance of the poem.[51]) This sense is however immediately followed by nonsense: while there may just be a reason for the appearance of the 'lebrel', I do not accept there is any logic behind the

---

[51] Pato discusses Cernuda's technique in *Un río, un amor* of ending poems with a single line, as is the case in 'Habitación de al lado', remarking that 'cierra el poema dándonos ... parte de la clave de su sentido' (*Los finales poemáticos en la obra de Luis Cernuda* (Boulder, Colorado: Society of Spanish and Spanish-American Studies, 1988), p. 39). In this case, the last line may in itself be open to interpretation. The last word, 'profundamente', could suggest that the lifelessness expressed in the phrase 'sin vida' is that state of pleasurable 'olvido' for which Cernuda often yearned, but this is not really tenable: the existence 'sin vida' is surely the incomprehensible, nonsensical world, from which the persona wishes to escape.

'terciopelo'.[52] Furthermore, even if the 'lebrel' is significant, that significance is deflated by linking the 'cazador' with 'terciopelo'.[53] Is this Surrealist caprice in its most blatant form for an effect which is a mystery to all but the poet? We have nevertheless already commented that the first two lines and the last line do provide a clue. This is in fact a poem about the meaninglessness of the persona's life. The meaningless images are there *precisely because they are quite literally meaningless*. In the poem we are being drawn into a state of confusion, where the signifier does not appear to refer to any signified at all. While we may appear to be able to attempt to make connections and thus interpret images (at least as far as the 'lebrel' is concerned), this ability is deliberately withheld from us by the juxtaposition with something completely nonsensical. It is a linguistic illustration of the state of the persona's own existence,[54] a deliberate demonstration of lack of meaning. The importance of the semantic void is then stressed further in the third stanza of the poem, when yet more arbitrary connections are made:

> Pero ningún lebrel acompaña a la muerte.
> Ella con mucho amor sólo ama los pájaros,
> Pájaros siempre mudos, como lo es el secreto (151)

If we take 'hunters hunting velvet' in stanza two to be deliberately nonsensical, used as a linguistic illustration of the meaninglessness of life, then it becomes rather less disconcerting when we are suddenly confronted in this stanza with death being in love with birds. It is a ludicrous concept, it is true, but if life is ludicrous, why should the words used to describe it not be ludicrous too? It is in fact not so much a ludicrous concept as not a concept

---

[52] Soufas argues that the 'hunting-dogs' are 'vaguely reminiscent of the moon goddess Diana' ('Agents of Power', p. 80), but, if this is the case, it seems capricious and teasing, for there is no evocation of a classical world. Soufas also suggests that 'terciopelo' is 'symbolic of the soft, mildly pleasant life ... for which men opt in exchange for their true freedom' (p. 81), but I find this a little speculative. Harris on the other hand contends that 'En la leyenda el lebrel es uno de los acompañantes de Nimrod y conduce a los muertos al reino de la muerte' ('La escritura surrealista de *Un río, un amor*, de Luis Cernuda', *Ínsula*, Año 44, No. 515 (1989), 16). Certainly this is more plausible than Soufas' argument, but, even if this is the case (and it is admittedly a very obscure allusion), the line reads '*No* la acompaña *ningún* lebrel': does this suggest that traditional legends do not apply?

[53] Harris himself concedes that 'el texto vuelve a la arbitrariedad' ('La escritura surrealista', 16).

[54] This is rather more far-reaching than Harris' comment that 'Al yuxtaponer dos elementos diferenciados, el poeta despierta asociaciones nuevas' ('Ejemplo de fidelidad poética: El superrealismo de Luis Cernuda', *La Caña Gris*, Nos. 6–8 (Otoño de 1962), p. 106).

at all, just empty words. More decisive still for the argument of the poem is the third line 'Pájaros siempre *mudos*, como lo es el *secreto*'. In the context of meaningless, nonsensical words and expressions, might not the 'secret' which is silence be this: that silence is preferable because there is nothing to be said or even nothing which *can* be said? If, in turn, nothing can be said, there is no reason for us as readers to attempt to 'refill', as it were, the empty words on the page with symbolic meanings. Language, at worst, is no more than a series of empty signifiers.

There is however a tension in 'Habitación de al lado' which is not particularly well resolved: the hopeless confusion of arbitrariness on the one hand and the two clues ('la muerte', line 2, and 'sin vida', line 21) which help to explain that arbitrariness on the other. It is not however in this poem that Cernuda's use of language in his Surrealist poetry is at its most subtle and accomplished. Elsewhere there is a more complex interweaving of meaning and non-meaning, where it is the *gap* between signifier and signified which is paramount. 'Dejadme solo' at first sight would appear to support Capote Benot's claim that it is 'muy cerca de la técnica automática'.[55] The poem is a bitter rejection of love,[56] but it is much more far-reaching than that:

Una verdad es color de ceniza,
Otra verdad es color de planeta;
Mas todas las verdades, desde el suelo hasta el suelo,
No valen la verdad sin color de verdades,
La verdad ignorante de cómo el hombre suele encarnarse en la nieve.
(163)

The most obvious feature of these lines is the lack of logic. Our initial reaction is one of confusion: how can 'color de ceniza' and 'color de planeta' have any bearing on a concept such as 'truth'? Whereas in 'Habitación de al lado' a series of highly arbitrary images are *framed* by the clues to their general significance, here concept and image are *juxtaposed*. The repetition of 'verdad' highlights that this concept is the primary concern. In lines one and two, by equating two arbitrary images with the notion of 'verdad', the concept of truth is 'deconstructed'. Since the two images make no real sense, this 'non-sense' is transferred to the word 'verdad'. In terms of this poem, there is no such thing as truth. The arbitrary images illustrate that the word 'verdad' is no more than an empty signifier, and that the signified itself

---

[55] Capote Benot, p. 130.
[56] This is seen, not only in the title, but also in the first line of the second stanza, 'En cuanto a la mentira, basta decirle «quiero»' (163).

does not exist. In addition, the phrase 'desde el suelo hasta el suelo' appears to be a deliberate deflation of a Platonic-type progression: we should expect it to read 'desde el suelo hasta el *cielo*', but here there is no movement: the persona is entirely earth-bound.[57] The result is the demonstration of signifiers' lack of validity. The three remaining lines of the stanza then serve to reiterate and intensify this concept. This reminds us of the apparent meaninglessness in the poems 'Vieja ribera' and 'La canción del oeste', and the similarities are unquestionably present. There was however something which was passed over without comment at that stage, but which by now may be easily surmised, namely the fact that we are still able to make sense of the poems. The lack of meaning is made explicit. This is a very 'ordered' kind of semantic void, illogical as that might sound. It is this process which I suggest is at work in a particularly accomplished way in 'Dejadme solo'. The word 'verdad' does have a significance in the poem, but it is not the one we expect. The presence together of the apparently meaningful and the apparently meaningless confuses our expectations. What we took to be a meaningful concept is revealed as absurd. This means that there is no void, but rather something different.[58]

The discussion has so far concentrated exclusively on *Un río, un amor* and ignored *Los placeres prohibidos*. *Los placeres prohibidos* is less overtly Surrealist. It is also semantically less obscure. Let us take just one example, from 'Qué ruido tan triste':

> Qué ruido tan triste el que hacen dos cuerpos cuando se aman,
> Parece como el viento que se mece en otoño
> Sobre adolescentes mutilados,
> Mientras las manos llueven,
> Manos ligeras, manos egoístas, manos obscenas, (177)

These lines are not really obscure or even ambiguous: there is a sense of despair, bitter cynicism and total disillusionment with love. They are not particularly 'Surrealist' either: the style is certainly free, and there is little in the way of conventional versification, but there is no sign of the chaotic outpourings of the subconscious or of the subtle experimentation with

---

[57] See also Bruton, 'The Developing Expression in the Poetry of Luis Cernuda', p. 122. This irony of lack of movement is underlined by the fact that 'suelo' and 'cielo' are phonologically similar, especially in Cernuda's Seville accent.

[58] Jacques Ancet agrees in general terms that Cernuda's use of Surrealism 'se está lejos del irracionalismo triunfante de algunos contemporáneos' ('El deseo, lo negro. (Sobre Luis Cernuda)', *Cuadernos Hispanoamericanos*, Nos. 514–15 (1993), 216), but does not take his argument any further.

semantics. What *Los placeres prohibidos* marks is no more than a flirtation with Surrealism, as Cernuda steadily develops his poetic expression.

To sum up, then, meaning for Cernuda, at least at this stage in his poetic development, is something fluid, not static, and there is a gap between signifier and signified. What he does is to demonstrate the existence of that very gap and show us where it lies in a given situation. Thus it is not the case that Cernuda is completely 'deconstructing' meaning or claiming that the concept of meaning is a philosophical nonsense. Rather, when we are presented with images and juxtapositions of terms which appear, in the Surrealist mode, illogical and even absurd, we are prompted to see a principle at work (although it must be admitted that there are both varying degrees of success and times when the poetry may be deemed more genuinely 'Surrealist'). Clues and hints, rather than explicit statements, show us the fact that individual words and concepts may not have their conventional signification, or may even be absurd. This is however more radical than a Surrealist search for striking new images, for there is a probing and questioning of the inherent meaningfulness of words, where, paradoxically, a completely meaningless concept may be part of the very 'message' of an individual poem. This is nevertheless still a kind of meaning, and definitive evidence that there is still plenty there for us to interpret. Cernuda's use of Surrealism allowed him to experiment with his ideas about language and meaning. The fact that he retains a commitment to poetic meaning, even when writing poetry which was by its nature obscure, to say nothing of the obvious evidence of ordering and structuring, means that it perhaps comes as less of a surprise when in his later poetry he actually attempts to write more clearly rather than obscurely. In this way, Cernuda's account of the disintegration of meaning actually anticipates an increased commitment to meaning, indeed, to an, albeit qualified, *re*-integration of meaning in his later poetry.

The Reintegration of Meaning: The Triumph of Literary Order?

We have seen that, at its most subtle, the poetry of *Un río, un amor* is not meaningless, even if it does unsettle our expectations. It nonetheless seems curious to posit the idea that meaning can then become 'reintegrated'. If conventional relationships between signifier and signified are being broken down, this is not a process which can suddenly stop and be reversed. A lack of belief in meaning is based on a philosophical standpoint (consciously or unconsciously) and, after such doubts have manifested themselves, language cannot be 'mended' and broken signifier-signified relationships repaired. It would therefore appear that the idea of a reintegration of meaning is either a blatant contradiction, or an attempt doomed to failure from the start. To what extent, then, is it possible to speak of meaning as being 'reintegrated' in the more mature poetry of *La realidad y el deseo*?

It is difficult to discuss Cernuda's theory of poetry in abstract terms, because, apart from the brief lecture 'Palabras antes de una lectura', Cernuda was very unwilling to write down any cohesive argument as to the nature of poetry. In the vast majority of his non-creative writings, there is an extremely limited amount which even refers directly to the poet himself, let alone to how he writes poetry. Even his autobiographical essay 'Historial de un libro', which gives plenty of useful details about the various circumstances under which the poetry was produced, offers very little in the way of insight into Cernuda's understanding of the nature of language and meaning. It is nonetheless possible to glean one or two pointers as to his ideas, and perhaps the clearest expression of these in his mature years is to be found in the 'Entrevista con un poeta', originally published in *Índice Literario* in 1959 and subsequently collected in *Poesía y Literatura II*. In response to a question regarding Cernuda's 'tabla de valores' when reading poetry, Cernuda says:

> – Me limitaré a decirle que si un gran poeta me aparece como tal, es: 1.°) por la fusión melódica en su verso de palabra, sentido y ritmo; 2.°) por la precisión y hermosura de su lengua; 3.°) por la amplitud de su visión; 4.°) por la riqueza y flexibilidad de su pensamiento. Pero además, y por encima de lo antes dicho, hace falta en el poeta la presencia de lo que llamaría la parte de Dios: el elemento imponderable, el toque mágico que anime y vivifique la materia sobre la cual trabajan sus demás cualidades.[59]

What is striking here is the conventionality of the ideas: Cernuda does not seem to strike any new philosophical or ideological ground whatsoever. With such conventional ideas, the nature of language and meaning does not really seem to come into question. This would appear to be confirmed yet further by his fourth point regarding 'la riqueza y flexibilidad de su pensamiento'. This implies that the 'pensamiento', the discursive content, is ultimately 'knowable', and that, while the form which is the poem is always quite unique, nevertheless that discursive content can still be discovered and understood by reading the poem. There appears to be none of the equivocation that is inherent in the obscure Surrealist-influenced poetry. Furthermore, the comment about 'el elemento imponderable' is particularly interesting: this would appear to be the element of divine or quasi-divine in-

---

[59] *Prosa I*, p. 812.

spiration, the influence of the Muses, as it were, which makes poetry live.[60] There seems to be little indication of a fear that the poetry is not capable of being understood.

This would appear to be a complete reversal of Cernuda's earlier stance and consequently a total logical inconsistency. What about the poetry itself? Does it confirm or deny this attitude? On a purely formal, structural level, it is interesting to note that strict versification, a key feature of poetry as conventional in its approach as that suggested in 'Entrevista con un poeta', is largely lost. In *Primeras Poesías* and *Égloga, Elegía, Oda* there is rigorous employment of traditional verse forms, but these two collections precede, not only Cernuda's poetic maturity, but also the 'chaos' of *Un río, un amor*. The mature poetry of *Donde habite el olvido* onwards would, in terms of verse form, appear to occupy some kind of 'middle ground'. The near-abandonment of versification in the Surrealist-influenced poetry is itself abandoned.[61] There is however never any return to the conscious traditionality of the early poetry. What does happen is that there is a *kind* of versification, but it tends not to be regular or conventional. Sometimes there are poems which follow a clear stanza pattern, such as 'El intruso' from *Vivir sin estar viviendo* (391–92), but often poems mix stanza lengths (for example 'El prisionero' (395) from the same collection).[62] What is more, while assonance is a frequent stylistic feature, rhyme is extremely rare. Obviously there is something of a tension between this freer type of versification and the very conventional theoretical ideas of 'Entrevista con un poeta'. Complete confidence in meaning would cause us to expect very traditional verse forms, since free verse is a modern innovation, and irregularity and disorder go 'hand-in-hand' with a world view characterised by disintegration, and, by extension, with meaning which has lost the 'invariable presence' which guarantees it. In this way, then, there is at least a hint, however small, that Cernuda's practice could be appearing to be falling away from a state of total linguistic security.

Still on a formal level, it is worthwhile also considering the use of rhythm and metre within stanzas. Again, in the earliest poetry, the metrical structure is carefully controlled and conforms to the traditional verse forms being employed, and, thereafter, there is sporadic use made of regular metres. Despite this, in the same way that, in the later poetry, stanza lengths are more variable, so too there is no overall consistent pattern as far as

---

[60] Compare this with 'Desolación de la Quimera' (527–30).

[61] Oddly enough, even in *Un río, un amor* there are poems where metre and versification are very traditional: 'Cuerpo en pena', for example, is written in regular Alexandrines, which fits very uncomfortably with Surrealism.

[62] See also Maristany, pp. 78 and 80.

rhythm and metre are concerned. Thus 'El prisionero', while having an irregular stanza structure, is nonetheless written in regular heptasyllabic lines,
while 'Vereda del cuco' from *Como quien espera el alba* has lines which
vary considerably in length and rhythm, for example:

> Extático en su orilla,
> Oh tormento divino,
> Oh divino deleite,
> Bebías de tu sed y de la fuente a un tiempo,
> Sabiendo a eternidad tu sed y el agua. (377)

The changes in metre which characterise this poem are used to good effect.
They do not conform to a neat stanza pattern (although a number of the
stanzas are very roughly similar), but rather change to reflect the mood of
the poem or the state of excitement of the persona. This is illustrated here in
the way that the short lines help convey something of the stimulation and
excitement of the experience, while the longer lines form more of a meditation on the experience and the persona's life. When used in this way, the
breaking of traditions is liberating and can be used to enhance the meaning
of the poem. On the other hand, entire poems, such as '*Birds in the Night*'
from *Desolación de la Quimera*, can be so 'liberated' as to produce line after line as gloriously unmemorable as 'Ojalá nada oigan: ha de ser un alivio
ese silencio interminable' (497). It is thus difficult to draw any definitive
conclusions about structure within stanzas, but that in itself causes us to
wonder how successful this 'triumph of literary order' might prove to be.

What about Cernuda's use of language in his mature poetry? While the
verse forms are freer, the language, in common with the conventional ideas
of 'Entrevista con un poeta', seems much more overtly comprehensible. After the crisis of *Un río, un amor*, signifier and signified seem to have moved
much closer together. The desire to deconstruct words and concepts appears
to have vanished. A good example of this new-found confidence is 'El
poeta' from *Vivir sin estar viviendo*, where Cernuda explores the nature of
his poetic career:[63]

> Mucho nos dicen, desde el pasado, voces
> Ilustres, ascendientes de la palabra nuestra,
> Y las de lengua extraña, cuyo acento

---

[63] In the course of the poem reference is made to 'él' and 'tú'. While 'tú' is once again
Cernuda's preferred means of addressing himself (the distance between poet and persona
is minimal here), 'él' apparently refers to Juan Ramón Jiménez (see *Poesía completa*, p.
810), although for much of the poem it could refer to any accomplished poet.

> Experiencia distina nos revela. Mas las cosas,
> El fuego, el mar, los árboles, los astros,
> Nuevas siempre aparecen. (404)

The first thing that is surely striking here after the poems of *Un río, un amor* is the clarity and simplicity of the language. The previous gap between signifier and signified has not so much diminished as completely vanished. It is particularly significant that Cernuda here talks about language itself, and especially 'lengua extraña'. Here if nowhere else we might expect there to be voiced a degree of confusion, a certain barrier to comprehension. On the contrary: the verb which is directly linked to foreign languages is 'revelar', the exact converse of obfuscation, and a total contradiction of the linguistic processes which were evident in *Un río, un amor*. The only area of doubt might surround the words 'Mas las cosas .../Nuevas siempre aparecen', but this is far from new and unexpected meanings. This bespeaks an enhancement of personal experience. The later part of the poem then proceeds to explore more fully the relationship between the poet and his world:

> Nuevas y arcanas, hasta que al fin traslucen
> Un día en la expresión de aquel poeta
> Vivo de nuestra lengua, en el contemporáneo
> Que infunde por nosotros,
> Con su obra, la fe, la certidumbre
> Maga de nuestro mundo visible e invisible. (404)

The first line of this stanza refers to 'las cosas' of the previous stanza, but now stating that what is 'arcane' or 'enigmatic' about 'las cosas' does not stay a mystery when transformed into poetry. Quite the reverse: it is the poet's 'expresión' of them which causes them to become comprehensible. Language is no longer the barrier to communication but the fundamental source of meaning. This has much in common with the Romantic perception of the poet as someone with heightened consciousness revealing the mysteries of the world to ordinary people. The poem continues in a similar vein, with the presence of Juan Ramón Jiménez (or any significant precursor) coming to the fore in the penultimate stanza:

> Agradécelo pues, que una palabra
> Amiga mucho vale
> En nuestra soledad, en nuestro breve espacio
> De vivos, y nadie sino tú puede decirle,
> A aquel que te enseñara adónde y cómo crece:
> Gracias por la rosa del mundo. (405)

There is a strong feeling of gratitude in these lines to Juan Ramón for the supreme gift of poetry which has been given to him.[64] The beauty of poetry is summed up in the last line as 'la rosa del mundo' (the demons and disasters having been conveniently forgotten), and is explored further in the closing stanza:

> Para el poeta hallarla es lo bastante,
> E inútil el renombre u olvido de su obra,
> Cuando en ella un momento se unifican,
> Tal uno son amante, amor y amado,
> Los tres complementarios luego y antes dispersos:
> El deseo, la rosa y la mirada. (405)

The second line here seems to cast doubt on the value of writing for the benefit of others, favouring instead the benefit to the poet of creating a perfect poem. This is certainly egocentric, but at the same time such an image of perfection means that the poetry itself is not called into question, and by extension there can be no suggestion of placing meaning in an enigmatic light. In fact, when we consider that 'amante, amor y amado' are for Cernuda three of the most basic elements of his poetry anyway, then this 'rosa del mundo' in which 'los tres complementarios se unifican' emerges as an idealised image, not just of poetry in general, but of Cernuda's poetry in particular. Not only that, since these three 'complementarios' are said to be united in his ideal poetry, we are not left to wonder about the poetry's basic content. It therefore has both a form and a meaning. Cernuda appears to have 'reintegrated' meaning totally.

We saw earlier how, in 'La canción del oeste', the 'jinete', as symbol of the Wild West, is exploited and deconstructed to show its sheer lack of meaning. How is symbolism used in the later poetry? A good example of the extent to which Cernuda reacts against his earlier stance of doubt about meaning is to be found in 'Cordura' from *Las nubes*. This poem was discussed above in relation to Cernuda's flirtation with Christianity[65] and is one of the rare expressions of hope in the dark and dismal poetry from the early time of exile.[66] The crux of the poem is the fourth stanza from the end:

> Duro es hallarse solo
> En medio de los cuerpos.

---

[64] Presumably this indicates a feeling of spiritual affinity rather than significant direct influence.

[65] See above, pp. 54–57 and 64–65.

[66] It dates from 1938. See *Poesía completa*, p. 796.

> Pero esa forma tiene
> Su amor: la cruz sin nadie. (286)

'La cruz sin nadie' is, as Harris comments, 'the [Christian] image of the empty cross'.[67] The empty cross is one of the most potent symbols of the last two thousand years, and is known and instantly recognisable throughout the Western world, irrespective of whether individuals are religious or not. By invoking it, there is almost no need for the remaining three stanzas, for they do little more than explain its value for Cernuda: the ability to find 'comunión con los hombres' and the hope that 'La noche será breve' (286). Most important here however is the very fact that it has been used, with its conventional significance. There is no attempt to deconstruct the symbol of the Cross or suggest that it is meaningless. On the contrary, Cernuda exploits its Christian resonances to prove the poem's fundamentally religious import. Without the Christian significance, the poem falls apart.[68]

It may be possible to counter that Cernuda could have recourse to a traditional symbol in 'Cordura' because he was himself exploring the idea of faith in Christianity. It is not however an isolated example. A further illustration is to be found in 'Urania' from *Como quien espera el alba*. This poem is primarily about order in love:

> Ella está inmóvil. Cubre aéreo
> El ropaje azulado su hermosura virgen;
> La estrella diamantina allá en la frente
> Arisca tal la nieve, y en los ojos
> La luz que no conoce sombra alguna. (328)

The symbolism of the poem does not centre on a linguistic construct *per se*, but rather on the mythological figure of Urania herself. She is used as a symbol of Platonic love and order.[69] What is remarkable is that it is exclusively the symbol which is there in the poem, and what she represents has to be known by the reader as part of a common stock of Western knowledge.

---

[67] Harris, *Luis Cernuda. A Study*, p. 81. Like Harris (p. 81, note 33), I do not agree with Silver's interpretation that it is 'the agony of desire' (*Et in Arcadia Ego*, p. 112).

[68] The fact that the symbol is still recognisable as such and not merely as one intertextual resonance among many is one of the illogicalities inherent in modern literary theory. Logically we should be able to understand nothing, but nevertheless we do: this is a basic premise of M. H. Abrams' counter-argument to radical Post-Structuralism ('The deconstructive angel', in Lodge, pp. 264–76). The point here however is that a poet cannot simultaneously doubt meaning as a definable entity and still use language as if he believed in it. Cernuda's usage necessarily entails his belief.

[69] See above, pp. 114–15.

The symbol thus very vividly exists in its own right within the poem. There is however a subtle difference between this poem and 'Cordura'. The Cross of Christ can only be symbolic of salvation from sin and rebirth in union with Christ, but there is a greater range of possible signification with the figure of Urania, relating to beauty, order, divinity, etc. Cernuda in this case has therefore selected those aspects of the figure which best suit his purpose. There is consequently a degree of invention on Cernuda's part. Nonetheless this does not alter the fact that, first, the range of significations is limited, and second, those significations must be known by the reader. If 'Urania' as a poem is not placed specifically within the context of Greek mythology, the poem falls apart. As the Cross of Christ confirms the religious significance of 'Cordura', so the presence of Urania here confirms an image of mythological order. Once again there is no attempt to deconstruct the symbol or take away any of its Greek mythological resonance. This in turn reiterates the degree to which Cernuda has returned to a traditional understanding of the use of language and symbolism.[70]

Cernuda does not however see himself constrained to follow only the line of standard Western symbols. The degree of invention noted in 'Urania', albeit limited in that poem, increases substantially elsewhere. Cernuda is able to make use of symbols which have special relevance to his own situation and tailor them accordingly. One symbol which recurs time after time is the beautiful boy. Not an uncommon symbol in itself in Western poetry,[71] nonetheless Cernuda uses it entirely according to what it means to him (unlike a symbol like the empty Cross, which *has* to be symbolic of Christ's sacrifice for redemption). A good example is 'A un muchacho andaluz', from *Invocaciones*.[72] There are actually at least three symbols in this poem: the boy himself, the sea and the boy's lips. After opening the poem with a statement of the persona's devotion to the beautiful boy, the second stanza explores the boy's relationship to the sea:

> ¿Eras emanación del mar cercano?
> Eras el mar aún más

---

[70] We are perfectly entitled to argue that such symbolism is arbitrary (although it is dubious how illuminating such an analysis would be). That however is *our* decision. What matters most is that it is not something proposed by the text itself, unlike 'La canción del oeste', which *implicitly propounds* such a process of deconstruction.

[71] For a detailed account of the topic, see Camille Paglia, *Sexual Personae. Art and Decadence from Nefertiti to Emily Dickinson* (Harmondsworth: Penguin, 1992), especially chapters 20 and 22.

[72] Despite its being contemporaneous with 'Palabras antes de una lectura', there is not really any satisfactory evidence in this poem that 'las palabras ... traicionan'.

Que las aguas henchidas con su aliento,
Encauzadas en río sobre tu tierra abierta,
Bajo el inmenso cielo con nubes que se orlaban de rotos
    resplandores. (221)

In this poem the 'muchacho' functions as the primary symbol and then the sea and the lips are used as secondary symbols dependent on that primary symbol. The primary symbol exists entirely in its own right. We are eventually told in the seventh stanza that the boy represents 'verdad de vida' (222), but for much of the poem this is left for us to assume. Not only that, it is unduly restrictive to interpret the symbol purely as 'verdad de vida'. All the various positive images which revolve around the symbol 'boy' (e.g., beauty, vitality, innocence) are brought together, not in the word 'muchacho', but in the physical being which the Andalusian boy is. The signifier 'muchacho' is then the linguistic representation of that physical being. For Cernuda, signifier correlates directly with signified, which is not any Andalusian boy, but *his* Andalusian boy. This however causes a small problem to arise. While there is no question as to what the 'muchacho andaluz' signifies here, the fact that it is taken primarily from Cernuda's own personal experience, rather than traditional Western symbolism in more general terms, implies a difference of approach. It is pointlessly pedantic to insist that 'the Cross' *need* not symbolise Christ's act of salvation; we know that it does. If however the symbol of Urania has a broader range of possible meanings, although still very limited, the potential range of meanings is much wider here. It is much more difficult to be adamant that 'un muchacho andaluz' absolutely has to symbolise beauty, vitality, innocence, etc. This is because the symbol has been constructed specifically for the poem, and its exact meaning is only contained in that poem. Another writer referring to the Cross cannot avoid Christ, but another writer referring to an Andalusian boy could easily project his own significance on to it. The construction of a personal, specific, individual symbol is therefore not quite as confident as the use of more generalised traditional symbols, since it forces us to be much more dependent on specific textual evidence. That said, the textual evidence of 'A un muchacho andaluz' grants us a clear interpretative line.[73]

Bearing this slight difference in semantic confidence in mind, we may consider now the two secondary symbols in the poem. The secondary symbol of the sea operates as an adjunct to the symbol of the boy. The basic process is the same. The sea is a physical entity invested with certain significance by the poem, drawn to a certain extent from convention, certainly, but

---

[73] Contrast this with the 'lebrel' of 'Habitación de al lado'. (See above, pp. 149–51.)

also from the poet's individual experience. It is not however up to us to speculate endlessly as to what the sea may or may not represent, because there is rather more in the way of explanation, with the sea's energy and vitality in particular highlighted in the stanzas quoted above. The need to provide an explanation in itself of course infers that an exact correlation cannot be relied upon. Much the same is then true of the secondary symbol of the lips, revealed in stanza four:

> Y tus labios, de bisel tan terso,
> Eran la vida misma,
> Como una ardiente flor
> Nutrida con la savia
> De aquella piel oscura
> Que infiltraba nocturno escalofrío. (221)

The lips are symbolic of sensual love, vitality, beauty, 'la vida misma'. Again the symbol is not merely a word but something with its own autonomous existence to which the word 'labios' clearly refers. To attempt to interpret the symbol in any other way is effectively to judge it by applying our own understanding. The theoreticians would of course contend that this is inevitable, first, because the mind of the poet is ultimately unknowable to all but himself, and second, because no reader can avoid bringing his/her own culture and ideas to a literary text. The symbol of the lips, as with the boy and the sea, does offer scope for varying interpretations, but such scope is still relatively limited. Differences of interpretation are only likely to lie in the details. Not only that, Cernuda clearly believes his symbols point directly to a coherent and ultimately finite set of significations. There is no self-reflexive proposition of the problems of language and interpretation. Cernuda's use of symbolism therefore necessarily entails his belief in the inherent meaningfulness of language.

Any doubt in the inherent meaningfulness of language has thus far been very small. Is the same true of more purely formal concerns? It was mentioned in passing above that Cernuda in his mature poetry can make use of rhythm and metre when it reflects the mood of the individual poem. We can however examine this technique further. Even although in much of his poetry versification, rhythm, etc., are irregular, there are times when there is a very specific, conscious effort to co-ordinate the elements of the poem's form in order to assist in the communication of the meaning. Evidence of this can be seen in *Un rio, un amor*: for example, the repetition of 'verdad', in 'Dejadme solo', juxtaposed with arbitrary images, demonstrates that the word 'verdad' means nothing.[74] It is therefore the *form* of the poem which helps gives the clue to its meaning. Thus when meaning is seen to be disintegrating, Cernuda is able to exploit the form to make the meaning more clear. But we can go further still. There is evidence that even the sound of the words can be employed to reflect the meaning, which, in conjunction with all the various stylistic features, form a poem which is an entirely 'integrated whole'. An interesting poem is 'El arpa' from *Como quien espera el alba*:

> Jaula de un ave invisible,
> Del agua hermana y del aire,
> A cuya voz solicita
> Pausada y blanda la mano.
>
> Como el agua prisionera
> Del surtidor, tiembla, sube
> En una fuga irisada,
> Las almas adoctrinando.
>
> Como el aire entre las hojas,
> Habla tan vaga, tan pura,
> De memorias y de olvidos
> Hechos leyenda en el tiempo.
>
> ¿Qué frutas del paraíso,
> Cuáles aljibes del cielo
> Nutren tu voz? Dime, canta,
> Pájaro del arpa, oh lira. (343)

Personally, I think an evocation of the music of the harp is the principal theme of this poem.[75] The harp produces a very gentle, 'floating', ethereal sort of sound. This is to a certain extent reflected in Cernuda's choice of words: in the first stanza especially there is a predominance of 'a' vowels, which is the most open of the vowels, and there are surprisingly few consonants, the only really harsh sound being the very first one, the velar fricative of 'Jaula'. While this is admittedly in a strong position as the first sound,

---

[74] See above, pp. 151–52.

[75] Silver argues that the 'bird-harp sings because it is in consonance with the natural world' (*Et in Arcadia Ego*, p. 41), while Bruton contends that the poem is about 'the struggle to write poetry' ('The Developing Expression in the Poetry of Luis Cernuda', p. 373). I find such ideas to be no more than secondary to the main theme of the music itself.

nevertheless it is over very quickly, allowing the majority of the stanza to dwell on the softer, more 'ethereal' sounds which attempt to imitate the sound of a harp. There are many soft sounds throughout the poem, and frequent juxtapositions of two vowel sounds which merge into one another. This imitation of the harp creates a soft, gentle, harmonic poem which in turn echoes and reinforces the main theme of music.[76] Furthermore, the use of regular octosyllabic lines and four-line stanzas creates a regular, rhythmical, 'musical' sort of poem.

Virtually all of the evidence we have analysed thus far relating to the post-Surrealist poetry illustrates how strong Cernuda's adherence to meaning is: only the slightly less traditional verse forms really suggest a discordant note (the invention of symbols is only very slightly discordant); otherwise Cernuda's mature poetry could, from the point of view of the creation of literary order, inhabit a world before *Un río, un amor*. This is of course nonsensical. We found plenty of evidence to demonstrate Cernuda's doubts about language and meaning in *Un río, un amor*. The mature poetry does *not* invalidate the early poetry. So how can this be reconciled? Purely as a contradiction? Contradictions are not, of course, something new in *La realidad y el deseo*, but it is not so simple. There are definite cracks and holes in Cernuda's apparent total reintegration of meaning. 'Silla del rey', from *Vivir sin estar viviendo*, is a meditation on Philip II's building of 'El Escorial'. Since the palace is perceived as an artistic creation, it is in fact on a deeper level Cernuda's reflection on his own creative *œuvre*.[77] Most of the poem is in 'exultant, arrogant mood':[78]

> Una armonía total, irresistible, surge;
> Colmena de musical dulzor, resuena todo;
> Es en su celda el fraile, donde doma el deseo;
> En su campo el soldado, donde forja la fuerza;
> En su espejo el poeta, donde refleja el mito. (420–21)

---

[76] For further analysis of the 'musicality' of Cernuda's poetry, see Ruiz Silva, *Arte, amor y otras soledades*, pp. 83ff.

[77] For a detailed and illuminating study of the poem, see Harris, *Luis Cernuda. A Study*, pp. 102–03, 107–08 and 113–14. Concha Zardoya concentrates on the issue of Spain and the progress of history ('El Escorial' was in Franco's Spain a symbol of the Establishment and traditional Spanish values), pointing out that we do not know if Cernuda 'siente amor o desprecio por ellas' ('Imagen de España en la poesía de Luis Cernuda', *Sin Nombre*, 6, No. 4 (1976), 39).

[78] Harris, *Luis Cernuda. A Study*, p. 113.

The positive images of poetry here are obvious. The implication from the basic parallel of Escorial/poetry is that Cernuda's poetry is just as impressive and magnificent as the king's palace. But there is a problem. Cernuda's edifice is not necessarily as steadfast as it might be:

> La mutación es mi desasosiego,
> Que victorias de un día en derrotas se cambien.
> Mi reino triunfante ¿ha de ver su ruina?
> O peor pesadilla ¿vivirá sólo en eco,
> Como en concha vacía vive el mar consumido? (421–22)

Like any building, there is a danger that the 'structure' of Cernuda's poetry will disintegrate and collapse.[79] If Cernuda's poetry is similar to 'El Escorial', then it must be the pinnacle of artistic creation, and yet the seeds of destruction are there.[80] At its most basic level, Cernuda's poetry consists of words on a page put together in such a way that they become 'meaningful'. What then must be happening if it changes to 'derrotas' (line two)? The consignment to obscurity was always a fear for Cernuda and certainly has a part to play in this. There is however something more fundamental at work. If the poetry is a 'derrota', then it must mean nothing to future generations. It loses its meaning. *Literary order is once again becoming literary chaos.* This is admittedly not exactly the same as a 'deconstruction' of meaning, but it nevertheless illustrates that there is still

---

[79] See also Luis Martínez Cuitiño, 'El reflejo del mundo en la obra de Luis Cernuda', *Revista de Literatura,* 45 (1983), 131–32.

[80] Harris argues that Cernuda is putting forward his own belief that the poet ought to be the redeemer of the world (*Luis Cernuda. A Study*, p. 107), while both Coleman (p. 128) and Jiménez-Fajardo (*Luis Cernuda*, p. 113) emphasise lines from the stanza after the one quoted, to support the claim that the poem stresses the *absence* of the threat of destruction:

> Mi obra no está afuera, sino adentro,
> En el alma; y el alma, en los azares
> Del bien y el mal, es igual a sí misma:
> Ni nace, ni perece. Y esto que yo edifico
> No es piedra, sino alma, el fuego inextinguible. (422)

Javier Almodóvar and Miguel A. Márquez also compare these lines with Heraclitus to prove the same thing ('Heráclito en *La realidad y el deseo*', *Estudios Clásicos*, 30, No. 93 (1988), 46). Luis Maristany likewise asserts that 'la obra es para [Cernuda], esencialmente, algo interior' ('La complacencia ante la obra', in Cortines, p. 191). What all these arguments do however is fall into the same trap as the king himself, and ignore the very real doubts which are actually voiced. Not only that, the king's arrogance is such as to make him supremely unlikeable, which in turn distances us from him and makes us less inclined to be persuaded by him.

something problematic about it: for all that the poet tries to construct
meaning, he cannot guarantee the effect it will have on the reader. This is
stressed again in the second question in this stanza, where it is a 'peor
pesadilla' (a strong expression indeed) that to future generations the 'reino
triunfante' will be no more than an echo like the sound of the sea 'en concha
vacía', i.e., something which is entirely without the substance of the original.
Poetry cannot mean something if it does not mean something *to someone*.
Not only that, it could even become corrupted by careless or unsympathetic
readers. Just how terrified the king is of things going wrong is then illustrated in the fourth-last stanza:

> No puedo equivocarme, no debo equivocarme;
> Y aunque me equivocase haría
> Él que mi error se tornara
> Verdad, pues que mi error no existe
> Sino por Él, y por Él acertando me equivoco. (422)

The first line encompasses two frantic, desperate denials that he might be
wrong, illustrating just how much he requires to try to persuade himself. The
second line is then dangerously close to an open admission that he is wrong,
and is followed by a ludicrously illogical appeal to God: if the king is wrong,
so he says, God will put things right, because the building of the Escorial
was for the glory of God. So if the king has made a mistake, he has made it
with the very best of intentions. Even if the king is persuaded by this, no-
body else could possibly be. The building of the Escorial is for the king's
glory and his glory only, as an expression of his arrogance. He has after all
explicitly told us that he is afraid of the ruin of '[su] reino triunfante'. By
extension, given the parallels with Cernuda's own situation and the
'structure' of his poetry, the poet's disquiet is conveyed with singular precision.

What is evident, then, from this analysis of Cernuda's use of language in
his poetry after his 'chaotic' overtly Surrealist phase, is something very close
to a total reintegration of meaning. Overtly comprehensible language and the
use of traditional symbols and conventionally symbolic language are so
clearly apparent that it is difficult to tell that the mature poetry follows a
phase which casts very strong doubts on the possibility of universal meaning.
This is a contradiction, and again demonstrates the quite remarkable complexity of *La realidad y el deseo*. There is however one further element: as
the final analysis of the disintegration of meaning points towards meaning-
*ful*ness, so too the final analysis of the reintegration of meaning points
towards meaning*less*ness. It is thus finally to an attempt to bring these conflicting elements together which we now must turn.

Synthesis: Chaotic Order and Ordered Chaos

If the analysis of language and meaning thus far has taught us anything, it is what we have seen so often already, namely how closely allied order and chaos are. This time it is the tension between the order of meaningfulness and the chaos of meaninglessness which is at issue. In order to proceed to a more complete (if inevitably imperfect) understanding of the way that the two interact, it is profitable to consider three further poems which deal with the act of writing itself and the poet's and poetry's relationship to the future. A poem which takes a humorous look at the act of writing and the relationship of author to creation is 'Divertimiento' from *Vivir sin estar viviendo*. This is a slight, trivial poem, but it nevertheless does provide a useful starting-point for our discussion. It is a sonnet, and takes the form of a dialogue between the poet and the sonnet itself:

> «Asísteme en tu honor, oh tú, soneto.»
>   «Aquí estoy. ¿Qué me quieres?» «Escribirte.»
>   «Ello propuesto así, debo decirte
>   Que no me gusta tu primer cuarteto.»
> «No pido tu opinión, sí tu secreto.»
>   «Mi secreto es a voces: advertirte
>   Le cumple a estrofa nueva el asistirte.
>   Ya me basta de lejos tu respeto.» (403)

This poem is more a literary exercise, even a game, than a serious exposition of the problems of creation. Nonetheless it does highlight one crucial factor: poetry is a two-way process. It is not exclusively for the poet to decide exactly what will be communicated. When we were analysing the use of symbols in the later poetry, we laid heavy emphasis on the fact that Cernuda treats his symbolic language as working within a finite range of definable interpretations. That however does not stop the poem from being a living entity where, within that range of definable interpretations, there is still scope for divergence of understanding, especially in the hands of the careless or unsympathetic reader. While 'Divertimiento' does not postulate such a profound and intimate relationship between poem and reader, nevertheless it does conceive of the poem as a living entity. If we recall 'Palabras antes de una lectura', then we remember that 'las palabras están vivas, y por lo tanto traicionan'.[81] Here 'las palabras' could not be more 'vivas', and they certainly do 'betray' the poet, even to the point of criticising his handling of writing. Not only that, the final line of the second quatrain, 'Ya me basta de

---

[81] *Prosa I*, p. 605. See also above, p. 144.

lejos tu respeto' is deceptively simple. The key phrase is 'de lejos': it may well be unintentional here, but this does hit upon the fact that there will inevitably be a degree of distance, conscious or not and willed or not, between poet and poem. In elevating the poem above the poet, this is pointing tentatively to the poet's lack of ultimate control over its interpretation. The irony of all of this is that this poem is extremely easy to understand. As a lucid (if banal) exploration of the problematic poet-poem-reader relationship, it therefore combines the two conflicting ideas of meaning and non-meaning: it speaks in an overtly meaningful way of the potential inability to communicate effectively.

Just how fragile it is possible for the poet's control over his poetry to be is seen rather more clearly in the bitter poem '*Malentendu*' from *Desolación de la Quimera*. This poem deals explicitly with the relationship between the poet and his readers. The title, French for 'misunderstood', says it all: the reader has distorted what the poet wanted to express. This is highlighted by the choice of a French word as the title rather than Spanish. The reader's distortion is such that he has effectively transposed it, not into a real foreign language, but into a 'new' language, i.e., forcing the poem to speak a language alien to the one which the poet intended. The poem is actually substantially less profound even than 'Divertimiento', and is in intent primarily an opportunity for Cernuda to settle old scores by launching an angry attack on Pedro Salinas, who had dared to refer to Cernuda as a 'Licenciado Vidriera',[82] meaning that he is a 'delicate, timid, solitary creature'.[83] Despite the tediously polemical and petulant tone of the poem, it does have a serious point to make:

> Fue tu primer amigo literario
> (¿Amigo? No es la palabra justa), el que primero
> Te procuró experiencia en esa inevitable
> Falacia de nuestro trato humano:
> Ver cómo las palabras, las acciones
> Ajenas, son crudamente no entendidas.
>
> Pues no quería o no podía entenderte,
> Tus motivos él los trastocaba
> A su manera: de claros
> En oscuros y de razonables

---

[82] Pedro Salinas, 'Nueve o diez poetas', in *Ensayos de literatura hispánica* (Madrid: Aguilar, 1958), p. 373.
[83] Harris, *Luis Cernuda. A Study*, p. 12.

> En insensatos. No se lo perdonaste
> Porque es imperdonable la voluntaria tontería. (524–25)

Harris is right to lay stress on Cernuda's revulsion at the way that someone could take some of his poems and use them as a means of painting a false picture of their author,[84] but there are also other factors which deserve to be taken into consideration. Just as in 'Divertimiento' 'respect' for the sonnet was 'de lejos', so too here 'las palabras', to the formulation of which Cernuda has devoted his life (a distinction between poet and persona here is well-nigh impossible to find), are described as 'las acciones *ajenas*'. Once something has been written down and published, it assumes a life of its own, over which the poet cannot exercise control, not even if the meaning is obvious. Salinas' misinterpretation of Cernuda's poetry is not regarded as justifiable confusion in the face of enigmatic expression, but rather as 'la voluntaria tontería' which is 'imperdonable'. Moreover, this is at the hands of someone who called himself an 'amigo'. What would happen when read by an enemy? Thus in the end it may not matter how philosophically committed to the concept of meaning the poet may be, for that unknown quantity, the reader, is free to do with the poetry whatever he or she chooses. On the other hand, this awareness does not stop the poet from writing: the poem itself is testimony to his inability to remain silent, despite the fear he must entertain that *'Malentendu'* will likewise be 'crudamente no entendido'.

'*Malentendu*' is however an aesthetically unsatisfactory poem. One poem which is much more aesthetically successful is 'A un poeta futuro' from *Como quien espera el alba*. Cernuda confronts again the, for him, very vexed question of what will happen to his work, not just while he is still alive, as in '*Malentendu*', but once he has died and it has departed completely from his control. While 'Silla del rey' however is at least largely characterised by arrogance and self-assurance, despite the doubts which were seen as present, and, while '*Malentendu*' is a violent tirade which asserts the poet's right to a fair hearing, the tone of 'A un poeta futuro' is much more negative and uncertain. The first thing that is striking about the poem is that each of the first four stanzas (out of a total of only eight) starts with a negative: 'No conozco a los hombres', 'No comprendo a los ríos', 'No comprendo a los hombres', 'Mas no me cuido de ser desconocido' (339–41). These in themselves create a very self-doubting impression, an impression of a man who is a stranger in the world. Particularly interesting is the fourth of these, which consists of two negatives in the one line: 'no' and

---

[84] Harris, *Luis Cernuda. A Study*, p. 167.

the prefix 'des-' of 'desconocido'. The irony of this line is that, while the adage is that 'two negatives make a positive', in this case the positive is the verb 'cuidarse de', which means 'mirar por su salud', 'atender', 'ocuparse' or *'preocuparse'*.[85] It is most likely that it is 'preocupación' which dominates the persona's view as he looks towards the future, despite the superficial optimism of this fourth stanza:

> Sólo quiero mi brazo sobre otro brazo amigo,
> Que otros ojos compartan lo que miran los míos.
> Aunque tu no sabrás con cuánto amor hoy busco
> Por ese abismo blanco del tiempo venidero
> La sombra de tu alma, para aprender de ella
> A ordenar mi pasión según nueva medida. (341)

The first line here has rather erotic overtones, but we have to remember that this is the 'brazo' of a 'poeta futuro', which is crucial to an understanding of the following line. What the persona's eyes are perusing is not a person but his own poetry. The eyes of the friend are to 'share' it in the sense that they are to understand it as he intends, not according to his/her own set of pre-established criteria (as Salinas is accused of doing). The fact that he is looking for the future friend 'con amor' does sound optimistic, but the reference to the future itself as 'ese abismo blanco' is much more unsettling. The unsettling tone is confirmed in the fifth stanza:

> Yo no podré decirte cuánto llevo luchando
> Para que mi palabra no se muera
> Silenciosa conmigo, y vaya como un eco
> A ti, como tormenta que ha pasado
> Y un son vago recuerda por el aire tranquilo. (341)

Despite its being entitled 'A un *poeta* futuro', this is assuredly addressed to any future reader, not necessarily a poet (although our own readings are in themselves creative and therefore we are 'poets' too[86]). What is most important is the self-doubt, for a poet is nothing without his audience. The crux of these lines is unquestionably 'Para que mi palabra no se muera/Silenciosa'. It is at this point that the poem concentrates on the essence of poetry, and that is 'la palabra'. A word, if it 'dies silently', can have no meaning whatsoever.

---

[85] *Larousse Diccionario de la lengua española*, ed. Ramón García-Pelayo y Gross (Barcelona: Ediciones Larousse, 1987), p. 228.

[86] Bloom makes a similar comment, namely that (p. 3), 'As literary history lengthens, all poetry necessarily becomes verse-criticism, just as all criticism becomes prose-poetry.'

It represents the total destruction of meaning. It is interesting to recall again the comment in 'Palabras antes de una lectura' that 'las palabras *están vivas*, y por lo tanto traicionan' (my emphasis).[87] If 'las palabras' are 'muertas', then this is the final nadir of linguistic chaos: absolute meaninglessness. Nevertheless, even here there is a tiny glimpse of the resurgence of some semblance of meaning: the last line here speaks of 'un son vago'. It is surely something highly equivocal, but nevertheless the conviction that the meaning of his poetry will still be salvaged, that it will still speak to someone. Doubt and affirmation are *coexisting*. In the light of this, let us consider now the closing stanza:

> Cuando en días venideros, libre el hombre
> Del mundo primitivo a que hemos vuelto
> De tiniebla y de horror, lleve el destino
> Tu mano hacia el volumen donde yazcan
> Olvidados mis versos, y lo abras,
> Yo sé que sentirás mi voz llegarte,
> No de la letra vieja, mas del fondo
> Vivo en tu entraña, con un afán sin nombre
> Que tu dominarás. Escúchame y comprende.
> En sus limbos mi alma quizá recuerde algo,
> Y entonces en ti mismo mis sueños y deseos
> Tendrán razón al fin, y habré vivido. (342–43)

Doubt comes first here: the poet envisions his 'versos' as 'olvidados'. Particularly significant is the choice of the verb 'yacer', which has definite connotations of the gravestone inscription 'Aquí yace ...'. Without an audience, literature is dead. At the same time however it is highly ironic that this is itself a poem: the very act of writing is an expression of the conviction that the poet has something meaningful to impart. The definitive statement of the relationship of meaning to non-meaning comes in the second half of this stanza. Meaning has to be a two-way process.[88] For all that the poet be-

---

[87] *Prosa I*, p. 605. See also above, p. 144.

[88] I can see little justification in María Victoria Utrera's reference to 'el triunfo del poeta' in this poem ('La estructura temporal de *La realidad y el deseo* en *Como quien espera el alba*', *Archivo Hispalense*, 74, No. 225 (1991), 143). Martha LaFollette Miller meanwhile deals with similar ideas, although she chooses, quite legitimately, to concentrate more on the 'intertextual' concepts of the 'past and future texts that help create his own text' rather than on the direct relationship between Cernuda and individual future readers ('Society, History, and the Fate of the Poetic Word in *La realidad y el deseo*', in *The Word and the Mirror*, ed. Jiménez-Fajardo, especially pp. 171–72).

lieves that what he writes means something to him (which in itself explains how he can return to the traditional 'meaningful' modes of language discussed as the cornerstone of his mature poetry), its status is highly equivocal and precarious until it enters 'en tu entraña', until the reader has completed the process. It is once that process is complete that the poet can say 'habré vivido'. The final irony lies in the facts that, first, he cannot know if this will ever happen, and second, and more disturbingly, if, as was seen in the fifth stanza, it is no more than an 'eco', a 'son vago', the poet cannot guarantee how it will live 'en nuestra entraña'.[89] That depends on *us*.[90] Therefore ultimately what Cernuda seems to seek to do in his most accomplished poetry is to find a mode of language which will time and again hold together, and *in tension*, both elements of meaning and non-meaning. That is why his overtly meaningless so-called Surrealist poetry still has meaning. That is why his overtly meaningful poetry contains the seeds of a new destruction. In short, meaning is chaotic order – meaning which stands on precarious foundations – *and* ordered chaos – non-meaning which desperately tries to build or rebuild its foundations. And *we* as readers have ultimately to act to bring order too.

[89] Soufas argues, in terms of 'Luna llena en Semana Santa' from *Desolación de la Quimera*, that 'the text is not fulfilled in itself but in another form of resurrection, Cernuda's, in the reader' ('«*Et in Arcadia Ego*»: Luis Cernuda, Ekphrasis, and the Reader', *Anales de la Literatura Española Contemporánea*, 7 (1982), 105), but this clearly does not take account of the problem of *how* Cernuda will be 'resurrected'.

[90] This is a theme to which Cernuda returns yet again in the extremely bitter (and artistically not very successful) poem 'A sus paisanos' in *Desolación de la Quimera* (546–48). See also Douglas Barnette, 'Luis Cernuda y su Generación: La creación de una leyenda', *Revista de Estudios Hispánicos*, 18 (1984), 125–26.

CONCLUSION

'Order in a world of chaos': to lose faith in God as the ultimate ordering force behind the universe is to be confronted with a world which has no ultimate purpose, where the concept of 'absolute order' has no significance. Since the existence of God (or any kind of Absolute) cannot be proved or disproved by rational argument, both theism and atheism can only be matters of individual belief. What has characterised the modern age has been a gradual falling away from faith in God, either to active atheism or to a more complacent disregard for religious matters. This loss of faith has found its expression in literature, and is a prominent feature of the poetry of Luis Cernuda.

There is little to be gained from replicating the arguments of this study here. There are however certain crucial aspects which should be borne in mind. In the first place, the loss of faith in an Absolute, in transcendent order, is paramount. Furthermore, the decline from order into chaos is seen as irrevocable. The age of order can be represented as no more than a distant, primitive, almost mythical 'Golden Age', totally divorced from the contemporary world. For Cernuda, this is a world of chaos, where life is characterised by alienation, *Angst*, meaningless relationships, problem after problem.

The response to the world of chaos is what then comes to the fore. Clearly there are two principal options: either to face despair, or to seek order and attempt to make life once more make sense. There is certainly despair present in the poetry we have studied, but there is also a desire to conquer this despair. In all of the attempts to find order, however, what is always apparent is the continuing threat of chaos. On the one hand, there is a desire to find an Absolute, but the quest ends in failure. On the other hand, there is a desire for order within this world, but, when it is sought in 'love', there is above all the problem of the chaos of base eroticism. Similarly, when order is sought in art, attempting to produce art can alienate the artist from life, or even, when Cernuda is at his most Romantic, *ought* to alienate the artist from life and yet paradoxically have the potential to guide him towards the divine. The experience of art meanwhile is indisputably positive, and is closer to a saving power than God or Christ in *La realidad y el deseo*, but nonetheless is still at best no more than a temporary, fleeting experience which cannot last. Furthermore, the ability to create literary order is fraught with the problems of the very meaning of the words which the writer uses.

The coexistence of order and chaos: that is what seems to be a hallmark of *La realidad y el deseo*. What we witness in Cernuda's poetry is a stance of ambivalence and ambiguity. We are presented with a variety of problems, we see the various attempts to find solutions, but those solutions are not definitive. (Indeed, these attempts can lead to a greater degree of chaos than before, as is all too painfully the case for the Magi at the end of 'La adoración de los Magos'.) What his art seeks to do is to bring together in literary form the two opposing poles of order and chaos, where the dialectic itself is portrayed, even though there may be no end to the tension which exists between them. The lack of definitive solutions may ultimately be a source of despair, but if nothing else there is always the honesty of a picture which does not shrink from seeing both sides of the situation and which never pretends to reconcile the irreconcilable. It is up to us to cope with the paradoxes and complexities as boldly as did Cernuda himself, without attempting to force a semblance of unity where there is none.

There is one thing which follows from this process of bringing together and interweaving differing and conflicting ideas, and that relates to the style of writing. The style copes with these contradictions by allowing them to coexist, but also, and more fundamentally, by *reflecting* the tension in the use of language itself. Language which appears meaningless, and yet which is still communicating something; language which is apparently meaningful, and yet which simultaneously communicates uncertainty about itself. *That* is the culmination of the process of decline from order into chaos, *and* of the search for order in a world of chaos. Within literature, it is language which is obviously paramount: the uncertainties about language mirror and parallel the crisis of faith, while the finding of a literary form parallels the search for order in life. While the first-hand experience of the search for order in the lives of Cernuda's personae must remain limited to the lives of those personae, the literary form which expresses it reaches out directly towards *us*. But that leaves us with a question: how will it live 'en *nuestra* entraña'?

LIST OF WORKS CONSULTED

Primary Literature

Cernuda, Luis. *Obra completa*. 3 vols. Ed. Derek Harris and Luis Maristany. Madrid: Ediciones Siruela, 1993–94.

Secondary Literature

Almodóvar, Javier, and Miguel A. Márquez. 'Heráclito en *La realidad y el deseo*.' *Estudios Clásicos*, 30, No. 93 (1988), 43–50.

Ancet, Jacques. 'El deseo, lo negro. (Sobre Luis Cernuda).' *Cuadernos Hispanoamericanos*, Nos. 514–15 (1993), 215–20.

Argullol, Rafael. 'Cernuda romántico.' *Quimera*, 15–I–1982, pp. 29–32.

Ballestero, Manuel. *Poesía y reflexión: La palabra en el tiempo*. Madrid: Taurus, 1980.

Barnette, Douglas. 'Luis Cernuda y su Generación: La creación de una leyenda.' *Revista de Estudios Hispánicos*, 18 (1984), 123–32.

Barón Palma, Emilio. *Luis Cernuda: vida y obra*. Sevilla: Editoriales Andaluzas Unidas, 1990.

Bellón Cazabán, Juan Alfredo. *La poesía de Luis Cernuda. Estudio cuantitativo del léxico de* La realidad y el deseo. Granada: Universidad de Granada, 1973.

Bellver, Catherine C. 'Luis Cernuda's Paragons of Mythical Beauty.' *Revista Hispánica Moderna*, 43 (1990), 32–41.

Bruton, Kevin J[ohn]. ' "El joven marino": a Landmark in Cernuda's Poetic Development.' *Quinquereme*, 4, No. 1 (1981), 85–92.

— — —. ' "La mirada" in the Poetry of Luis Cernuda–The "Hedgehog on the Prowl".' *Anales de la Literatura Española Contemporánea*, 21 (1996), 27–40.

— — —. 'Luis Cernuda and the Poetics of Desire.' *Ibero-Romania*, 27 (1988), 61–78.

— — —. 'Symbolical Reference and Internal Rhythm: Luis Cernuda's Debt to Hölderlin.' *Revue de Littérature Comparée*, 58 (1984), 37–49.

— — —. 'The Cemetery Poems of Luis Cernuda.' *Anales de la Literatura Española Contemporánea*, 13 (1988), 189–209.

— — —. 'The Developing Expression in the Poetry of Luis Cernuda: The Rôle of Image and Symbol.' Unpublished thesis London 1980.

— — —. 'The Romantic and Post-Romantic Theme of Poetic Space as Exemplified in the Poetry of Luis Cernuda.' In *Space and Boundaries in Literature*,

Vol. III of *Proceedings of the Twelfth Congress of the International Comparative Literature Association*. Ed. R. Bauer, D. Fokkema and M. de Graat. München: Iudicum, 1990, pp. 351–56.

Cacheiro, Maximino. 'La problemática del escrito en "La realidad y el deseo".' *Cuadernos Hispanoamericanos*, No. 316 (1976), 54–60.

Caminero, Juventino. 'Luis Cernuda como poeta comprometido en la guerra civil española.' *Letras de Deusto*, 16, No. 35 (1986), 53–70.

Capote Benot, José María. *El surrealismo en la poesía de Luis Cernuda*. Sevilla: Universidad de Sevilla, 1976.

Coleman, J. Alexander. *Other Voices: A Study of the Late Poetry of Luis Cernuda*. Chapel Hill: The University of North Carolina Press, 1969.

Cortines, J., ed. *Actas del primer congreso internacional sobre Luis Cernuda (1902–1963)*. Sevilla: Universidad de Sevilla, 1990.

Curry, Richard K. *En torno a la poesía de Luis Cernuda*. Madrid: Pliegos, 1985.

Debicki, Andrew P. *Estudios sobre poesía española contemporánea. La generación de 1924–1925*. Madrid: Gredos, 1968.

De Laurentis, Shelley A. 'Luz y sombra en la poesía de Cernuda.' *Sin Nombre*, 6, No. 4 (1976), 8–18.

Delgado, Agustín. *La poética de Luis Cernuda*. Madrid: Editora Nacional, 1975.

Fernández Bañuls, Juan Alberto. 'Bécquer y la creación poética del 27: el caso de Cernuda.' *Archivo Hispalense*, 54, No. 165 (1971), 40–76.

García-Devesa, Consuelo. 'Cuatro poemas de amor o un poema de Luis Cernuda a la luz de Bécquer, Rosalía y A. Machado.' *Romance Notes*, 33 (1992–93), 197–206.

Gariano, Carmelo. 'Aspectos clásicos de la poesía de Luis Cernuda.' *Hispania*, 48 (1965), 234–46.

Gil de Biedma, Jaime, Juan Gil Albert and Luis Antonio de Villena. *3 Luis Cernuda*. Sevilla: Universidad de Sevilla, 1977.

Harris, Derek. 'A Primitive Version of Luis Cernuda's Elegy on the Death of Lorca.' *Bulletin of Hispanic Studies*, 50 (1973), 357–73.

— — —. 'Ejemplo de fidelidad poética: El superrealismo de Luis Cernuda.' *La Caña Gris*, Nos. 6–8 (Otoño de 1962), 102–08.

— — —. 'La escritura surrealista de *Un río, un amor*, de Luis Cernuda.' *Ínsula*, Año 44, No. 515 (1989), 15–17.

— — —, ed. *Luis Cernuda*. Madrid: Taurus, 1977.

— — —. *Luis Cernuda. A Study of the Poetry*. London: Tamesis: 1973.

Hughes, Brian. 'Cernuda and the Poetic Imagination: *Primeras Poesías* as Metaphysical Poetry.' *Anales de Literatura Española*, 1 (1982), 317–31.

— — —. *Luis Cernuda and the Modern English Poets. A Study of the Influence of Browning, Yeats and Eliot on his Poetry*. Alicante: Universidad de Alicante, 1987.

Ibáñez Avendaño, Begoña. *El símbolo en «La realidad y el deseo» de Luis Cernuda. El aire, el agua, el muro y el acorde como génesis literaria*. Kassel: Reichenberger, 1994.

Jiménez-Fajardo, Salvador. 'Ekphrasis and Ideology in Cernuda's *"Ninfa y pastor por Ticiano".*' *Anales de la Literatura Española Contemporánea*, 22 (1997), 29–51.

— — —. *Luis Cernuda*. Boston: Twayne, 1978.

— — —, ed. *The Word and the Mirror: Critical Essays on the Poetry of Luis Cernuda*. Toronto: Associated University Presses, 1989.

Ledford, Lorraine. 'Cernuda's *demonio*: Devil or Divinity?' In *Essays in Honor of Jorge Guillén on the Occasion of his 85th Year*. No ed. Cambridge, Massachusetts: Abedul, 1977, pp. 42–51.

López Castro, Armando. 'Ética y poesía en Cernuda.' *Cuadernos para Investigación de la Literatura Hispánica*, 8 (1987), 75–105.

McMullan, Terence. 'Luis Cernuda and the Emerging Influence of Pierre Reverdy.' *Revue de Littérature Comparée*, 49 (1975), 129–50.

Mabrey, María Cristina C. *La obra poética de Luis Cernuda: entre mito y deseo*. Madrid: Pliegos, 1996.

Mandrell, James. 'Cernuda's "El indolente": Repetition, Doubling, and the Construction of Poetic Voice.' *Bulletin of Hispanic Studies*, 65 (1988), 383–95.

Marcial de Onís, Carlos. *El surrealismo y cuatro poetas de la generación del 27*. Madrid: José Porrúa Turanzas, 1974.

Maristany, Luis. *La realidad y el deseo. Luis Cernuda*. Barcelona: Laia, 1982.

Martínez, David. 'Luis Cernuda, poeta existencial.' *Revista de la Universidad Nacional de Córdoba*, 5 (1964), 144–70.

Martínez Cuitiño, Luis. 'El reflejo del mundo en la obra de Luis Cernuda.' *Revista de Literatura*, 45 (1983), 127–48.

Martínez Nadal, Rafael. *Españoles en la Gran Bretaña. Luis Cernuda. El hombre y sus temas*. Madrid: Hiperión, 1983.

Montoro, Adrian G. 'Rebeldía de Cernuda.' *Sin Nombre*, 6, No. 4 (1976), 19–30.

Müller, Elisabeth. *Die Dichtung Luis Cernudas*. Genève: Romanisches Seminar der Universität Köln, 1962.

Newman, Robert K. 'Luis Cernuda: El hombre visto a través de su poesía.' *Ínsula*, Año 19, No. 207 (1964), 6 & 13.

— — —. '«Primeras Poesías». 1924–27.' *La Caña Gris*, Nos. 6–8 (Otoño de 1962), 84–99.

Nield, Brian Whittaker. 'Surrealism in Spain, with Special Reference to the Poetry of Alberti, Aleixandre, Cernuda and Lorca, 1928–1931.' Unpublished thesis Cambridge 1971.

Olivio Jiménez, José. 'Emoción y trascendencia del tiempo en la poesía de Luis Cernuda.' *La Caña Gris*, Nos. 6–8 (Otoño de 1962), 45–83.

Ortiz, Fernando. 'T. S. Eliot en Cernuda.' *Cuadernos Hispanoamericanos*, No. 416 (1985), 95–104.

Pato, Hilda. 'El «tú» (y el «otro») en la poesía de Luis Cernuda.' *Anales de la Literatura Española Contemporánea*, 11 (1986), 225–35.

— — —. *Los finales poemáticos en la obra de Luis Cernuda*. Boulder, Colorado: Society of Spanish and Spanish-American Studies, 1988.

Paz, Octavio. 'La palabra edificante.' In *Cuadrivio*. 2nd ed. México: Editorial Joaquín Mortiz, 1969, pp. 165–203.

Quirarte, Vicente. *La poética del hombre dividido en la obra de Luis Cernuda.* México: Universidad Nacional Autónoma de México, 1985.

Real Ramos, César. 'La raíz de *la diferencia* de Luis Cernuda: La visión mítica de la realidad.' *Anales de la Literatura Española Contemporánea*, 15 (1990), 109–27.

——. *Luis Cernuda y la 'Generación del 27'.* Salamanca: Ediciones Universidad de Salamanca, 1983.

Resina, Juan Ramón. 'La realidad y el deseo en la poesía de Luis Cernuda.' *Hora de Poesía*, 29 (1983), 72–83.

Romero, Francisco. 'El muro y la ventana: La "otredad" de Luis Cernuda.' *Cuadernos Hispanoamericanos*, No. 396 (1983), 545–75.

Ruiz, Mario E. 'La angustia como origen de *la realidad* y manifestación *del deseo* en Luis Cernuda.' *Revista de Estudios Hispánicos*, 5 (1971), 349–62.

Ruiz Silva, José Carlos. *Arte, amor y otras soledades en Luis Cernuda.* Madrid: De la Torre, 1979.

——. 'En torno a un poema de Luis Cernuda: "Mozart".' *Cuadernos Hispanoamericanos*, No. 316 (1976), 61–65.

——. 'La música en la obra de Luis Cernuda.' *Revista de Literatura*, 39 (1978), 53–98.

Ruiz Soriano, Francisco. 'Ejemplos coincidentes de los tópicos de "la ciudad estéril" y "los hombres vacíos" en T. S. Eliot, Luis Cernuda y Rafael Alberti.' *Anales de la Literatura Española Contemporánea*, 18 (1993), 295–308.

——. 'Eliot, Cernuda y Alberti: la ciudad vacía.' *Cuadernos Hispanoamericanos*, Nos. 539–40 (1995), 43–54.

Sahuquillo, Ángel. *Federico García Lorca y la cultura de la homosexualidad. Lorca, Dalí, Cernuda, Gil-Albert, Prados y la voz silenciada del amor homosexual.* Stockholm: Stockholms universitet, 1986.

Salinas, Pedro. 'Nueve o diez poetas.' In *Ensayos de literatura hispánica.* Madrid: Aguilar, 1958, pp. 359–75.

Sánchez Rosillo, Eloy. *La fuerza del destino. Vida y poesía de Luis Cernuda.* Murcia: Universidad de Murcia, 1992.

Silver, Philip W. 'Cernuda and Spanish Romanticism: Prolegomena to a Genealogy.' *Revista Hispánica Moderna*, 43 (1990), 107–13.

——. *De la mano de Cernuda: Invitación a la poesía.* Madrid: Cátedra, 1989.

——. *Et in Arcadia Ego: A Study of the Poetry of Luis Cernuda.* London: Tamesis, 1965.

Soufas, Charles Christopher, Jr. 'Agents of Power in the Poetry of Luis Cernuda.' Unpublished dissertation Duke 1979.

——. 'Cernuda and Daimonic Power.' *Hispania*, 66 (1983), 167–75.

——. *Conflict of Light and Wind: The Spanish Generation of 1927 and the Ideology of Poetic Form.* Middletown, Connecticut: Wesleyan University Press, 1989.

——. '«*Et in Arcadia Ego*»: Luis Cernuda, Ekphrasis, and the Reader.' *Anales de la Literatura Española Contemporánea*, 7 (1982), 97–107.

———— ——. 'Ideologizing Form: Anti-Mimetic Language Theories in the Early Poetry of Jorge Guillén and Luis Cernuda.' *Anales de la Literatura Española Contemporánea*, 16 (1991), 101–17.

Talens, Jenaro. *El espacio y las máscaras. Introducción a la lectura de Cernuda.* Barcelona: Anagrama, 1975.

Ulacia, Manuel. *Luis Cernuda: Escritura, cuerpo y deseo.* Barcelona: Laia, 1986.

Utrera, María Victoria. 'La estructura temporal de *La realidad y el deseo* en *Como quien espera el alba.*' *Archivo Hispalense*, 74, No. 225 (1991), 119–45.

Valender, James. *Cernuda y el poema en prosa.* London: Tamesis, 1984.

———— ——. 'Cernuda y sus "Poemas para un cuerpo".' *Revista de la Universidad de México*, 38, No. 15 (1982), 30–37.

———— ——, ed. *Luis Cernuda ante la crítica mexicana.* México: Fondo de Cultura Económica, 1990.

Wilson, Edward M. 'Cernuda's Debts.' In *Studies in Modern Spanish Literature and Art Presented to Helen F. Grant.* Ed. Nigel Glendinning. London: Tamesis, 1972, pp. 239–53.

Zardoya, Concha. 'Imagen de España en la poesía de Luis Cernuda.' *Sin Nombre*, 6, No. 4 (1976), 31–41.

Tertiary Literature

Aldana, Francisco de. *Poesías castellanas completas.* Ed. José Lara Garrido. Madrid: Cátedra, 1985.

Allen, R. E., ed. *The Concise Oxford Dictionary of Current English.* 8th ed. Oxford: Clarendon Press, 1990.

Anderson, Andrew A. *Lorca's Late Poetry: A Critical Study.* Leeds: Francis Cairns, 1990.

Bécquer, Gustavo Adolfo. *Rimas.* Ed. José Luis Cano. Madrid: Cátedra, 1983.

Bloom, Harold. *A Map of Misreading.* Oxford: Oxford University Press, 1975.

Breton, André. 'Premier Manifeste du Surréalisme.' In *Les Manifestes du Surréalisme* suivis de *Prolégomènes à un troisième Manifeste du Surréalisme ou non.* Paris: Éditions de Sagittaire, 1946, pp. 7–75.

Cardwell, Richard A. '*Don Álvaro* or the Force of Cosmic Injustice.' *Studies in Romanticism*, 12 (1973), 559–79.

Castro, Rosalía de. *En las orillas del Sar.* Ed. Marina Mayoral. 3rd ed. Madrid: Castalia, 1989.

Connell, Geoffrey W. 'Introduction.' In *Spanish Poetry of the Grupo Poético de 1927.* Oxford: Pergamon, 1977, pp. 1–25.

Eckermann, Johann Peter. *Gespräche mit Goethe in den letzten Jahren seines Lebens.* 2 vols. Ed. Fritz Bergmann. Frankfurt am Main: Insel, 1981.

Fray Luis de León. *Poesías.* Ed. Padre Ángel Custodio Vega. 7th ed. Barcelona: Planeta, 1992.

García Lorca, Federico. *Obras completas.* 4 vols. Ed. Miguel García-Posada. Barcelona: Galaxia Gutenberg, 1996–97.

García-Pelayo y Gross, Ramón, ed. *Larousse Diccionario de la lengua española.* Barcelona: Ediciones Larousse, 1987.

Gardiner, Patrick. *Kierkegaard.* Oxford: Oxford University Press, 1988.

Hannay, Alastair. *Kierkegaard.* London: Routledge, 1991.

Hölderlin, Friedrich. *Selected Verse.* Ed. and trans. Michael Hamburger. London: Anvil Press Poetry, 1986.

Howatson, Margaret C. and Ian Chilvers, eds. *The Concise Oxford Companion to Classical Literature.* Oxford: Oxford University Press, 1993.

Janaway, Christopher. *Schopenhauer.* Oxford: Oxford University Press, 1994.

Kierkegaard, Søren. *Kierkegaard's Writings.* 25 vols. Ed. and trans. H. V. Hong and E. H. Hong. Princeton: Princeton University Press, 1980.

Kleist, Heinrich von. *Werke in einem Band.* Ed. Helmut Sembdner. München: Carl Hanser, 1966.

Lodge, David, ed. *Modern Criticism and Theory: A Reader.* London: Longman, 1988.

Machado, Antonio. *Poesías completas.* Ed. Manuel Alvar. 17th ed. Madrid: Espasa-Calpe, 1993.

Miller, J. Hillis. 'Stevens' Rock and Criticism as Cure, II.' In *Theory Now and Then.* Hemel Hempstead: Harvester Wheatsheaf, 1991, pp. 117–31.

Morris, C. B. *A Generation of Spanish Poets 1920–1936.* Cambridge: Cambridge University Press, 1969.

— — —. *Surrealism and Spain 1920–1936.* Cambridge: Cambridge University Press, 1972.

Nicholls, Roger A. *Nietzsche in the Early Work of Thomas Mann.* Berkeley, Los Angeles: University of California Press, 1955.

Nietzsche, Friedrich. *Werke in drei Bänden.* Ed. Karl Schlechta. München: Carl Hanser, 1954–56.

Paglia, Camille. *Sexual Personae. Art and Decadence from Nefertiti to Emily Dickinson.* Harmondsworth: Penguin, 1992.

Petrarca, Francesco. *Canzoniere.* Ed. Roberto Antonelli, Gianfranco Contini and Daniele Ponchiroli. Torino: Einaudi, 1992.

Plato. *The Symposium.* Trans. Walter Hamilton. Harmondsworth: Penguin, 1951.

Predmore, Michael P. *La poesía hermética de Juan Ramón Jiménez. El 'Diario' como centro de su mundo poético.* Madrid: Gredos, 1973.

Pütz, Peter. *Friedrich Nietzsche.* Stuttgart: J. B. Metzlersche Verlagsbuchhandlung, 1967.

Rivas, Duque de. *Don Álvaro o la fuerza del sino.* Ed. Donald L. Shaw. Madrid: Castalia, 1986.

Sabugo Abril, Amancio. 'Teoría y práctica de la poesía. (De Juan Ramón a Cernuda).' *Cuadernos Hispanoamericanos,* No. 536 (1995), 131–38.

Salzberger, L. S. *Hölderlin.* Cambridge: Bowes and Bowes, 1952.

San Juan de la Cruz. *Poesía completa y comentarios en prosa.* Ed. Raquel Asún. 4th ed. Barcelona: Planeta, 1997.

Schopenhauer, Arthur. *Sämtliche Werke.* 7 vols. Wiesbaden: Eberhard Brockhaus, 1949.

Steiner, George. *Real Presences. Is There Anything in What We Say?* London: Faber and Faber, 1989.

Unamuno, Miguel de. *Niebla.* 18th ed. Madrid: Espasa-Calpe, 1980.

INDEX